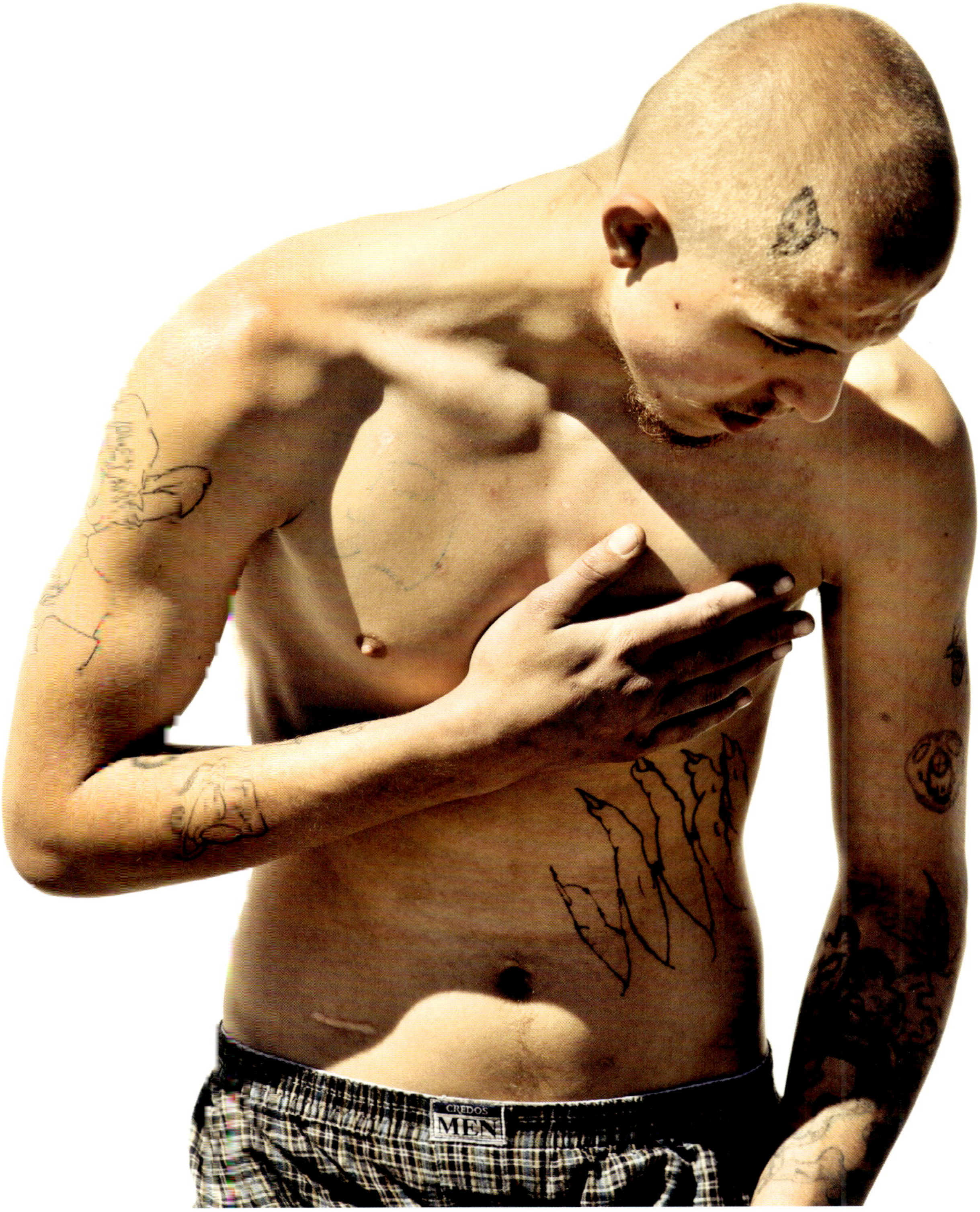

KATY GRANNAN, *Anonymous, Modesto, CA, 2012*

WORK BY KATY GRANNAN MAY BE FOUND AT **FRAENKEL GALLERY**, SAN FRANCISCO AND **SALON 94**, NEW YORK

Spring 2017

Opposite:
Alessandra Sanguinetti,
*Young Ho-Chunk girl
arrives for portrait
session. Black River Falls,
Wisconsin*, 2014
Courtesy the artist

Front cover:
Gregory Halpern,
Untitled, 2003–16
Courtesy the artist

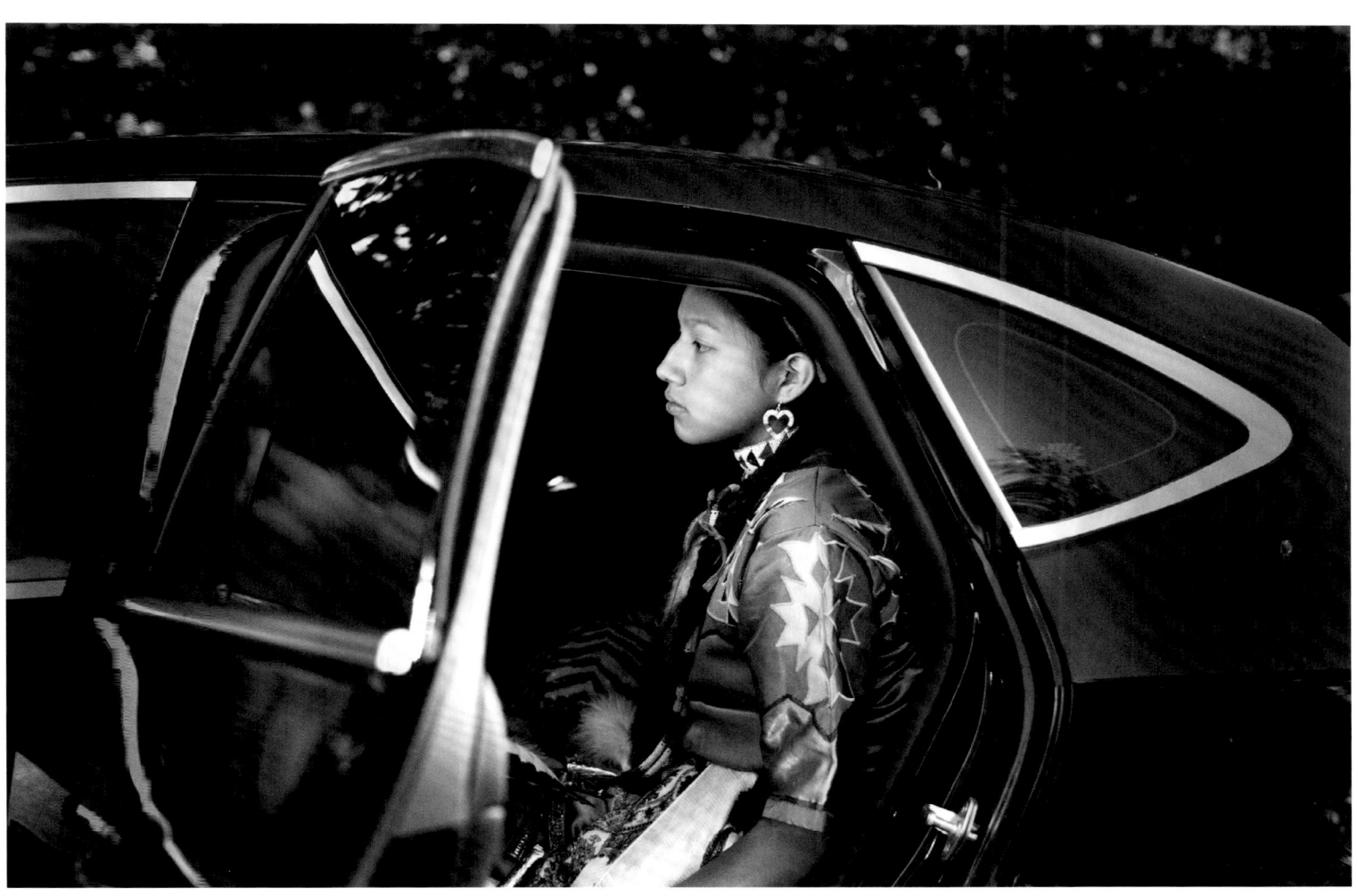

Aperture, a not-for-profit foundation, connects the photo community and its audiences with the most inspiring work, the sharpest ideas, and with each other—in print, in person, and online.

Aperture (ISSN 0003-6420) is published quarterly, in spring, summer, fall, and winter, at 547 West 27th Street, 4th Floor, New York, N.Y. 10001. In the United States, a one-year subscription (four issues) is $75; a two-year subscription (eight issues) is $124. In Canada, a one-year subscription is $95. All other international subscriptions are $105 per year. Visit aperture.org to subscribe. Single copies may be purchased at $24.95 for most issues. Subscribe to the Aperture Digital Archive at aperture.org/archive. Periodicals postage paid at New York and additional offices. Postmaster: Send address changes to Aperture, P.O. Box 3000, Denville, N.J. 07834. Address queries regarding subscriptions, renewals, or gifts to: Aperture Subscription Service, 866-457-4603 (U.S. and Canada), or email custsvc_aperture@fulcoinc.com.

Newsstand distribution in the U.S. is handled by Curtis Circulation Company, 201-634-7400. For international distribution, contact Central Books, centralbooks.com. Other inquiries, email orders@aperture.org or call 212-505-5555.

Help maintain Aperture's publishing, education, and community activities by joining our general member program. Membership starts at $75 annually and includes invitations to special events, exclusive discounts on Aperture publications, and opportunities to meet artists and engage with leaders in the photography community. Aperture Foundation welcomes support at all levels of giving, and all gifts are tax-deductible to the fullest extent of the law. For more information about supporting Aperture, please visit aperture.org/join or contact the Development Department at membership@aperture.org.

Library of Congress Catalog Card No: 58-30845.

ISBN 978-1-59711-418-9

Printed in Turkey by Ofset Yapimevi

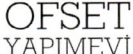

OFSET
YAPIMEVİ

Lead funding for the "American Destiny" issue of Aperture magazine is provided by the Henry Luce Foundation. Further generous support for Aperture magazine is provided in part by the Anne Levy Fund, and by public funds from the New York State Council on the Arts with the support of Governor Andrew M. Cuomo and the New York State Legislature, and the New York City Department of Cultural Affairs in partnership with the City Council.

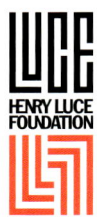

HENRY LUCE
FOUNDATION

Statement of Ownership, Management, and Circulation (Required by 39 U.S.C. 3685). 1. Publication Title: Aperture; 2. Publication no.: 0003-6420; 3. Filing Date: September 30, 2016 4. Issue Frequency: Quarterly; 5. No. of Issues Published Annually: 4; 6. Annual Subscription Price: $75.00; 7. Complete Mailing Address of Known Office of Publication: Aperture Foundation, 547 West 27th Street, 4th Floor, New York, NY 10001-5511; Contact Person: Dana Triwush; Telephone: 212-946-7116; 8. Complete Mailing Address of Headquarters or General Business Office of Publisher: Aperture Foundation, 547 West 27th Street, 4th Floor, New York, NY 10001-5511; 9. Full Names and Complete Mailing Addresses of Publisher, Editor, and Managing Editor: Publisher: Dana Triwush, Aperture Foundation, 547 West 27th Street, 4th Floor, New York, NY 10001-5511; Editor: Michael Famighetti, Aperture Foundation, 547 West 27th Street, 4th Floor, New York, NY 10001-5511; Managing Editor: Brendan Wattenberg, Aperture Foundation, 547 West 27th Street, 4th Floor, New York, NY 10001-5511; 10. Owner: Aperture Foundation, Inc., 547 West 27th Street, 4th Fl., New York, NY 10001; 11. Known Bondholders, Mortgagees, and Other Security Holders Owning or Holding 1 Percent or More of Total Amount of Bonds, Mortgages, or Other Securities: None; 12. Tax Status: The purpose, function, and nonprofit status of this organization and the exempt status for federal income tax purposes: Has Not Changed During Preceding 12 Months; 13. Publication Title: Aperture; 14. Issue Date for Circulation Data Below: Summer 2016 #223; 15. Extent and Nature of Circulation (Average No. Copies Each Issue During Preceding 12 Months; No. Copies of Single Issue Published Nearest to Filing Date): a. Total Number of Copies (Net press run): 16,547; 21,092; b. Paid Circulation; (1) Mailed Outside-County Paid Subscriptions Stated on PS Form 3541: 6,333; 6,087; (2) Mailed In-County Paid Subscriptions Stated on PS Form 3541: 35; 35; (3) Paid Distribution Outside the Mails Including Sales Through Dealers and Carriers, Street Vendors, Counter Sales, and Other Paid Distribution Outside USPS: 4,404; 7,161; (4) Paid Distribution by Other Classes of Mail Through the USPS: 38; 45; c. Total Paid Distribution: 10,809; 13,328; d. Free or Nominal Rate Distribution: (1) Free or Nominal Rate Outside-County Copies included on PS Form 3541: 309; 287; (2) Free or Nominal Rate In-County Copies Included on PS From 3541: 0; 0; (3) Free or Nominal Rate Copies Mailed at Other Classes Through the USPS: 179; 103; (4) Free or Nominal Rate Distribution Outside the Mail: 625; 700; e. Total Free or Nominal Rate Distribution: 1,113; 1,090; f. Total Distribution: 11,922; 14,418; g. Copies not Distributed: 4,625; 6,674; h. Total: 16,547; 21,092; i. Percent Paid 90.7%; 92.4%; 16. Electronic Copy Circulation, a. Paid Electronic Copies: 789; 729; b. Total Paid Print Copies + Paid Electronic Copies: 11,598; 14,057; c. Total Print Distribution + Paid Electronic Copies: 12,711; 15,147; d. Percent Paid (Both Print & Electronic Copies): 91.2%; 92.8%; I certify that 50% of all my distributed copies (Electronic & Print) are paid above a nominal price. 17. Publication of Statement of Ownership: Will be printed in the Spring 2017 issue of this publication.; 18. I certify that all information furnished on this form is true and complete. I understand that anyone who furnishes false or misleading information on this form or who omits material or information requested on the form may be subject to criminal sanctions (including fines and imprisonment) and/or civil sanctions (including civil penalties). Signature and Title of Editor, Publisher, Business Manager, or Owner: Dana Triwush, Publisher, September 30, 2016

aperture

The Magazine of Photography and Ideas

Editor
Michael Famighetti
Managing Editor
Brendan Wattenberg
Editorial Assistant
Annika Klein
Copy Editors
Clare Fentress, Donna Ghelerter
Production Director
Nicole Moulaison
Production Managers
Nelson Chan, Bryan Krueger
Work Scholars
Allison Cooke, Emma Kennedy, Jasphy Zheng

Art Direction, Design & Typefaces
A2/SW/HK, London

Publisher
Dana Triwush
magazine@aperture.org

Partnerships and Advertising
Elizabeth Morina
917-691-2608
emorina@aperture.org

Executive Director,
Aperture Foundation
Chris Boot

Minor White, Editor (1952–1974)

Michael E. Hoffman, Publisher and Executive Director (1964–2001)

aperture.org

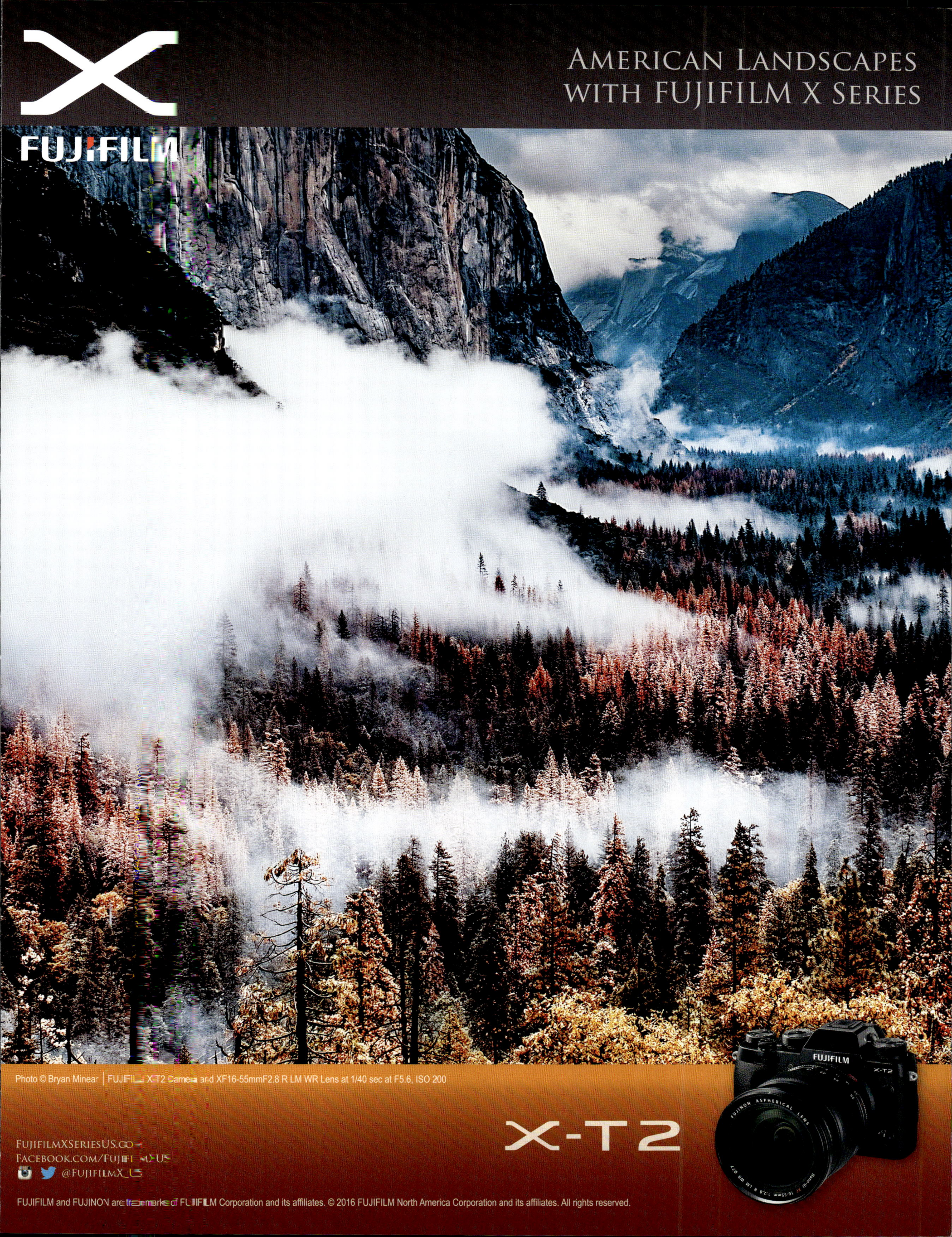

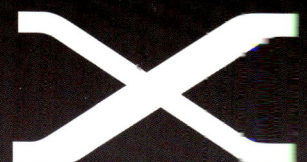

Photo © Bryan Minear | FUJIFILM X-T2 Camera and XF16-55mmF2.8 R LM WR Lens at 1/40 sec at F5.6, ISO 200

X-T2

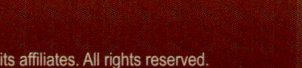

WE HAVE A DIFFERENT WAY OF LOOKING AT **AUCTIONS**

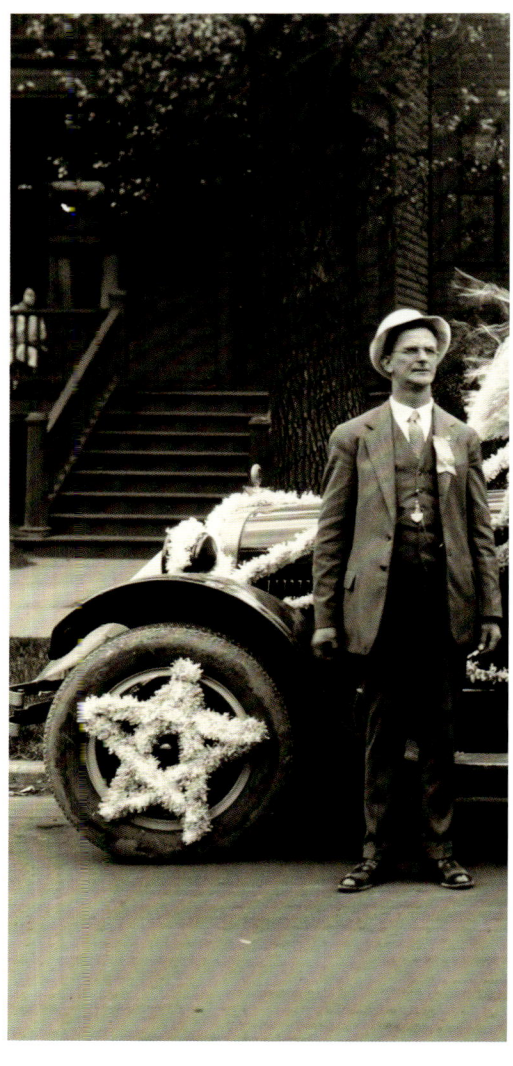
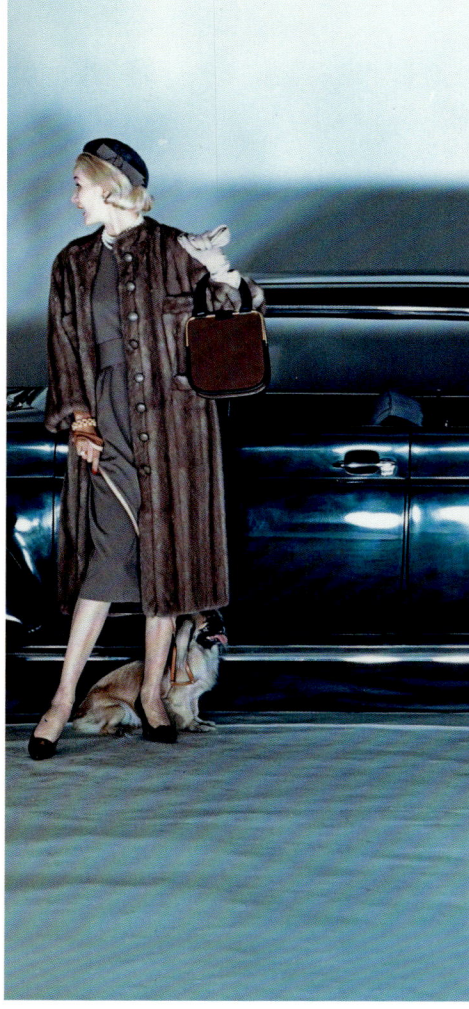
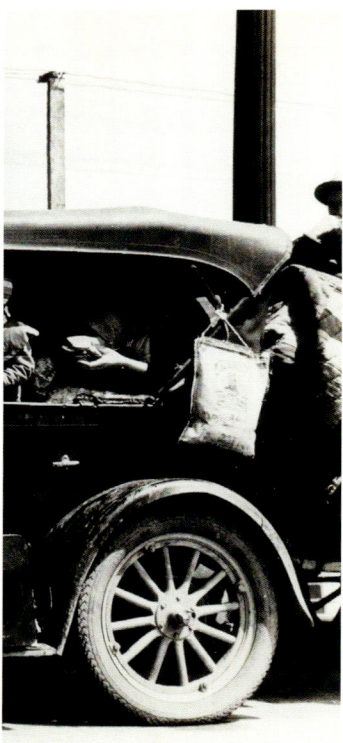

Find something new at Swann Auction Galleries. Our departments assemble sales that are unusually rich. n fact, we were the first American house to offer auctions of photographs, and our Photographs & Photobooks specialists remain innovators in their field. Swann understands more than art and books, we understand you, whether you're a lifelong collector, a first-time buyer, or looking to sell. We approach auctions with a blend of high-brow knowledge and low-brow fun. For a different perspective on auctions, come to Swann. We create our own culture.

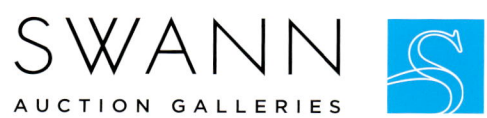

SWANN
AUCTION GALLERIES

104 East 25th St, New York, NY 10010 • 212 254 4710 • SWANNGALLERIES.COM/PHOTOGRAPHS

Redux
Rediscovered Books and Writings

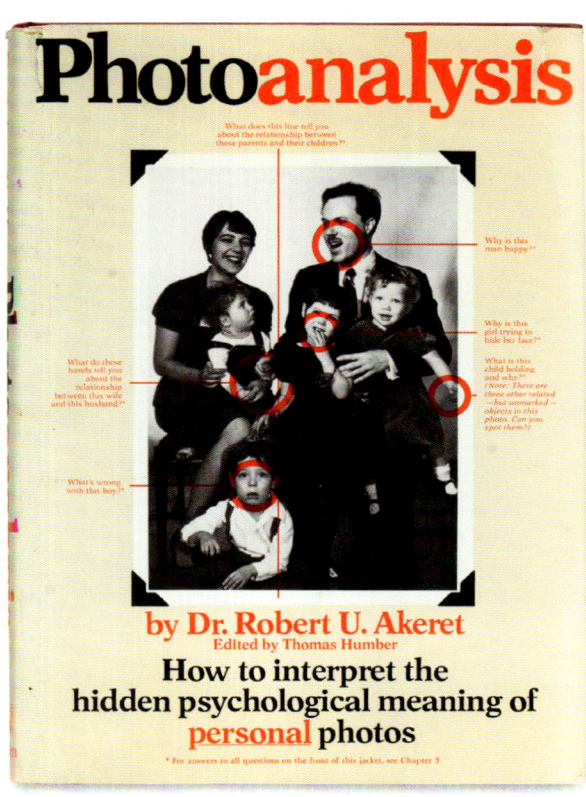

The how-to manual for reading a photograph
Sara Knelman

We have to learn to read, but looking, for most of us, just happens. So how do we know how to "read" what we see?

The history of photography is a matrix of codes and systems devised for drawing out meanings from pictures. It's hard to think of a discipline without this application: medicine, criminology, advertising, history, art history. Sorting out sincerity from agenda, disinterest from dogma, is part of what keeps images alive. With photography-as-mass-media continuing to accelerate, reading images—as opposed to just looking—is more and more urgent, a critical eye the sharpest counterweapon against seduction. This isn't a new idea: in his 1931 essay "A Small History of Photography,"

Walter Benjamin quotes an anonymous proclamation: "'The illiteracy of the future … will be ignorance not of reading or writing, but of photography.'"

Thirty-odd years later, "visual literacy" had become a specialist subject (the term was coined in 1969) and a fad—complete with how-to manuals. *Photoanalysis: How to Interpret the Hidden Psychological Meaning of Personal Photos*, published in 1973, was part of a slew of best sellers such as *Body Language* (1970) and *How to Read a Person Like a Book* (1971), marketed as "guides to understanding other people." Written by Dr. Robert U. Akeret, a Swiss-born psychoanalytic psychologist, *Photoanalysis* is a kind of inward-looking, pop version of

Roland Barthes's 1964 essay "Rhetoric of the Image" (though peculiarly devoid of discussion on the psychology of advertising). Spurred by the postmodern perception of identities as crafted projections, Akeret hurtles through a gamut of family snaps and press photography, his ongoing commentary cuing the reader on how to unravel the unconscious depths behind expressions, gestures, groupings, and postures. One sequence of images showing Marilyn Monroe in conflicting guises—as cheesecake, seductress, and newlywed—is uncannily close to Cindy Sherman's identity shifting in *Untitled Film Stills* (1977–80).

On the surface, it's photographic armchair psychology: helping readers investigate their own familial histories and hang-ups, and training them to be attentive to the potential foibles of fellow citizens. But Akeret's interpretations harbor their own hidden meanings. "Projecting yourself into photos," he writes early on, "provides an additional way of gaining insight into your own personality and unconscious feelings," though he seems strangely (or predictably!) blind to his own.

The paradox of the book, in other words, and what makes it interesting to us today, is its own myopia, hard to miss in hindsight. It's impossible to ignore the blatant gender stereotypes (one woman's strong hands, he notes, are "no stranger to washing, sewing, and cleaning") and retrospective predictions (childhood photographs of Hitler and mass murderer Charles Whitman ostensibly foretell the horrific acts of their futures).

Yet the exercise kicks up some interesting observations about the kind of assumptions we often make about pictures: that a photograph is a paradigmatic moment, automatically emblematic of a larger pattern of behavior, and, perhaps more dangerously, that everyone fits into a moral typology where goodness and evil, love and disinterest, confidence and uncertainty are mutually exclusive. If nothing else, it reminds us that we cannot separate our own fears and desires from what we choose to see.

Cover of *Photoanalysis: How to Interpret the Hidden Psychological Meaning of Personal Photos* (New York: Peter H. Wyden, Inc., 1973)

Sara Knelman is a writer, curator, and lecturer living in Toronto.

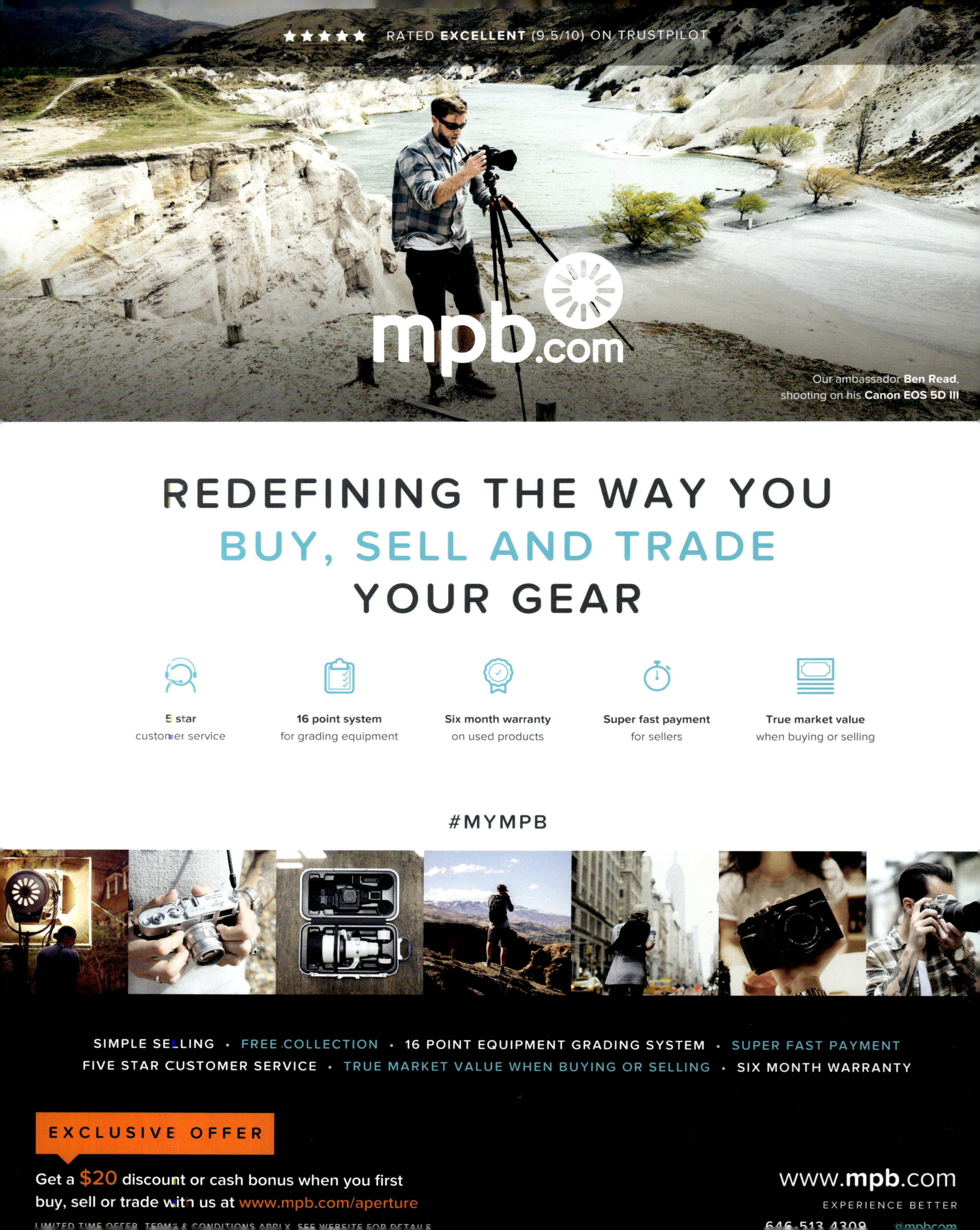

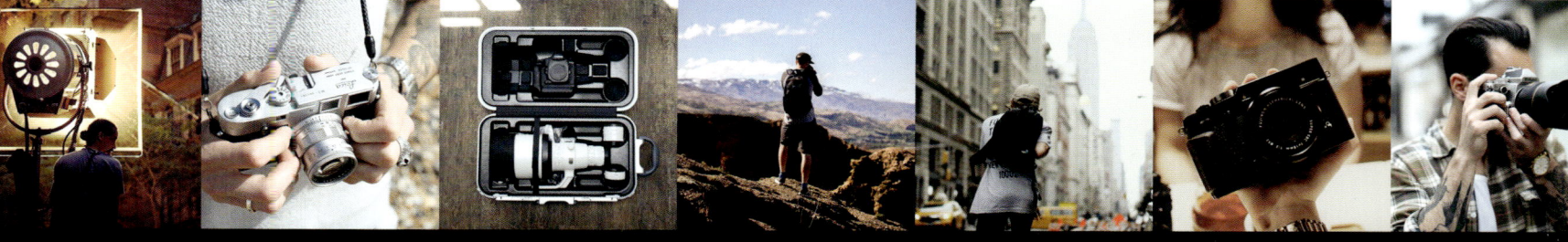

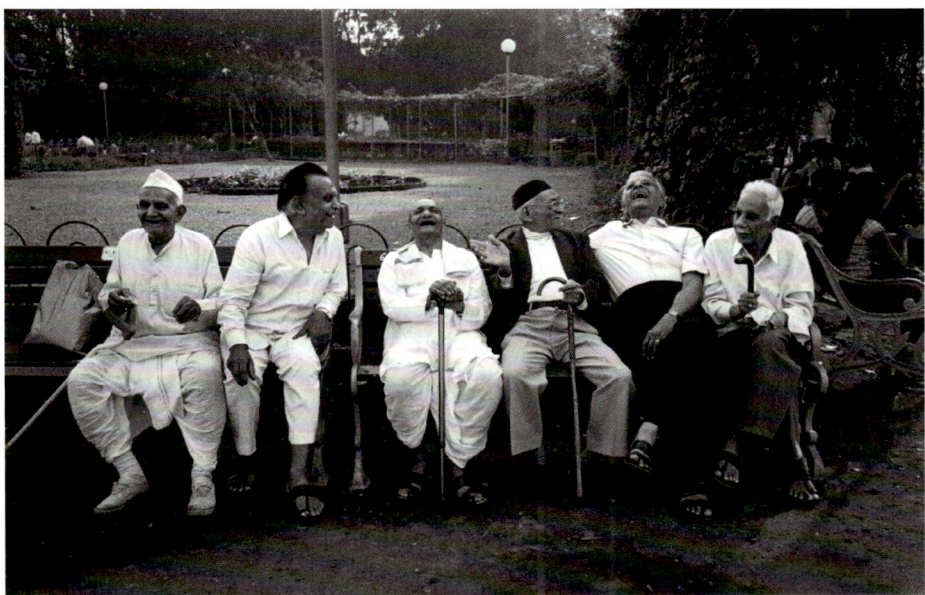

Betsy Karel, *Hanging Gardens*, 2006 © the artist and courtesy Howard Greenberg Gallery

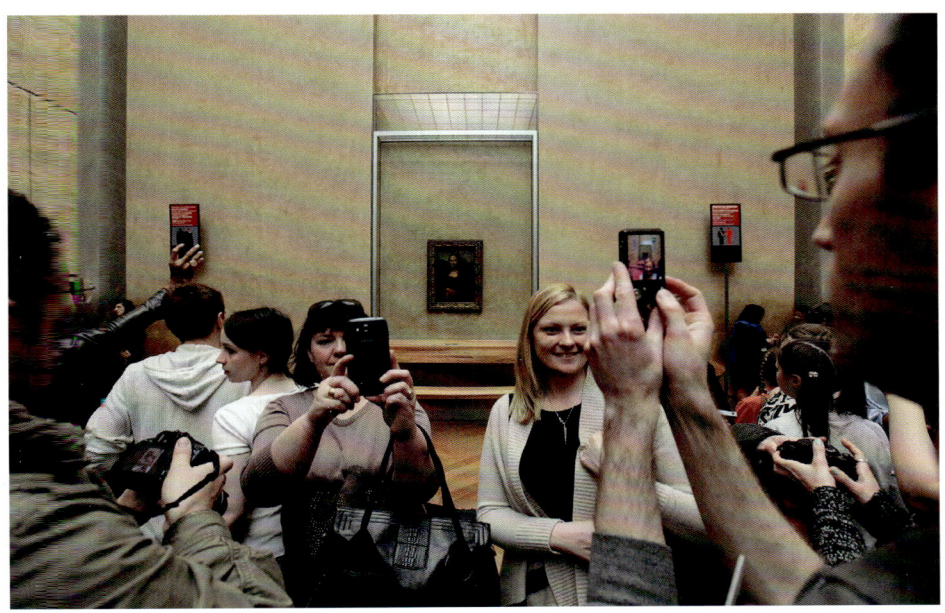

Steve Berman, *La Gioconda*, 2014 Courtesy the artist

Stephanie Rosenbloom

I go to Paris once a year and one of my favorite things to do is walk alone on quiet streets and through lesser-known museums. This photograph, by my friend and colleague Steve Berman, was taken in the Louvre, perhaps the city's busiest and best-known museum. Visitors who have come to see the *Mona Lisa* are gazing at camera lenses or at themselves rather than at the centuries-old da Vinci masterwork at their backs. In an age of Instagram and Twitter, this image, a gift to me from the photographer, serves as a personal reminder to look outward; to be present; to experience, not tweet, the moment.

Stephanie Rosenbloom writes the column "The Getaway" for the *New York Times*.

Suketu Mehta

I don't know the people in this photograph by Betsy Karel, which hangs in the living room of my Manhattan apartment, but I know them. They could be any of the groups of retired men that go for a daily walk: before the sun starts loaded for bear in the morning, or after it has admitted defeat and is sliding down the Bombay sky. The place is Hanging Gardens, green oasis of my boyhood. I can't listen to what's being said in the photograph, but I know the dialogue. The Parsi wit in the black cap has just cracked an off-color joke about a politician or film star. They've known each other for half a century now, and done what they've needed to in life. They can now leave their wives and their grandchildren behind to enjoy this daily constitutional, argue agitatedly about the state of the country, and laugh uproariously at the Bawa's remarks. On the right is a group of youngsters also hanging out, but not having half as much fun as the geezers. This is a photograph that makes me look forward to growing old.

Suketu Mehta is Associate Professor of Journalism at New York University and the author of *Maximum City: Bombay Lost and Found* (2004).

William Finnegan

I was in Bali for work, but the surf was big, so I borrowed a board. This photograph was taken at a fabled country spot called Padang Padang. It was my first wave of the morning. At the captured moment, I am about to make a mistake. Farther down the reef, Padang has two bowling sections—shallow spots where the wave becomes a violent barrel—and the correct line of attack for those sections is high on the wave's face. When I look at this image, my heels dig into the floor, my shoulders turn—what I should have done. But I was unfamiliar with the reef, and the board, and instead I held the low line you see, which did not work out well. What did work out well: several hours later, while I was hiking back to the road, a local teenager accosted me with a laptop computer. He had been shooting pictures from a cliff above the break, he said. He sold me this shot, on a flash drive, for eight bucks. It's been on my laptop, haunting me gently, for the year since.

William Finnegan is a staff writer at *The New Yorker* and the author, most recently, of *Barbarian Days: A Surfing Life* (2015).

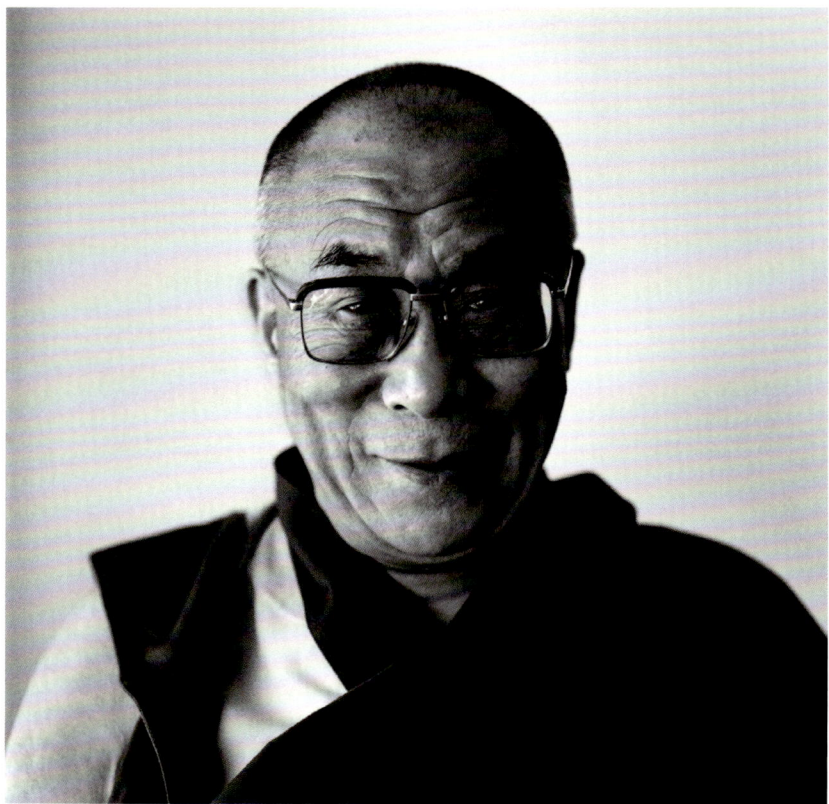

Brigitte Lacombe, *His Holiness the 14th Dalai Lama, Dharamsala, India*, **2003** Courtesy the artist

Pico Iyer

Every portrait is a self-portrait, so they say; I cherish that idea every time I look at the oversized photograph that beams down on my desk. As I chatted with the Dalai Lama in his home in 2003—I've been lucky enough to visit him there regularly since 1974—my old friend Brigitte Lacombe sat quietly on a sofa, taking everything in. Then she asked His Holiness if he'd mind stepping out onto his terrace for five minutes.

Silently, as relaxed and full of soft smiles as he was, she snapped a few frames on a small camera. When she sent me the result, I noticed one eye all kindness, one all penetration—on both sides of the lens. No amount of fancy equipment or elaborate setup can conjure something as piercing as this.

Pico Iyer is the author, most recently, of *The Art of Stillness: Adventures in Going Nowhere* (2014).

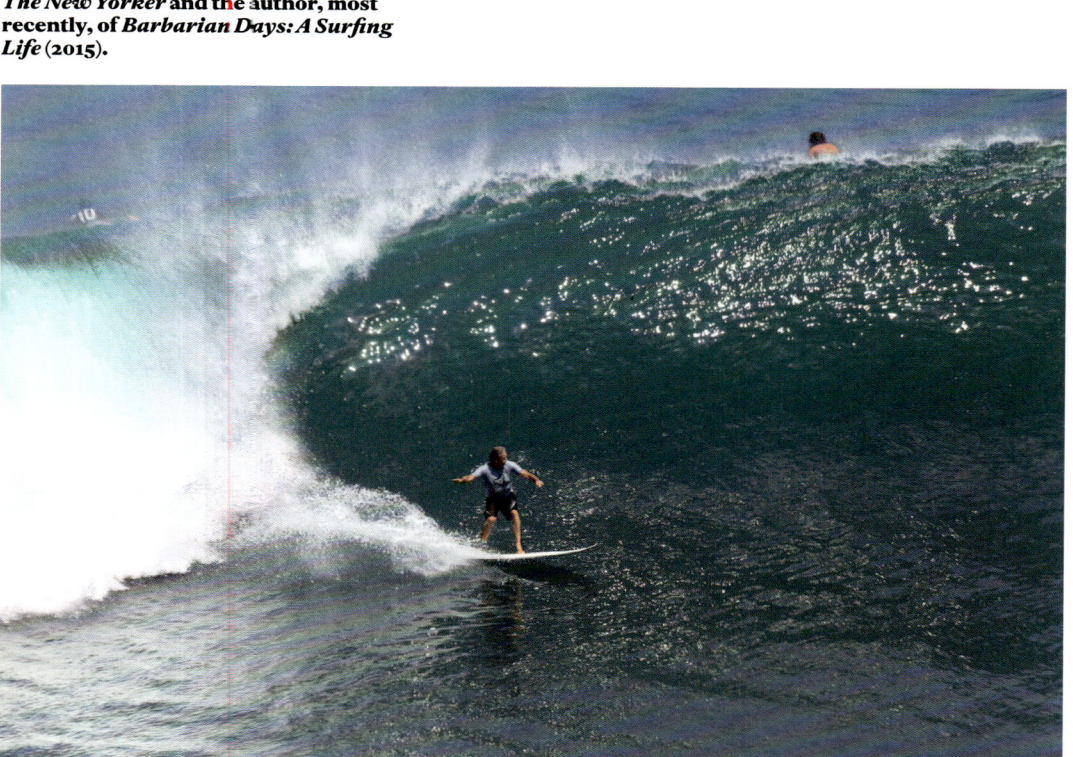

Photographer unknown, *William Finnegan, Padang Padang, Bali, Indonesia*, **November 6, 2015** Courtesy the author

Incoming by Richard Mosse
www.mackbooks.co.uk
February 2017

Heat Maps by Richard Mosse
Jack Shainman Gallery, NYC
February 2 - March 11, 2017

INCOMING

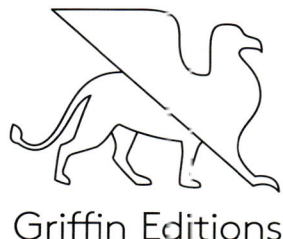

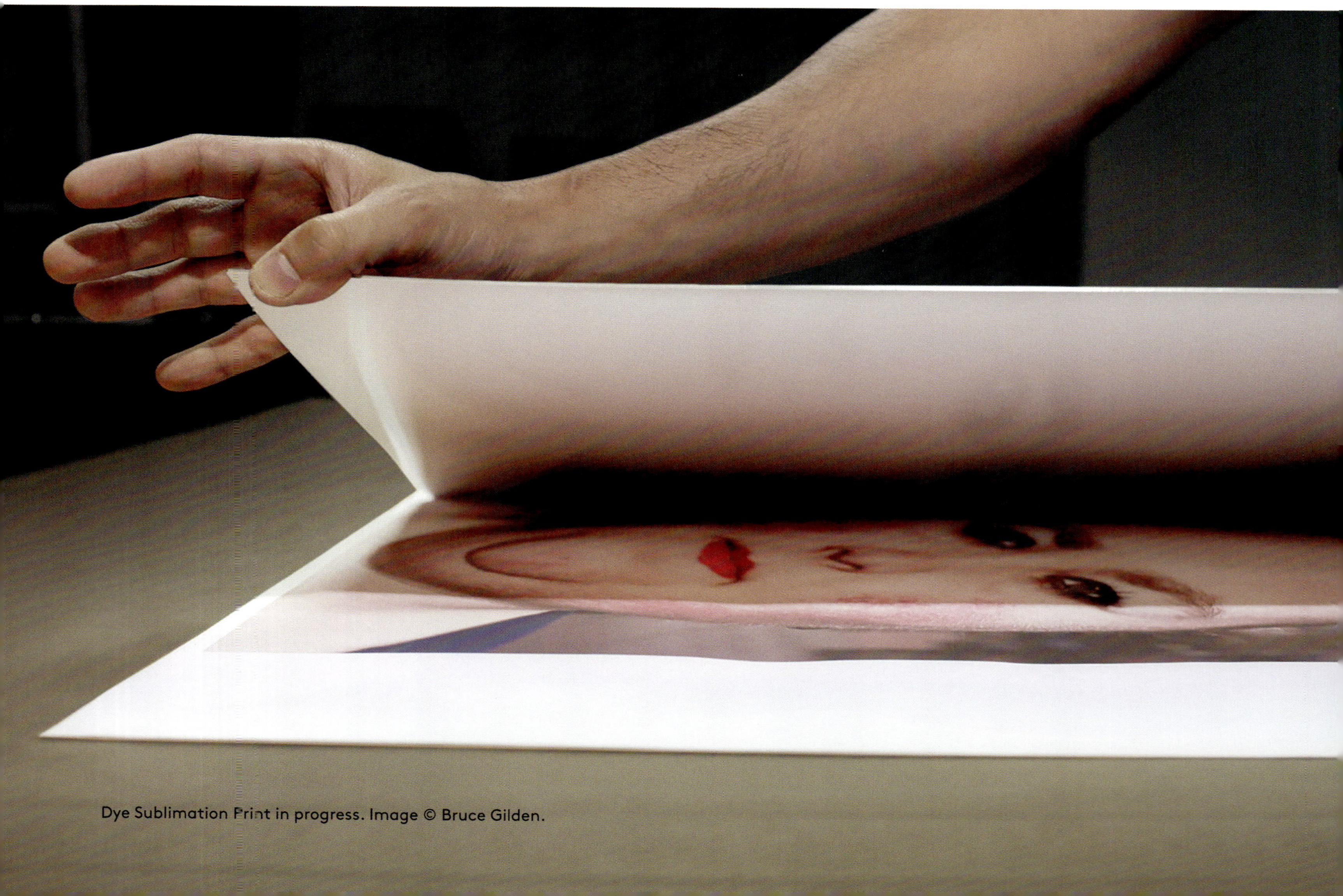

Dispatches
Istanbul

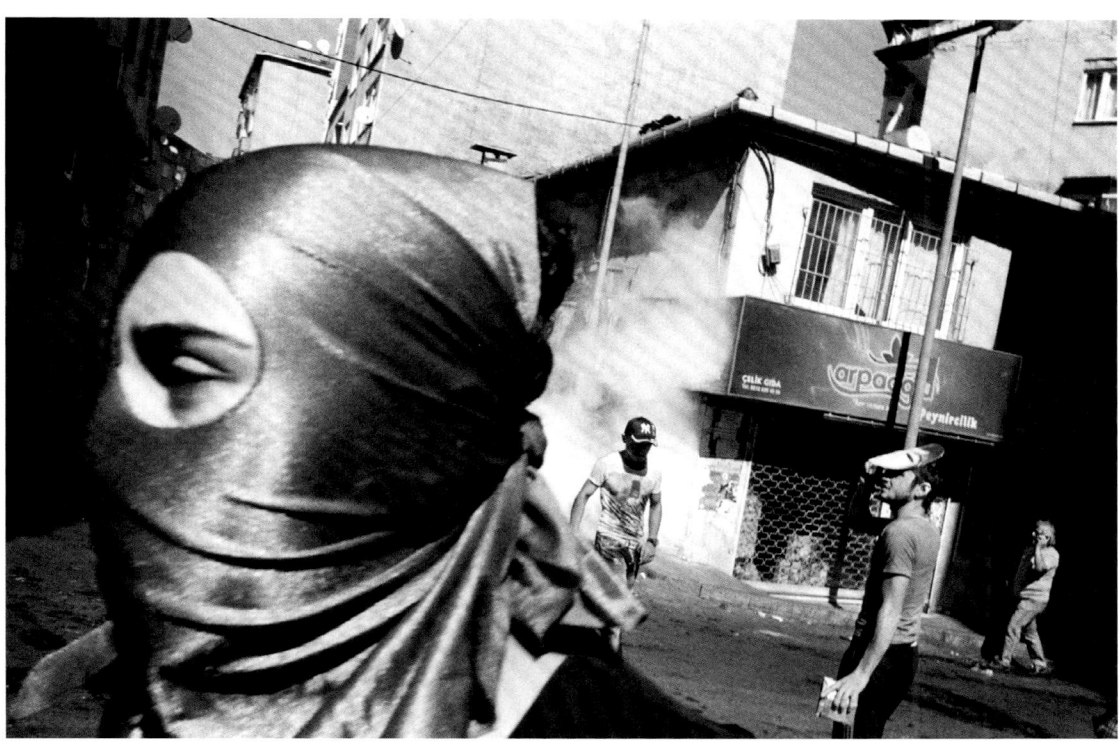

In Istanbul's photography scene, the anxious aftermath of a violent year
Kaya Genç

"A photograph can be incredibly intimidating for cops," Tuğba Tekerek, a Turkish journalist, told me recently. "They can use it to crush you."

The last twelve months have seen Turkey navigate an accumulation of violent incidents and growing surveillance; with them, the environment for photographers has changed for the worse. In this country, which occasionally tops the New York–based Committee to Protect Journalists's annual list of the world's leading jailers of journalists, taking pictures is an increasingly political and dangerous act.

Tekerek, arrested twice last year for photographing people in public spaces, was speaking from experience. When we met at a Caffè Nero one quiet morning last September, Istanbul had not fully awoken from the nightmares of 2016. ISIS suicide attacks on Istanbul's main shopping

avenue in March and in its airport last June, followed by a coup attempt by a religious cult that ended up killing hundreds of civilians in July, unsettled the city.

"Taking pictures here has turned into a big problem only in the past three years, following Gezi," she said, referring to violent protests around Istanbul's Taksim Gezi Park in 2013. Intent on documenting human rights violations, Tekerek often photographs in civic areas—the corridor of a courtroom, the garden of a police station. But these are the kinds of images likely to land the reporter behind bars. On the occasions Tekerek has been taken into custody, police officers have asked whether she is a terrorist studying the area for an attack. Twice, cops confiscated her camera and placed her in a locked room. Tekerek's supposed crime, meanwhile, stays the

same: her pictures contain images of uniformed or plainclothes police officers.

Charlie Kirk, a British photographer, made the same discovery when he arrived in Istanbul in the summer of 2012, following a career as a derivatives lawyer. "I was amazed by the number of protests on İstiklal Avenue," Kirk recalled. The 2013 protests at Gezi Park were a revelation for him. His first night photographing, on May 29, when tens of thousands packed the avenue and helicopters dropped tear gas on them, was burned onto his mind. Kirk produced a series of images using what the Australian photographer Rob Vallender describes as Kirk's gonzo style: an aggressive approach toward his subjects, whose unsuspecting faces he illuminates with an off-camera flash. With raw and clear-eyed realism, Kirk captured protests in the wake of the suppression

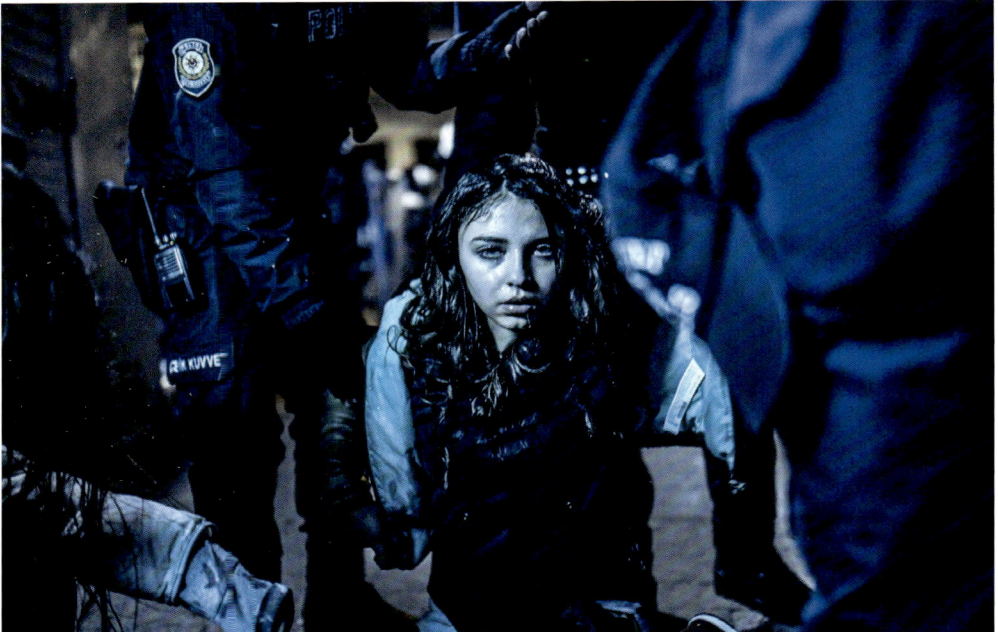

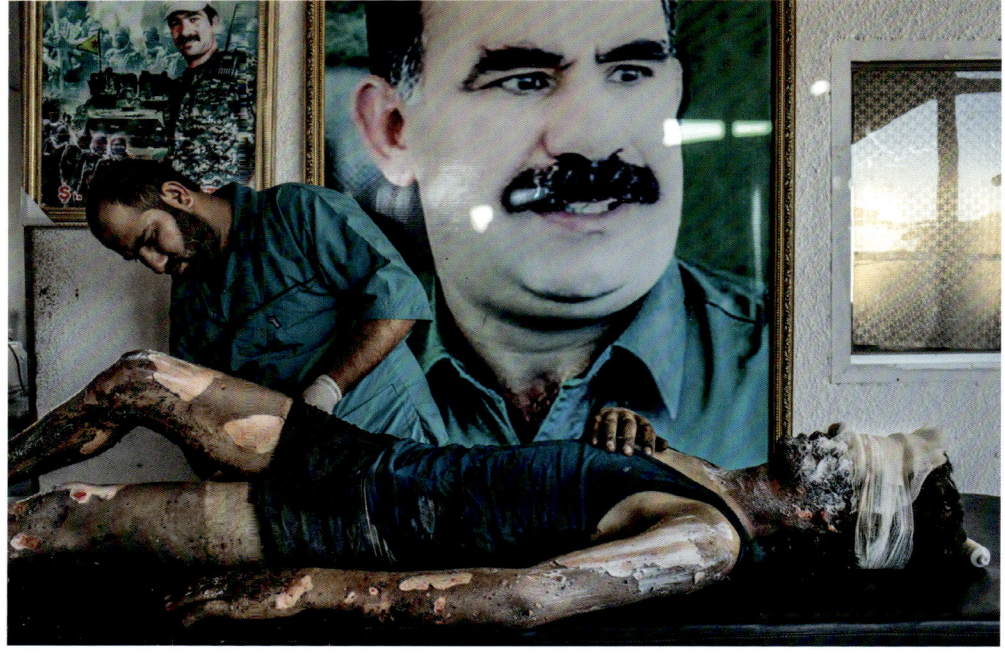

Previous page:
Charlie Kirk, *Okmeydani,
Istanbul, Berkin Elvan
protest,* 2013
Courtesy the artist

This page, top:
Bülent Kılıç, *A young
girl wounded with tear
gas after the funeral of
Berkin Elvan in Istanbul,*
March 12, 2014
© the artist/AFP/Getty
Images

This page, bottom:
Mauricio Lima, *A doctor
rubbing ointment on the
burns of a 16-year-old
Islamic State fighter
named Jacob in front of a
poster of Abdullah Öcalan,
the jailed leader of the
Kurdistan Workers' Party,
at a Y.P.G. hospital on
the outskirts of Hasaka,
Syria,* August 1, 2015
© and courtesy the artist

"The photography community here is used to attending the premiere every year at the end of August," Darendeliler said. "People were telephoning us to ask when the opening would be."

Akyüz and Darendeliler felt that the nonrenewal must have been political. In particular, they suspected the presence of a singular image by Mauricio Lima in the exhibition as possibly being the cause. Lima's photograph shows a doctor treating a sixteen-year-old ISIS militant at a hospital in northern Syria. A framed portrait of Abdullah Öcalan, the imprisoned leader of the Kurdish armed movement PKK, hangs in the background. (Turkish officials consider PKK—which routinely attacks Turkish security forces—and ISIS to be equally violent terrorist groups.) When Lima's photograph won the World Press Photo Contest's first prize in the general news category in February last year, Akyüz and Darendeliler received an email from the organization's Amsterdam office, inquiring whether the image would cause an issue. But World Press Photo, in response to my question about the exhibition, stated, "Our exhibition requires local partners for it to be organized in each location and local partners are not always available."

"We have never encountered censorship while editing our magazine," Akyüz said. "In 2007, we organized an exhibition in Bursa, with lots of nude images. The mayor, a member of the conservative ruling party, came to visit, looked at the images, and just walked by." In 2015, Bülent Kılıç's photograph of a young girl wounded during clashes in Istanbul received a World Press Photo Award and was exhibited without any problems.

Whether censorship or conservative caution was at play with the failure to present the exhibition in Istanbul, the atmosphere is more stark in eastern Turkey. Tuğba Tekerek told me of photographers who, when attempting to take pictures in war-ridden areas, were met with willful intimidation from military snipers. In one case, a photographer visibly shaken by the riot gear and machine guns was asked by a special operations police officer, "Why are you so scared of my machine gun? Your camera is more powerful than my gun, and much scarier."

of the Gezi uprising and the unrest in ethnically diverse Istanbul neighborhoods. He plans to publish his protest photographs in a book, but not in Turkey, where he fears censorship.

A few days after speaking with Kirk in September 2016, I paid a visit to the offices of Geniş Açı, a collective and formerly a prestigious photography magazine that ceased publication after producing fifty issues between 1997 and 2006. Refik Akyüz and Serdar Darendeliler, the duo who run the initiative, had sad news to share: the World Press Photo traveling exhibition, which they had been responsible for organizing at Forum Istanbul since 2009, usually opens every August, but there was no attempt by World Press Photo to renew the contract for an exhibition in 2016.

Kaya Genç, a novelist and
essayist based in Istanbul,
is the author of *Under
the Shadow: Rage and
Revolution in Modern
Turkey* (2016).

Art | Basel
Basel | June | 15–18 | 2017

UBS

Curriculum

A List of Favorite Anythings
by Moyra Davey and Jason Simon

Through her celebrated works in photography, video, and writing, Moyra Davey melds literary references—from Mary Wollstonecraft to Jean Genet—with personal histories. Her "mailer" project, made up of letters in the form of photographs, was exhibited at the 2012 Whitney Biennial. Her partner, Jason Simon, is a media and documentary artist. He took on the controversial 2002 shuttering of the Museum of Modern Art's Film Stills Archive, and presented both sides of the story in a multifaceted exhibition. Among the links between Davey and Simon is an expansive curiosity about photographs as material objects, evidence, and cultural history.

Boyd McDonald

Boyd McDonald (1925–1993), editor and publisher of the zine *Straight to Hell*, made the most eloquent sport of spotting social and sexual hypocrisy in films, watching black-and-white broadcast reruns via a rabbit-ear antenna in his SRO room for research. The result was *Cruising the Movies*, originally published in 1985. The prolific artist William E. Jones has recovered and rebuilt McDonald's story—contributing an introduction to the reprint of *Cruising* and a biography, *True Homosexual Experiences: Boyd McDonald and "Straight to Hell"* (2016)—as a waymark of lusting, watching, and the radically democratic force of smut.

Ydessa Hendeles

Ydessa Hendeles wears many hats: gallerist, collector, curator, writer, artist. *Partners* (2003–4), a monumental exhibition at the Haus der Kunst, Munich (the venue infamous for hosting Hitler's Degenerate Art show in 1937), consisted of works precisely staged to build an alternative history of the Holocaust. Hendeles's signature mark is showing traditional journalism and photography alongside cutting-edge contemporary art without making a distinction. *Partners*, now a book, contains Hendeles's renowned *Teddy Bear Project* and indelible images by photojournalists Malcolm Brown and Eddie Adams in dialogue with works by On Kawara, Hanne Darboven, and Maurizio Cattelan, to name a few. It is an erudite, multiform essay from the hand of an obsessive auteur.

Deana Lawson

The very "real" black bodies in Deana Lawson's photographs come with a strong element of theatricality. Posed in domestic settings or Edenic nature, Lawson's framings nonetheless evoke staged, enigmatic tableaux. Take *Cowboys* (2014), a cinematic night shot: two riders emerge from an inky sky; the horses exhibit the whites of their eyes; chaps, hat, and bandana are well worn. Lawson's statement about countering violent images of black men seen in today's media with celebrations of black rodeo riders makes us imagine the horse opera we're dying to see.

Billy Hough

Provincetown, Massachusetts, still feels like the artist colony it began as, thanks to a shrinking number of stalwarts, principally among them Billy Hough. His sessions at the piano, with ever present bassist Sue Goldberg and occasional guests, typically cover renditions of beloved albums or make studies of brilliant contrasts (one recent show mashed up Tom Waits and Eminem). His musical abilities alone would serve the scene, but Billy adds monologues that make every show feel like we've never understood a tune until he plays it.

Xavier Dolan

Xavier Dolan's films *I Killed My Mother* (2009) and *Mommy* (2014) both feature his star collaborator, Anne Dorval. They are heartbreaking and hilarious in equal measure. Dolan, a twenty-seven-year-old wunderkind, takes daring chances in his films. *Mommy*, the story of a mother's relationship with her delinquent, charismatic son, Steve, is shot in 1:1 aspect ratio, a square in the middle of the screen. The frame signals the ways Steve's world has boxed him in. Then, in moments of ecstasy, friendship, and bonding, the screen magically expands, a direct and totally unexpected use of a frame like we have never seen.

Hervé Guibert

Ghost Image (1996), Hervé Guibert's collection of short, idiosyncratic texts on photography, is particularly memorable for its essays on "lost" photographs—instances where the film did not advance or Guibert did not have his camera on hand. Guibert (1955–1991) was a prolific writer of criticism, novels, and diaries—*The Mausoleum of Lovers: Journals 1976–1991* (2014), for example—and a brilliant photographer: our favorites are of his desktop or couch, strewn with implements and evidence of writing, as though finding those same lost photographs in another state.

Janet Malcolm

The more photography rushes in to fill the gaps of an inflated art market, the more the air feels sucked out of its discourse. We consume Janet Malcolm's magazine articles with such greed and pleasure that we wonder at the missing critical currency of her writing on "the enigma of photography." Her essays from the 1970s, when she was a photography critic for *The New Yorker*, are full of air, and light, and jeweled insights. We return to her 1980 collection, *Diana and Nikon: Essays on the Aesthetic of Photography*, over and over, a reminder that the bond between photography and writing, more than combined powers of observation, is an essential imaginary.

Dayanita Singh and Aveek Sen

Dayanita Singh's books contain precisely chosen and sequenced photographs and are often accompanied by writer Aveek Sen's texts. Singh, who photographs mostly in black and white, has an incredible eye for light, texture, and framing, and an enviable ability to get in close on her human subjects. Recently, she has adopted the novel practice of exhibiting the books themselves, framed, or not, or inserted into freestanding sculptural units. Sen's writing is not "critical," but consists of highly imaginative texts that exist alongside Singh's work, sometimes intersecting, sometimes not. Singh and Sen together form a hugely seductive combination.

Billy Monk

Photography's lost practitioners regularly emerge through images recovered in flea markets, auctions, and abandoned storage. Billy Monk, a bouncer and photographer at the notorious Cape Town nightclub the Catacombs in the late 1960s, was one such discovery. In 1979, the photographer Jac de Villiers discovered Monk's negatives and contact sheets and immediately recognized their value. Three years later, Monk was murdered on his way to the first exhibition of his photographs, adding dramatic closure to a bizarre career. We live with a handful of Monk's astonishing images of barroom abandon: apartheid portraiture in its heyday, wasted working-class whites on benders, a decade before the liberation struggle in South Africa came knocking in force.

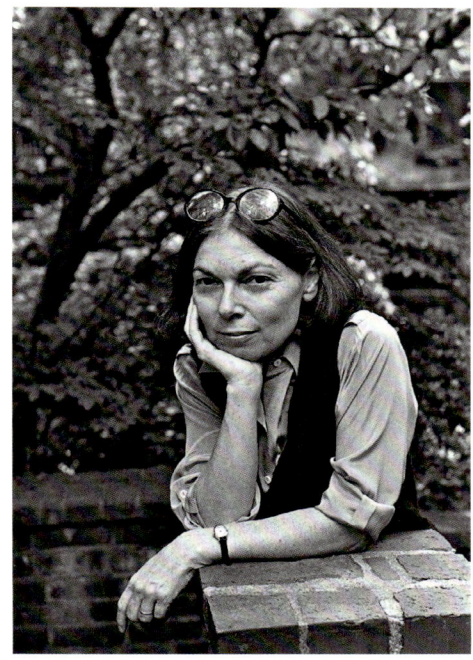
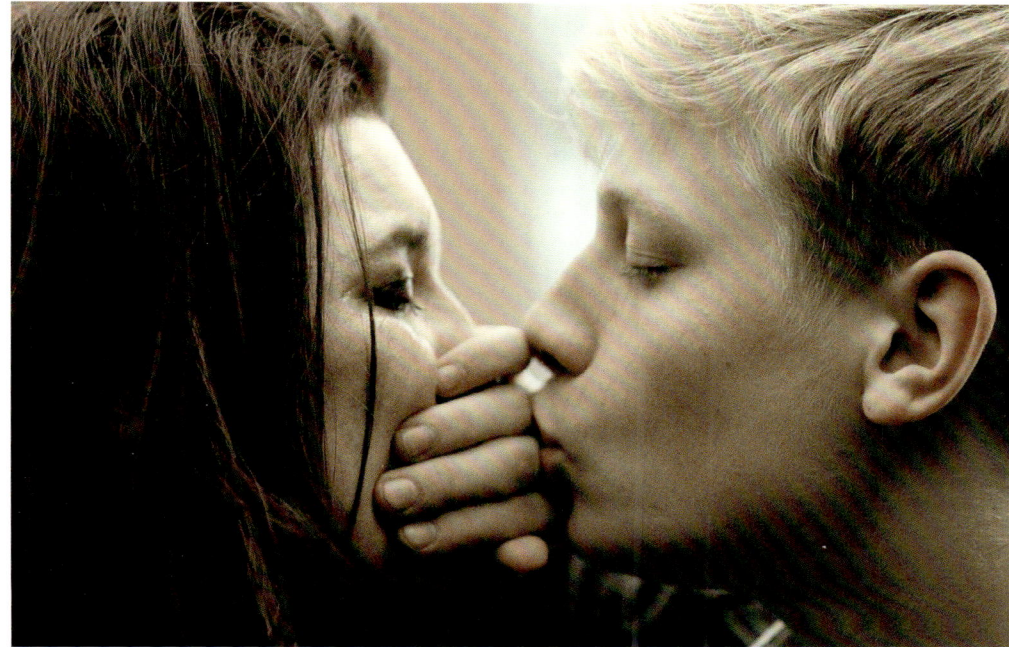
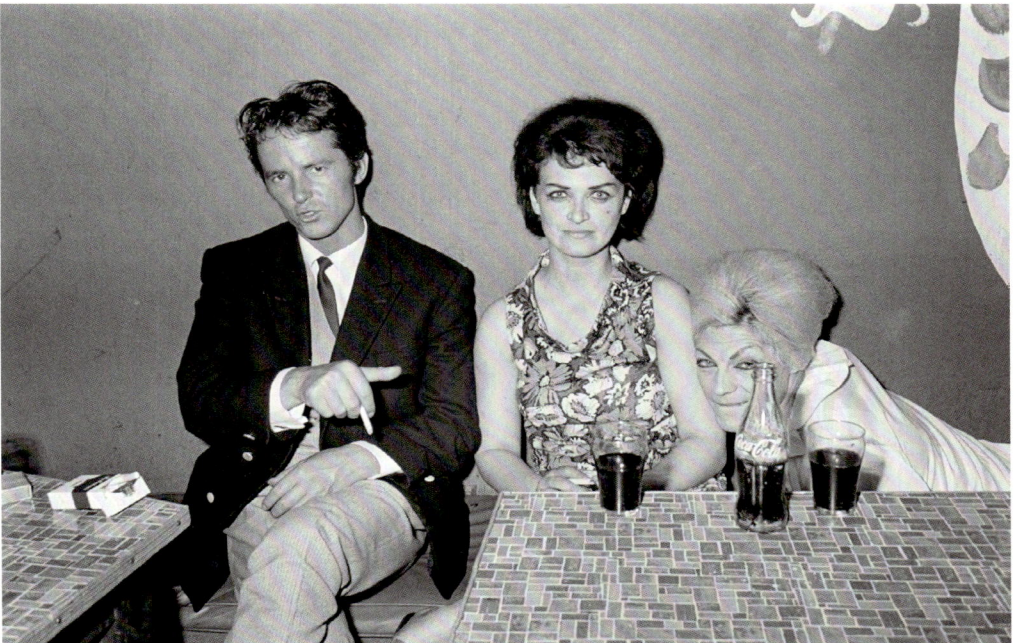
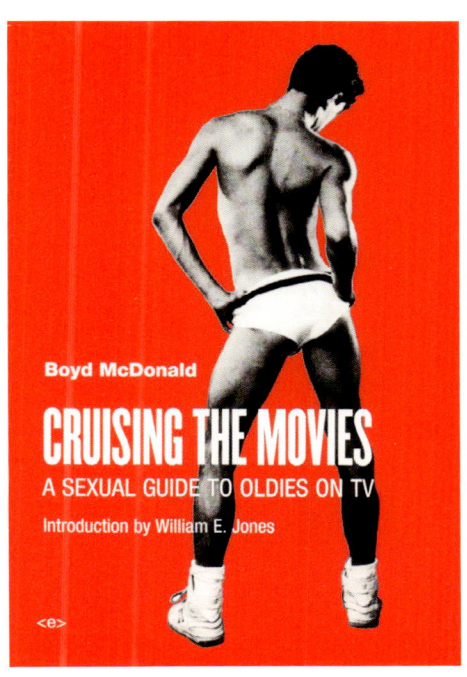
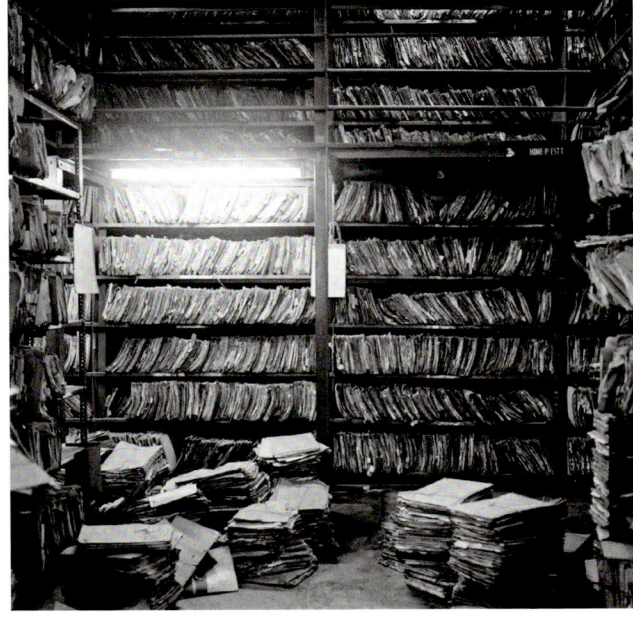
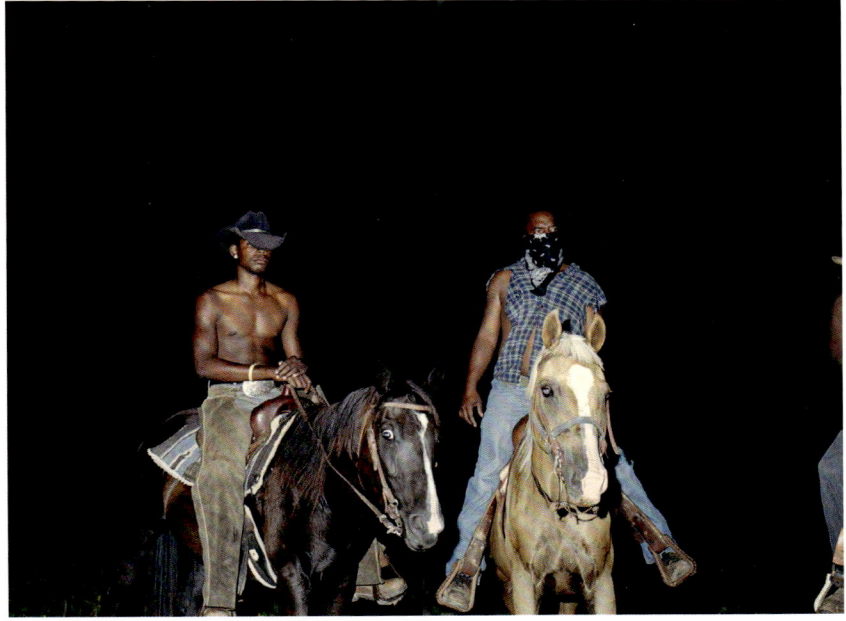

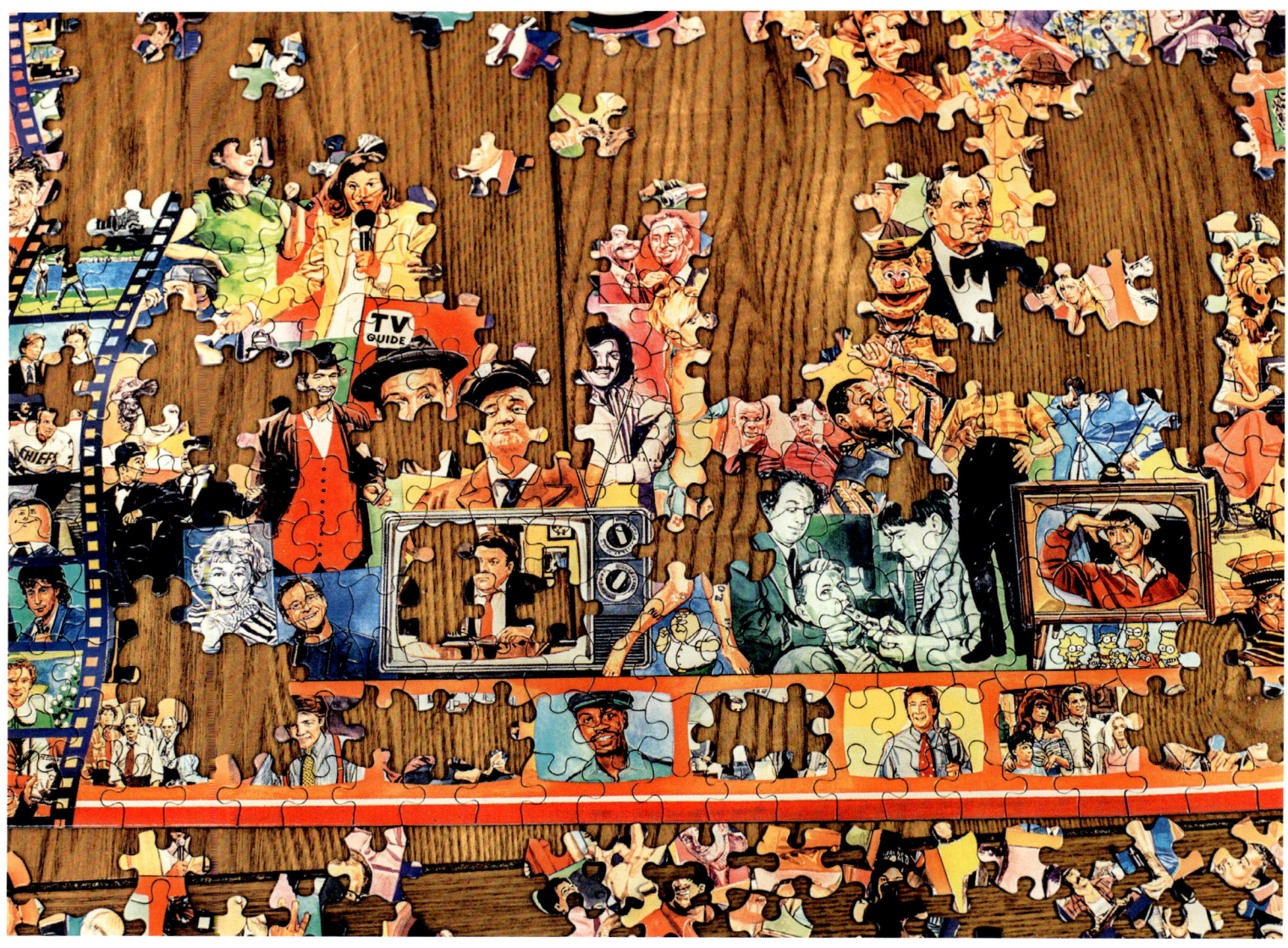

American Destiny

"In this contentious moment in history, the stories we tell are a social responsibility," novelist Sandra Cisneros writes in these pages, reflecting on Kathya Maria Landeros's images of Latino communities in the American West. From agricultural workers to those toiling on the factory floor, from regional cities weathering years of postindustrial decline to refugee populations assimilating into the heartland, the projects in this issue are bound by an urge to explore the social and political landscape of the United States.

The stories here take many forms. Some fuse art with urgent social conviction. Chauncey Hare, a former Standard Oil engineer and impassioned activist, crisscrossed the country in the 1970s to create an enduring record of American workers at home, before abandoning photography to become a therapist and advocate against abuse in the workplace. To tell the story of his father's unemployment from a major military contractor, Allan Sekula sought to reinvent documentary language and asked audiences to consider the state of the postwar American promise. A former president of a teachers' union, Fred Lonidier has taken his trenchant photo-based art into the union hall, far from the museum's rarefied white-cube spaces. Workers' health and safety, the freedom to protest, and the impact of NAFTA are topics that animate his rigorous output.

This issue maps geographies of economic promises unfulfilled, of wealth and opportunities that never trickled over to the other side of town. Mark Neville turns his lens on Pittsburgh to reveal how two Americas, divided by class and race, coexist in a region once dominated by the steel industry. Further north in the Rust Belt, Gregory Halpern captures the city of Buffalo in muted poetry. His hometown has seen its population and fortunes dwindle in recent decades, but life moves on despite an enduring frost. In New Haven, Connecticut, Jim Goldberg and Donovan Wylie trace highway infrastructure, individual stories, and the effects wrought by the loss of the city's manufacturing base.

From these eastern vantages, the West beckons. Halfway to there, Alessandra Sanguinetti meditates on the small agricultural community of Black River Falls, Wisconsin, providing quotidian glimpses of life in a town that helped deliver the traditionally Democratic state to Donald Trump. Katy Grannan deploys California's most famous feature—abundant sunlight—to illuminate communities that inhabit liminal zones and are all but invisible.

Grannan, like the other photographers in this issue, is highly aware of the problems that come with photographing social injustices, of the potential for exploitation, for reducing people to easy symbols. Like Walker Evans, who famously documented the lives of Alabama sharecroppers during the Great Depression, she refuses to romanticize. James Agee, collaborating with Evans on *Let Us Now Praise Famous Men*, wrote, "Understanding, and action proceeding from understanding and guided by it, is the one weapon against the world's bombardment, the one medicine, the one instrument by which liberty, health, and joy may be shaped or shaped towards, in the individual, and in the race."

Action and understanding are on our minds. As the pundits continue to prognosticate on an uncertain future—weighing how the interrelated factors of class, sexism, education, shifting demographics, racism, stagnant wages, and a failure to empathize with others have created our current political condition—how does the photographer navigate this new global order? The need for artists to offer persuasive, alternative visions is more urgent than ever.

As photographer LaToya Ruby Frazier and art historian Kellie Jones make clear in their wide-ranging conversation about the legacy of civil-rights-era photojournalism, photographers must bear witness to our times. Advocate for the vulnerable, the underrepresented, and the less powerful. Make contemporary racism visible. Counter pernicious narratives that are often borne and buttressed by images. Create work that informs our consciences.

Moving forward, *Aperture* will continue to encourage debates around pictures and social responsibility. To do so, as a not-for-profit publisher and independent voice, we need your help—as readers, as subscribers, as contributors. We sincerely value your support and engagement. —**The Editors**

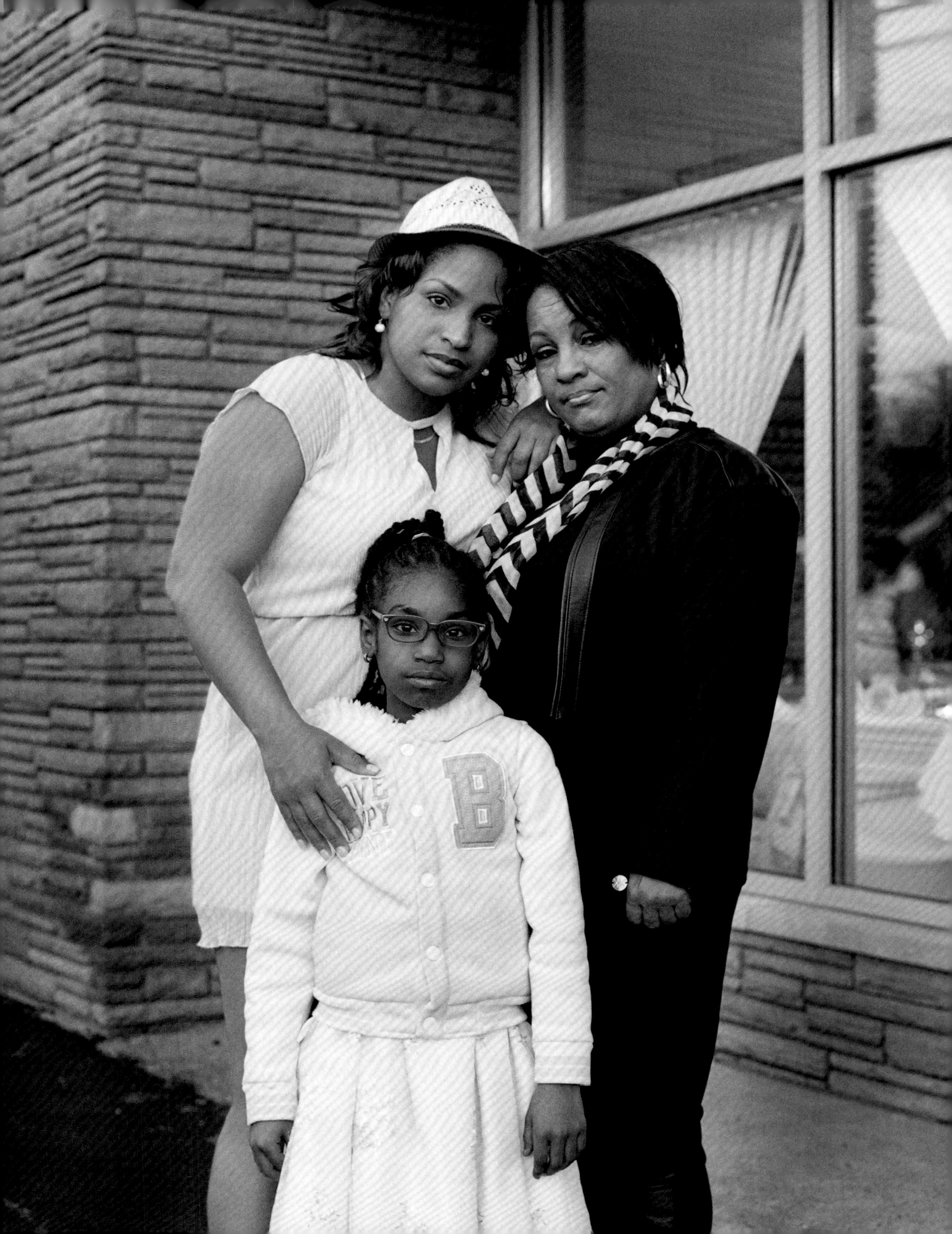

LaToya Ruby Frazier

Witness

The unfinished work of the civil rights movement
A Conversation with Kellie Jones

Shea Cobb with her
daughter, Zion, and
her mother, Ms. Renée,
outside the Social Network
banquet hall, 2016, from
the series *Flint is Family*

Kellie Jones: **Let's start with your book, *The Notion of Family* (2014). Did the popularity of *The Notion of Family* surprise you, especially given the subject matter? Members of your family have been supportive and willing subjects. Sometimes in such exposés we might feel victimhood. How have you crafted your approach differently?**

LaToya Ruby Frazier: Initially, when I started *The Notion of Family*, I knew that I needed to make something on behalf of my relationships with my mother and my grandmother, and something that was for me.

Growing up in the 1980s in the Rust Belt in Braddock, Pennsylvania—a time when cities are shrinking, all the factories have been outsourced, all your social services have been cut, the schools are closed, the library is barely functioning—I was already dealing with an invisibility complex. And I didn't really understand why we were next to this factory, caught in the shadow not only of the Edgar Thomson steel plant, but also caught in the shadow of Andrew Carnegie. What does that mean to have to measure yourself, or try to be seen, through an industrial capitalist?

Even though I was a teenager and I didn't have the language to articulate what I was seeing, I knew that I was dealing with shadows and invisibility, and dealing with toxicity and pollution, and then dealing with three generations—or really four, but I didn't meet my grandmother's mother—of women who grew up in three different social and economic periods. For my grandmother growing up in Braddock in the 1930s it was very different, because it was a bustling melting pot. None of us are fully black, but we've led our lives as black women. Then my mother growing up during the 1960s period of segregation, and then myself growing up there in the 1980s during the "war on drugs" and the abandonment.

The Notion of Family is the book of speaking to my younger self as an adult now, understanding what I know now, but also the coming-of-age story of what it means to grow up in a postindustrial, post-Fordist society, and the post-Reagan era. And what does it mean to be a black woman, inserting yourself, talking about the politics, talking about the toxicity, talking about industrial capitalism?

KJ: **How was it collaborating with your family?**

LRF: It's a precarious situation. Grandma didn't like to be photographed. She always said, "Go photograph yourself." That's what caused me to start doing self-portraits. My mother, as soon as I came in with the camera, instantly had ideas. But a lot of it revolved around surgery or operations, or having cancer removed from her breast, or just coming out of the hospital, and the same thing for my grandmother, except I didn't realize that she was dying from pancreatic cancer, because she never said anything. And I'm trying to figure out who I am between these two women, but at the same time our bodies are deteriorating in the landscape, because the three of us all have terminal illnesses.

KJ: **Has your practice always combined issues of environmentalism and race?**

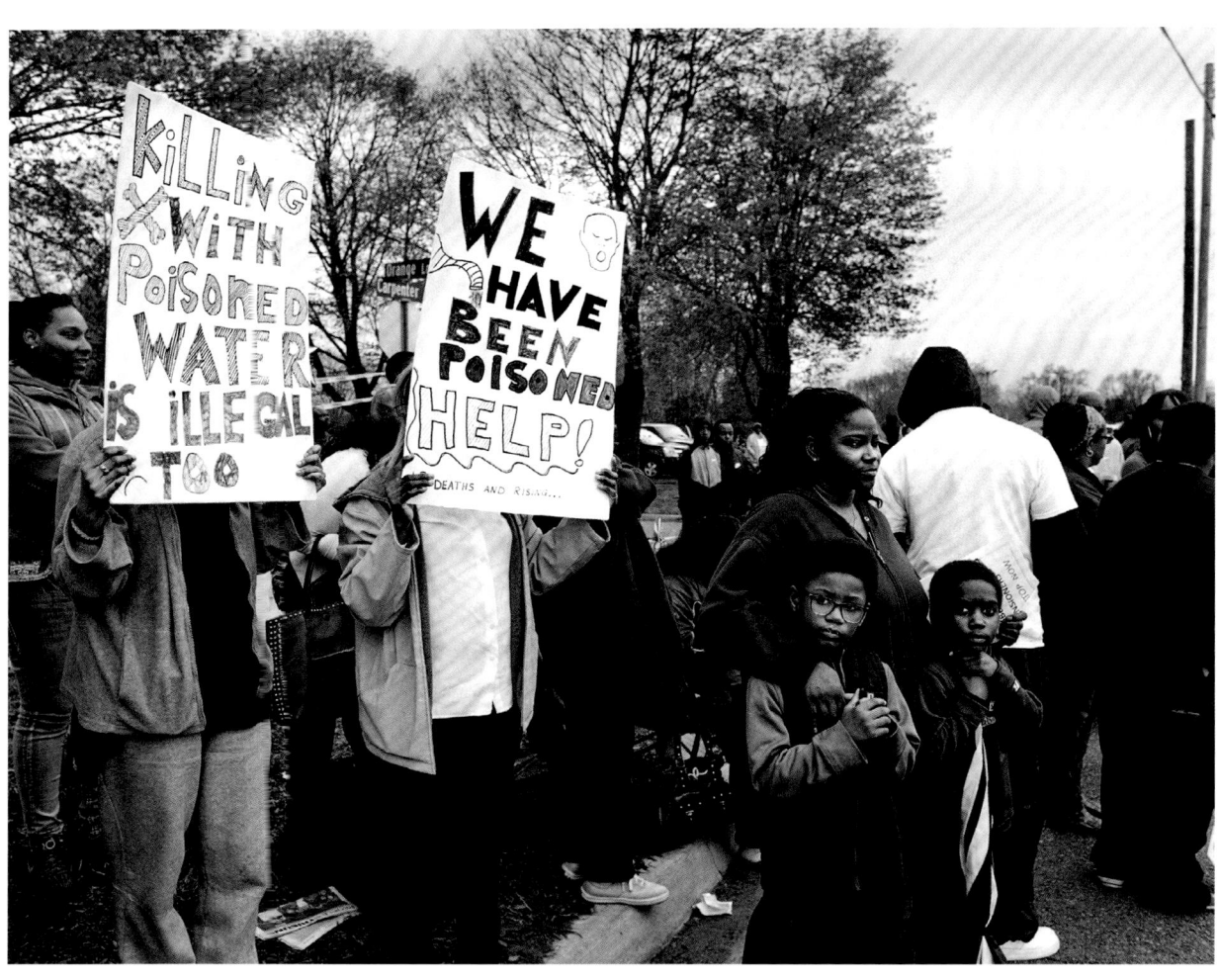

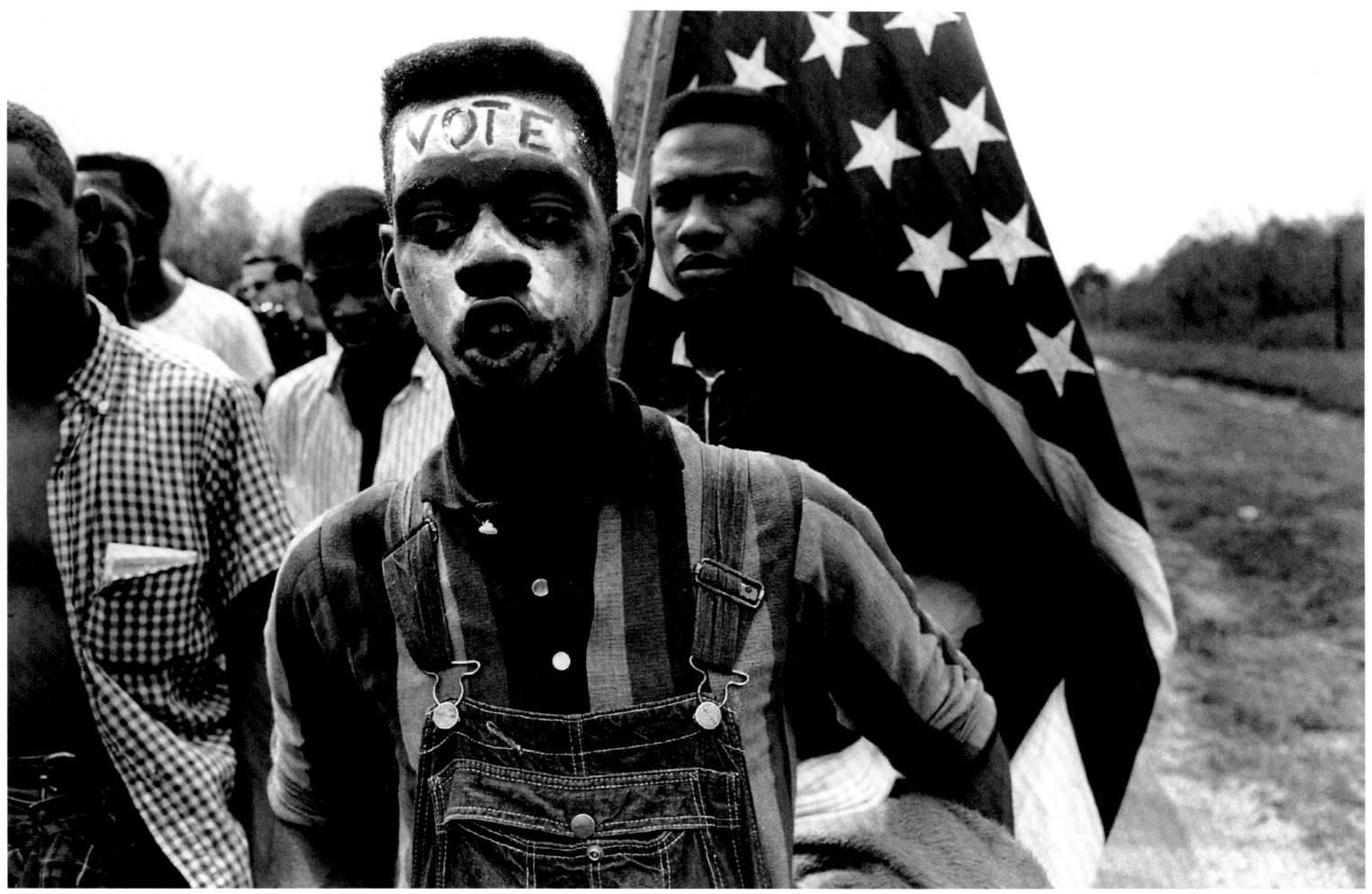

LRF: When you're a teenager making portraits, you don't realize that. You're just taking the class, trying to get the composition and the formal language. But it became very clear to me the day I went into the Carnegie Library. I pulled out this book, *Braddock, Allegheny County*. I took it back to my studio, and I'm turning through the pages. I knew the editor. I knew everyone who contributed to it. I knew everyone who wrote for it. And I got to the end and there wasn't a single African American in this book. And it was published in 2008 and I just couldn't understand how that was possible. So here I was innocently, quietly making these portraits of my mother and grandmother, and then it all changed when I saw the book. And it hit me: Okay, this has a bigger significance. This is not about you. You're in it, but really you're talking about how to rectify the fact that a large population of people has been omitted and erased from history, and continually silenced. So I felt intimidated by it, but I also was so outraged by it. I had a bigger mission.

And that's when *The Notion of Family* started to come into my mind, thinking about *The Family of Man* and what that show meant to American history, and the timing of the show in 1955, and thinking about Emmett Till being killed months later and the power of that photograph, and how images do spark memory, history. Activism starts to take place because images become available of something that wasn't visible.

KJ: **Can you talk about the impact of the MacArthur grant and how that changed your relationship to Braddock and Pittsburgh?**

LRF: Prior to the MacArthur I was seen as an angry, disgruntled little black girl who doesn't know what she is talking about, and doesn't have the right to talk about civic duty, and isn't allowed to point out how Braddock is being gentrified, and isn't allowed to

> I'm talking about being working class. I'm talking about being poor. I'm talking about being blue-collar. Our own presidents don't say "poor" or "poverty."

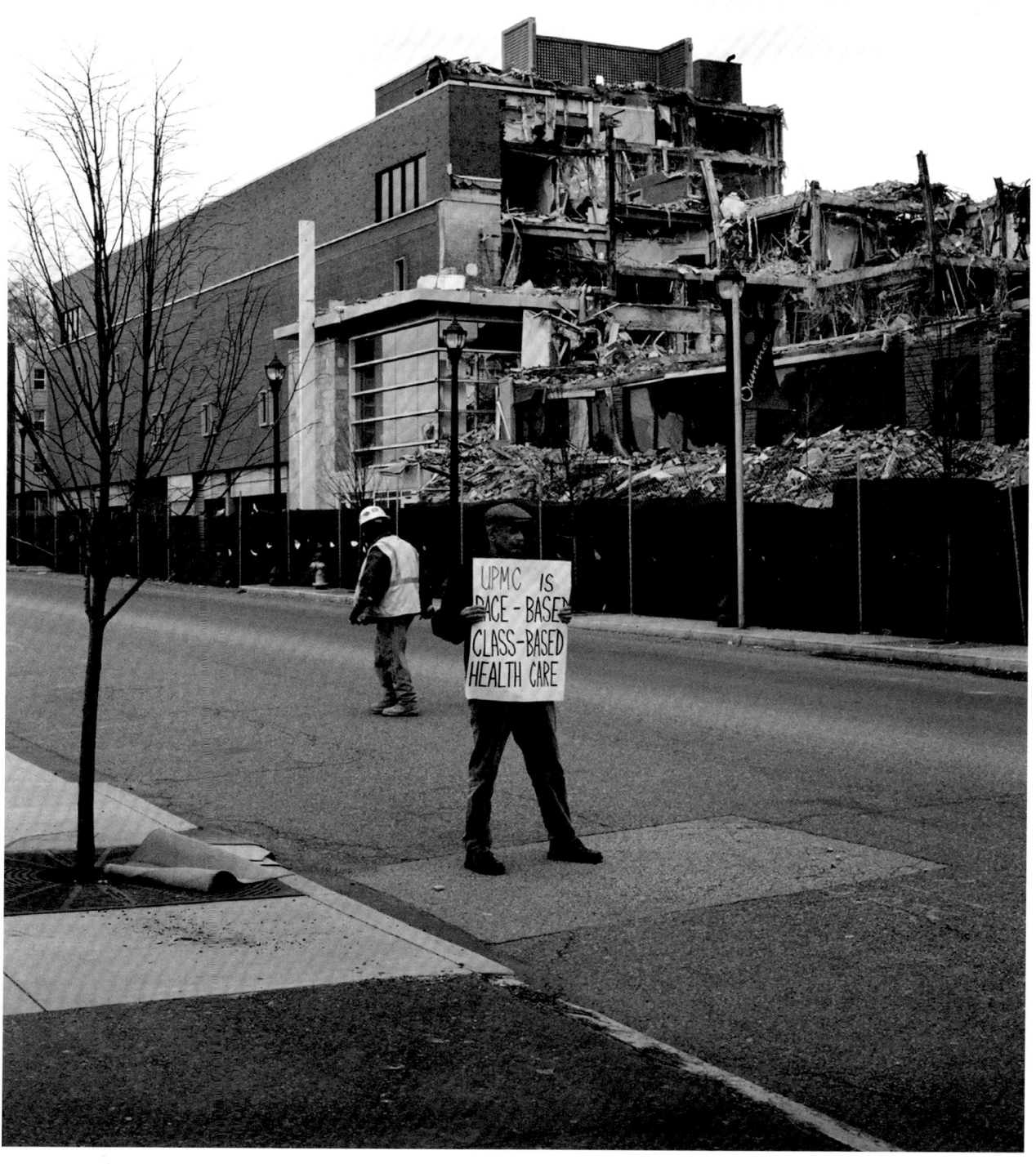

point out the rebranding of it, and how it's becoming homogenized and not including the people of color, and the working class, and the elderly, who have always occupied this community. I kept being reduced and dehumanized and silenced. It wasn't until I got the phone call that day and it became public, that all of a sudden Pittsburgh was proud. I was seeing my name in the paper. I had just moved to Chicago, but they were claiming it, and then so was Chicago. I was having to do interviews in both places. One time they said, "Well, is there anything left you would want to say, LaToya?" And I was like, "Yeah, I hope I make Pittsburgh proud." [*Laughter*]

August Wilson was on my mind when I received the MacArthur. And when I think about it, even though I'm using photography

and performance and video, it is speaking exactly to what he was doing, which was telling and narrating the daily stories and lives of working-class black people that are constantly overlooked. I really believe that if you can talk about the history of this country and the steel industry through Andrew Carnegie and all these other Scotsmen, then you can talk about America and its history through black women, through black men, and through black children.

I'm talking about being working class. I'm talking about being poor. I'm talking about being blue-collar. Our own presidents don't say "poor" or "poverty." They say "middle class," and I'm very agitated about that.

KJ: **You're certainly bringing that into view for a lot of people. I've taught your work in a course on Gordon Parks. I've seen you, along with Hank Willis Thomas and Mickalene Thomas, as heirs not only to his photography practice, but also to his sense of interdisciplinarity, as well as social justice. How does your interest in photography and video differ from his?**

LRF: Parks's *American Gothic* (1942) was one of the first images that I saw by him, in my photography class in undergrad, and it shook me up. To see Ella Watson standing there mimicking Grant Wood's *American Gothic* (1930)—I realized that this is a photographer in conversation with a painting, and a painter. Then I also noticed: Here is this woman, working in a government building in Washington, D.C., and nobody sees her, and she's the janitor who's cleaning and sweeping every night. But Gordon saw her, and it was the first time I realized that I can speak through a photograph. It's not about taking the picture. It's about making the image because you have something to say. She was only making what is equivalent now to $15,000 a year, and she had her children.

KJ: **And grandchildren.**

LRF: And that's how she was supposed to survive? So that image really pushed me to start to become more accountable and more responsible to what I wanted to say. But importantly, I learned about Gordon Parks from a homeless woman. I was photographing in a homeless shelter and when I handed this woman her portrait she said, "This reminds me of a photographer I saw on TV on PBS. Do you know Gordon Parks?" And I didn't, but as soon as I left I went and bought all of the books I could get my hands on. It was because of my encounter with all of his works and reading *A Choice*

I'm in pursuit of what Gordon Parks achieved. I'm trying to add to that legacy, but add to it as a young woman.

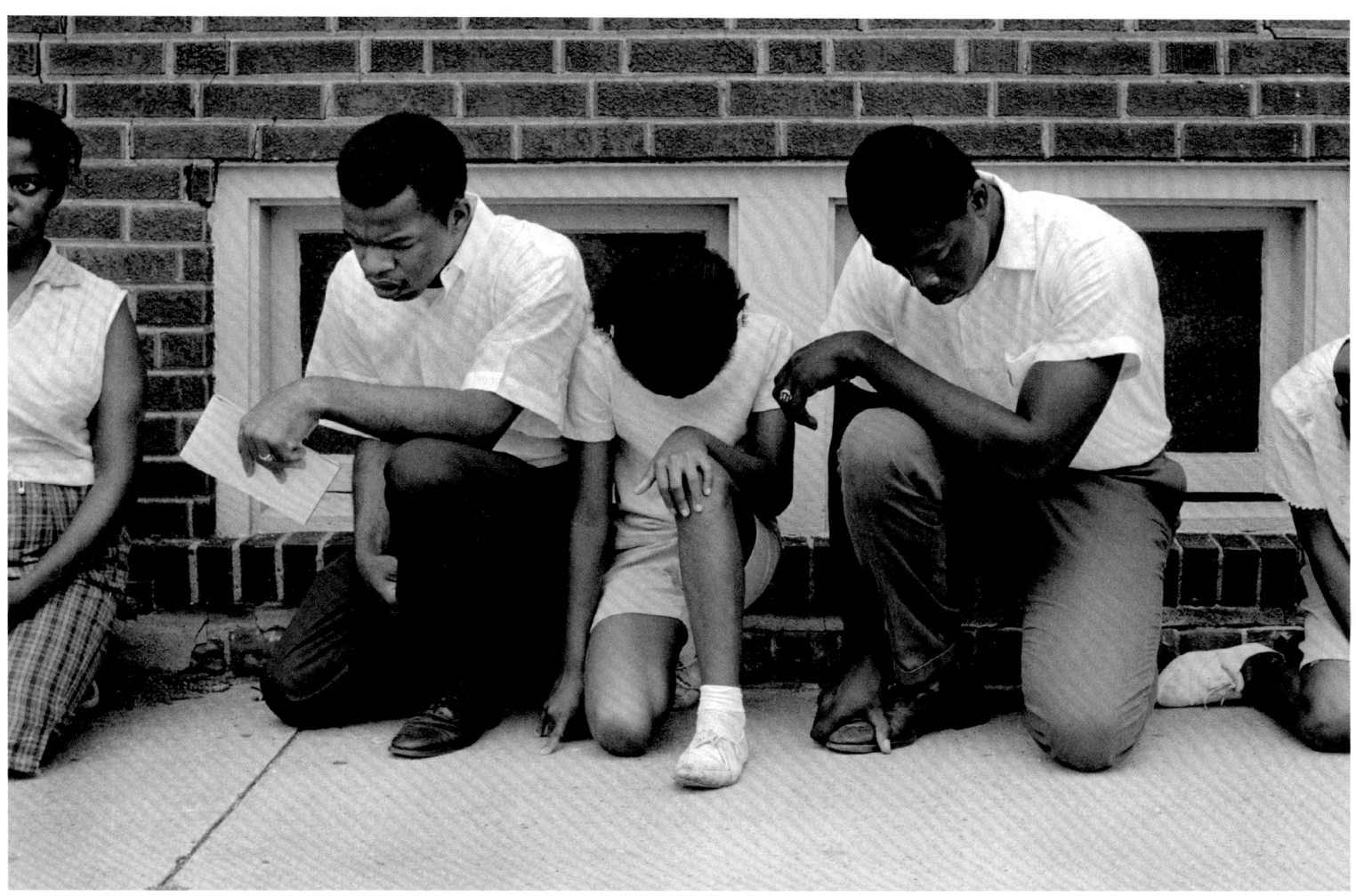

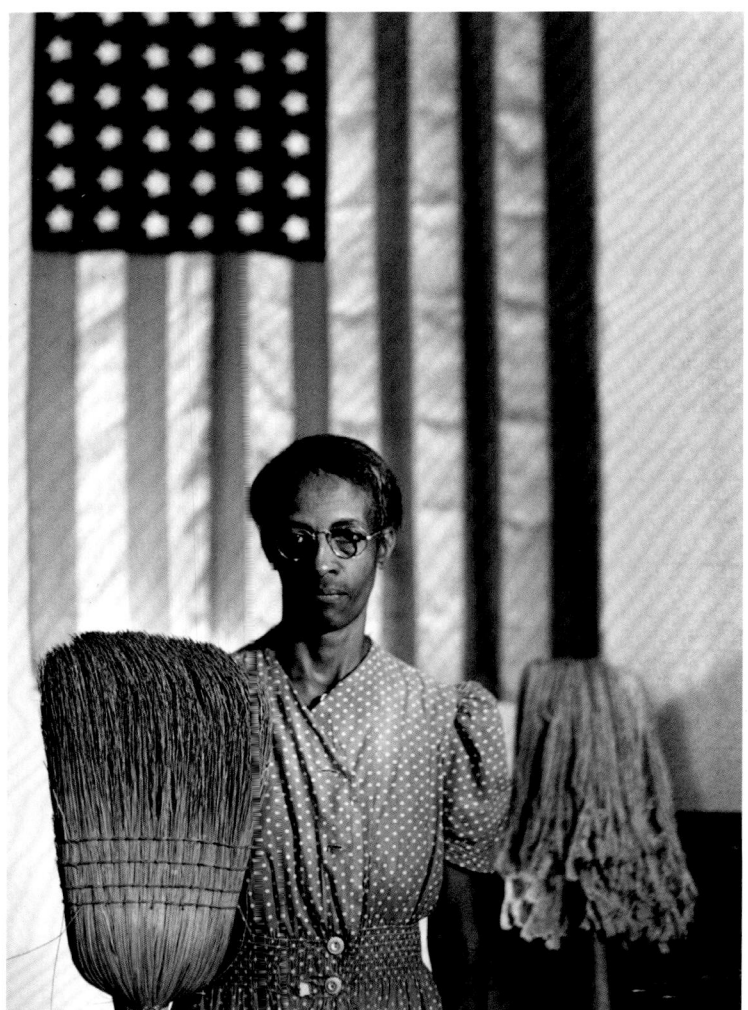

of Weapons (1966) that I changed. I'm in pursuit of what Gordon Parks achieved. I'm trying to add to that legacy, but add to it as a young woman and a young practitioner giving voice and collaborating with more women, more populations, but also seeing them as equals.

I want to ask you about *Witness: Art and Civil Rights in the Sixties*, the exhibition you curated at the Brooklyn Museum in 2014. When I came to *Witness* and saw the Bruce Davidson, the Gordon Parks, the Charles White, it all really started connecting for me in terms of what I was doing. I realized, Okay, LaToya, you are doing social activist work. I always had this feeling like it just wasn't enough. And then I saw the exhibition and I realized I was part of a long tradition and a long conversation, and it brought me so much more insight and confidence. Could you talk about the timing of the show and bringing this period, the 1960s, forward through the museum?

KJ: **Witness celebrates the fiftieth anniversary of the Civil Rights Act, which was about guaranteeing civil rights for all in this country, regardless of race, creed, or color. So we started with that 1964 date.**

What was exciting to me was to see so many interesting things that happened in that year artistically. It was Romare Bearden's breakout moment. He's been painting for years. He's in his fifties. People decide they love his collages. He's also using photographic material in these works.

One of the major things when we think about photography is that most people know the civil rights movement through it, through the photography of Danny Lyon, of Gordon Parks, and through television, but they didn't know about it through painting and sculpture.

LRF: I was definitely enlightened, and wish I got to study with you. When I was speaking earlier about being held accountable and responsible, not only was I challenging the narrative from my hometown and the narrative that we were all presuming to understand about how the Rust Belt is being developed, or the difference between working-class and creative-class theory, and our complacency as people from the creative sector and industry within that. I was also making it a point to bring people from my community into the institution.

So you have *Witness*, and *Now Dig This! Art and Black Los Angeles, 1960–1980* (2011), which you curated for the Hammer Museum in Los Angeles, happening right in the midst of this other burst as Obama's leaving, and you've got Black Lives Matter, and you've got "riots" coming out because of people resisting police brutality, understanding that the boys in blue could be a gang like the Bloods and Crips. All this realization happening in the American psyche. And the fact that everyone is having this meltdown, even considering Trump and Clinton. We're just so disillusioned and unhappy, and also desensitized at the same time about the history, the murderous onslaughts that we've done in this nation. Am I one of those artists contributing and being a witness to my time?

KJ: **You're definitely a witness to your time. You're telling us about Braddock. Many of us didn't know about it. And, like you said, it's representative of places all over the country, and really all over the world.**

LRF: I want to close on the Flint work. I had been tracking the Flint story, and then Mattie Kahn, who profiled me for *Elle* after the MacArthur, reached out and said she wanted me to cover the story. I initially said, "No way. This is *Elle*. It's fashion. Why in the hell

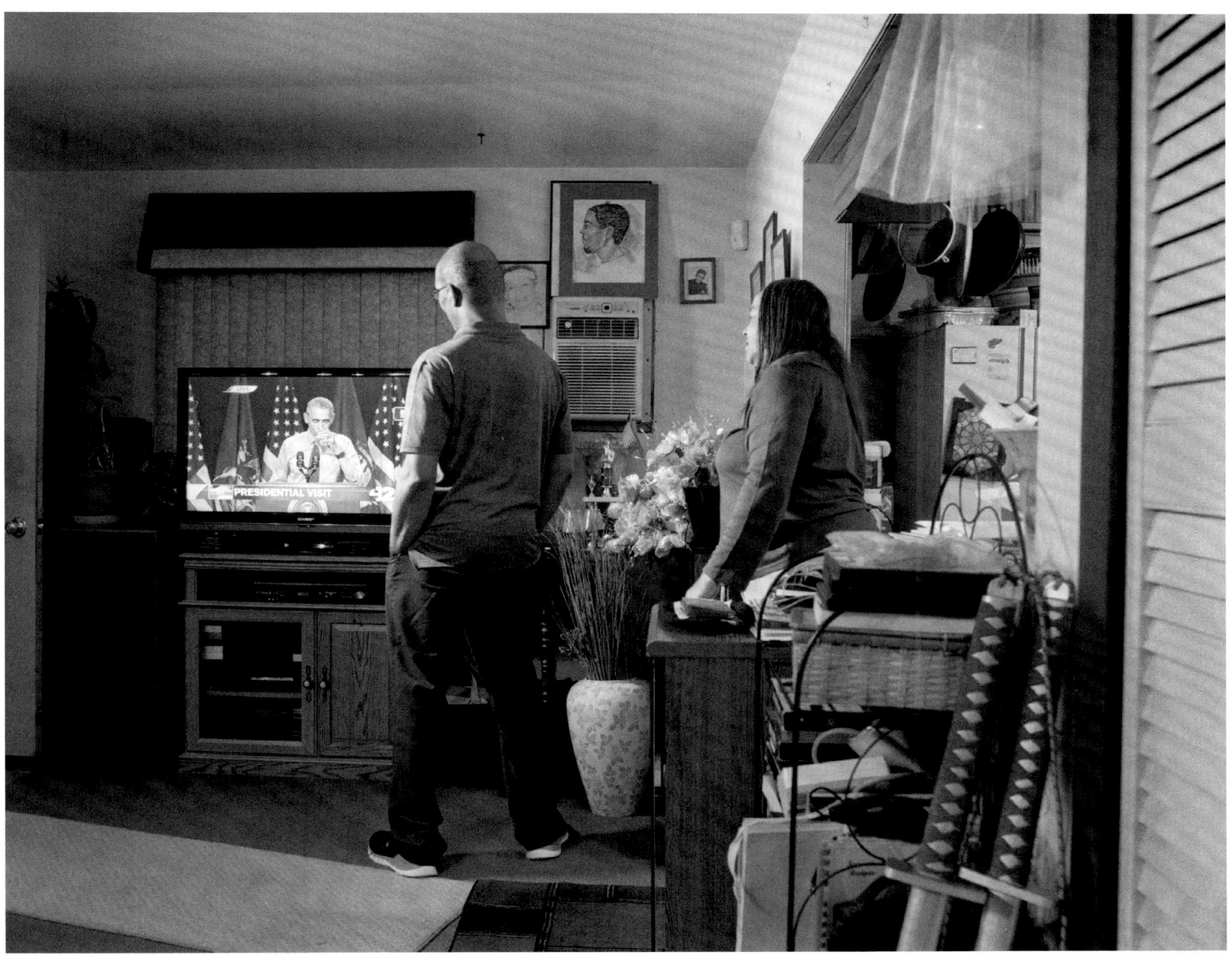

would I, of all people, want to deal with you?" Then I started thinking about Gordon Parks. Well, he was with *Life*; he was with *Vanity Fair* and *Vogue*. This is the next step, right? You want to impact mainstream culture, the masses. You want to get these things in front of them. So I decided to go.

And the fact that this is contaminated water: Water is a human right. Water is life. And the fact that no one's even looking anymore. Clinton is not there. Bernie Sanders is not there. No more free concerts to raise money. As I was packing up to leave, a kid grabbed this poster of Governor Snyder and brought it over to me. He wanted me to see something. He had something to say. He wanted me to document it, and I thought about *Witness*. I thought about all those photographs, because when I looked at him, I could see that language of the civil rights era, and I couldn't help but shoot it. Everything from that exhibition came forward and I thought, You have to shoot this. So I grabbed my camera back out and I shot it. I'm thinking about the fact that Gordon was also mindful. Just because people were living in what looks like squalor, which is really the landlord's fault, they were still educating themselves. They were reading; they were studying; and he was making photographs of people reading their books and studying, in addition to going through the whole system that keeps you trapped. Then there's the image of Obama drinking the Flint River water. I was dying to get that photograph. I kept asking, "Where is someone I can photograph watching him drinking the water?" I knew I needed it to be this historic image.

Denise and Rodney Clay, Shea's aunt and uncle, watch President Obama take a sip of Flint water on television, 2016, from the series Flint is Family

All photographs by LaToya Ruby Frazier courtesy the artist; Gavin Brown s Enterprise, New York/Rome; and Michel Rein, Paris/Brussels

This conversation is adapted from a public talk between LaToya Ruby Frazier and Kellie Jones at the Strand Book Store, New York, in October 2016.

Kellie Jones is Associate Professor in Art History and Archaeology and the Institute for Research in African American Studies at Columbia University and the author, most recently, of *South of Pico: African American Artists in Los Angeles in the 1960s and 1970s* (2017).

BUFFALO
Gregory Halpern

Brian Sholis

"I've never been able to make a successful picture of Manhattan," photographer Gregory Halpern says. "It feels like every inch of that island has been claimed." By contrast, Buffalo, New York, where Halpern has photographed often since 2003, has less than half its peak population. "There's an emptiness in the landscape that was compelling and intriguing."

He knows whereof he speaks: Halpern was raised in the city. After the completion of the Erie Canal in 1825, Buffalo grew rapidly as it helped connect the East with an expanding American West. By century's end it was one of America's ten largest cities, and played host to the Pan-American Exposition in 1901. (A major celebration of progress and industry in the Americas, the event is remembered today as the site of President McKinley's assassination.) The city's grain and steel industries kept Buffalo's economy afloat through much of the twentieth century. But its recent history mirrors that of other American Rust Belt cities and is marked by deindustrialization, suburbanization, and population shifts to the American South and West. The opening of the Saint Lawrence Seaway in 1959, which took shipping elsewhere, caused further difficulties.

Halpern grew up in the city confronting these developments. As a child in the 1980s, he explored Buffalo's abandoned buildings and vacant lots with his brother. They delighted in the imaginative possibilities of its rich history and unclaimed spaces. Halpern concedes this aspect of Buffalo may have helped him learn, as a young photographer, to leave room for interpretation. His photographs of the city create atmospheres rather than arguments. Overcast skies are prevalent and even interior scenes feature pallid light. There is little action, and often a sense of isolation: a solitary red bowling ball rolls down a lane; a solitary man pauses during a meal at a cheap café; a solitary building rises in the middle distance, beyond snowdrifts.

These are not showy pictures. Halpern frequently places his subjects at dead center. Nearly as often, his photographs also feature arresting, seemingly unrelated details that add surprising depth. A beaten-down passenger van, its door ajar and its interior piled high with beer cans, might be a story of lower-class despair. But the single balloon tied to the van's side-view mirror makes literal a contrasting sense of buoyancy.

Buffalo's economic slump defines the city in the popular imagination. That understanding is rooted in fact: Buffalo is one of the poorest large cities in America. And you can find that story in Halpern's photographs, which feature unkempt places and people with ragged edges. In March 1964, Walker Evans, another photographer who captured American poverty, delivered a lecture at Yale University titled "Lyric Documentary." In this talk Evans spoke at length about his collection of early twentieth-century postcards depicting cities like Buffalo in their era of rude health. He understood that from small moments comes profound understanding. "Those honest, direct little pictures have a quality today that is more than that of mere social history." So, too, Halpern recognizes through these pictures that, amid Buffalo's difficulties, "babies are born there. People fall in love there. Certain people would say the city is dying, but it's also continually being born."

Brian Sholis is executive director of Gallery TPW, Toronto.

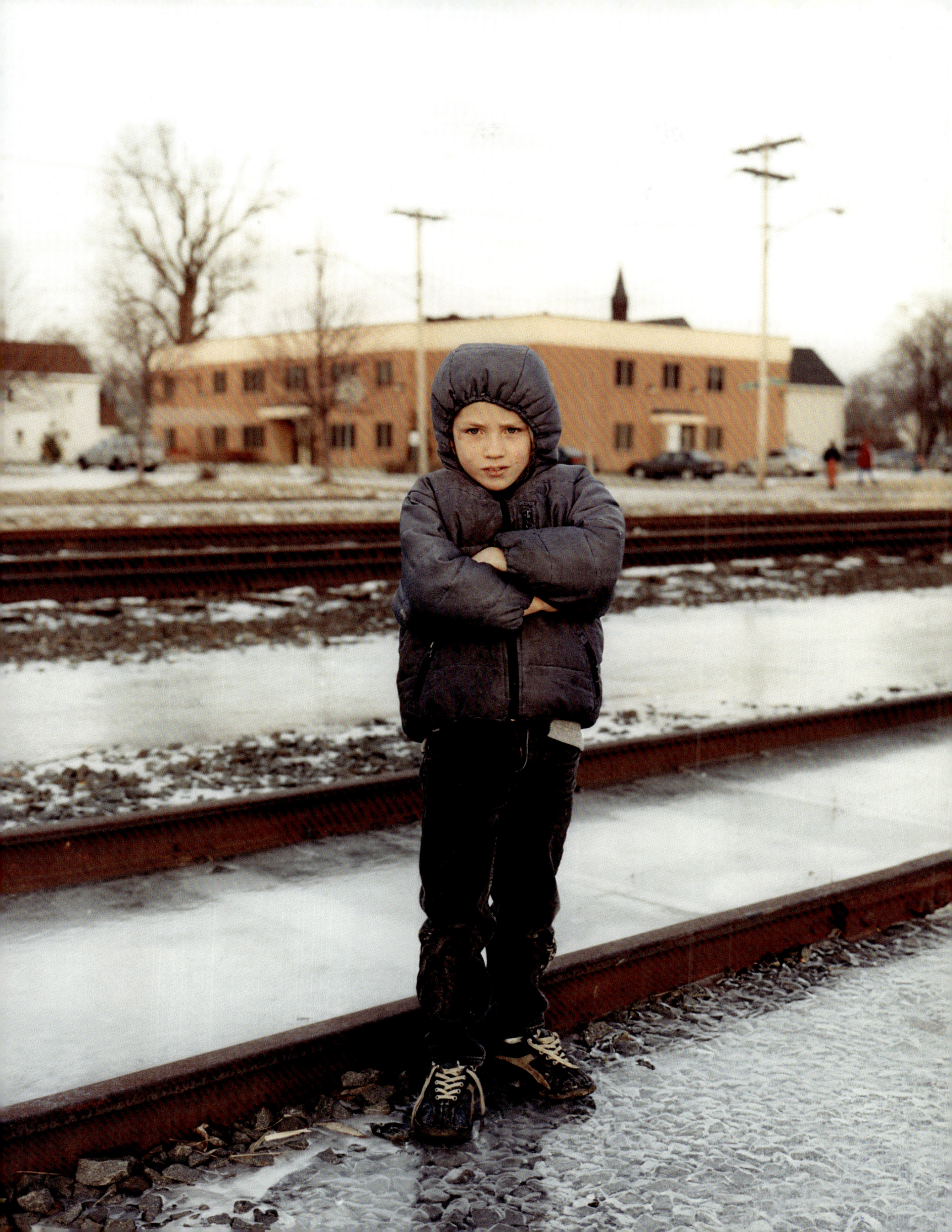

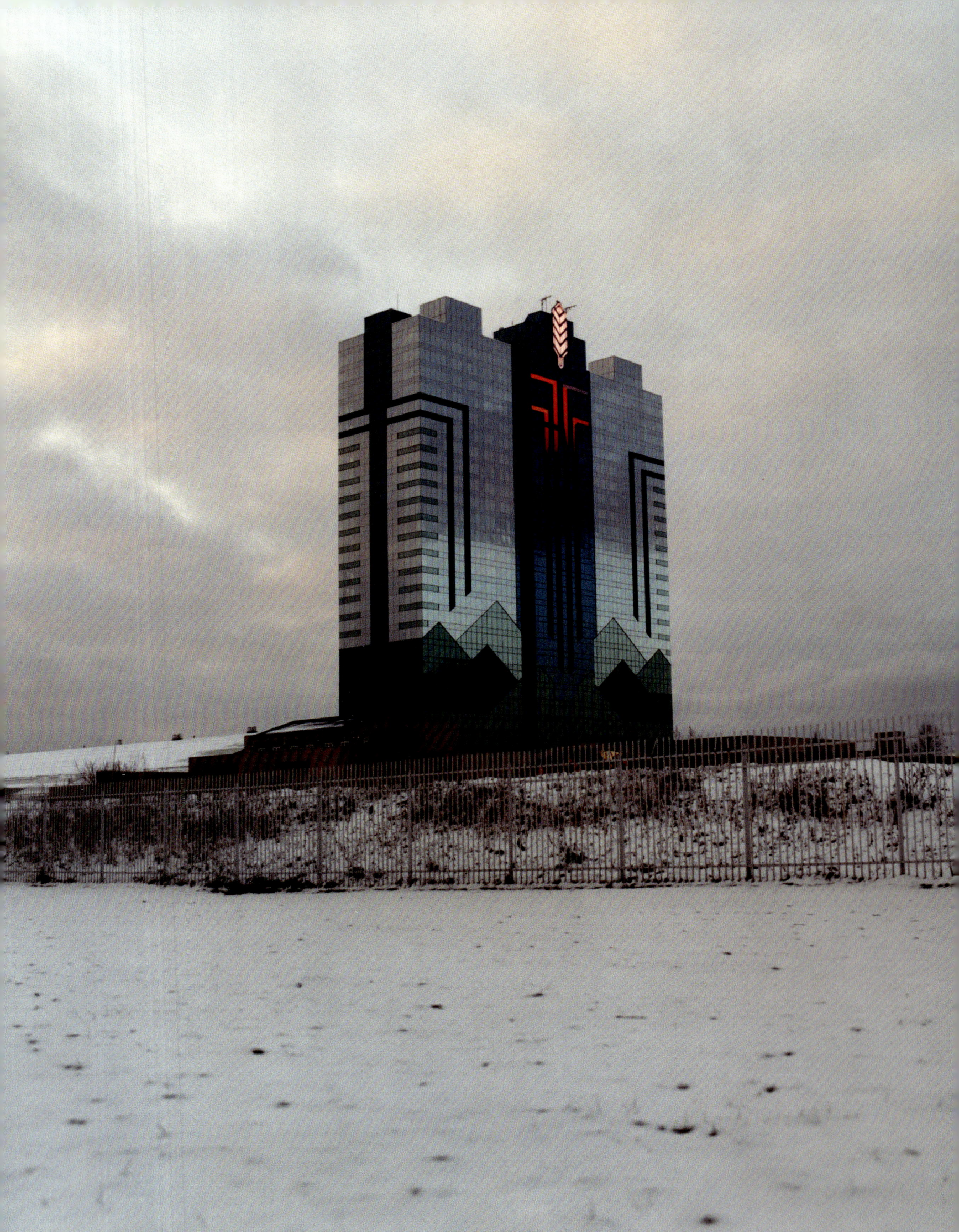

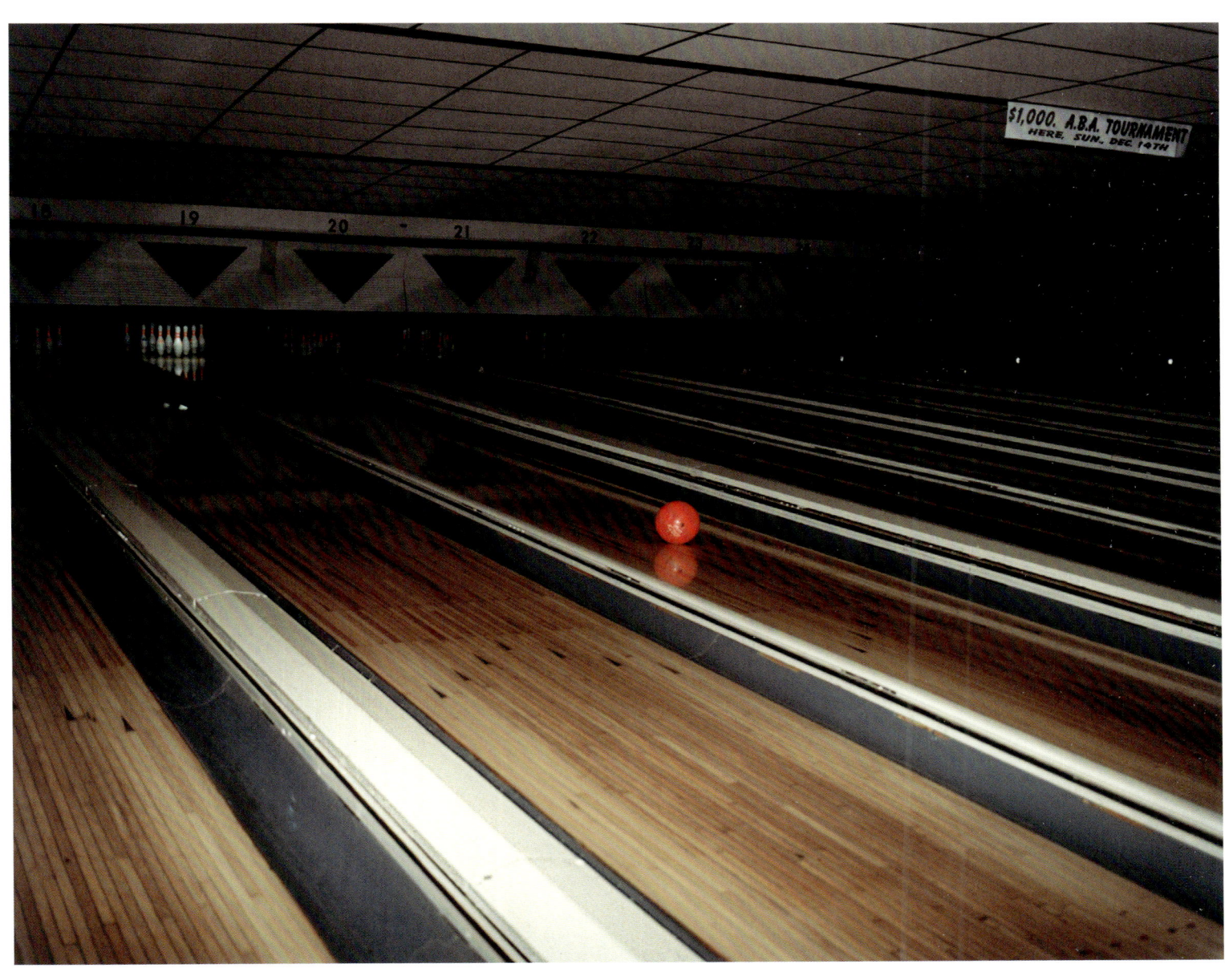

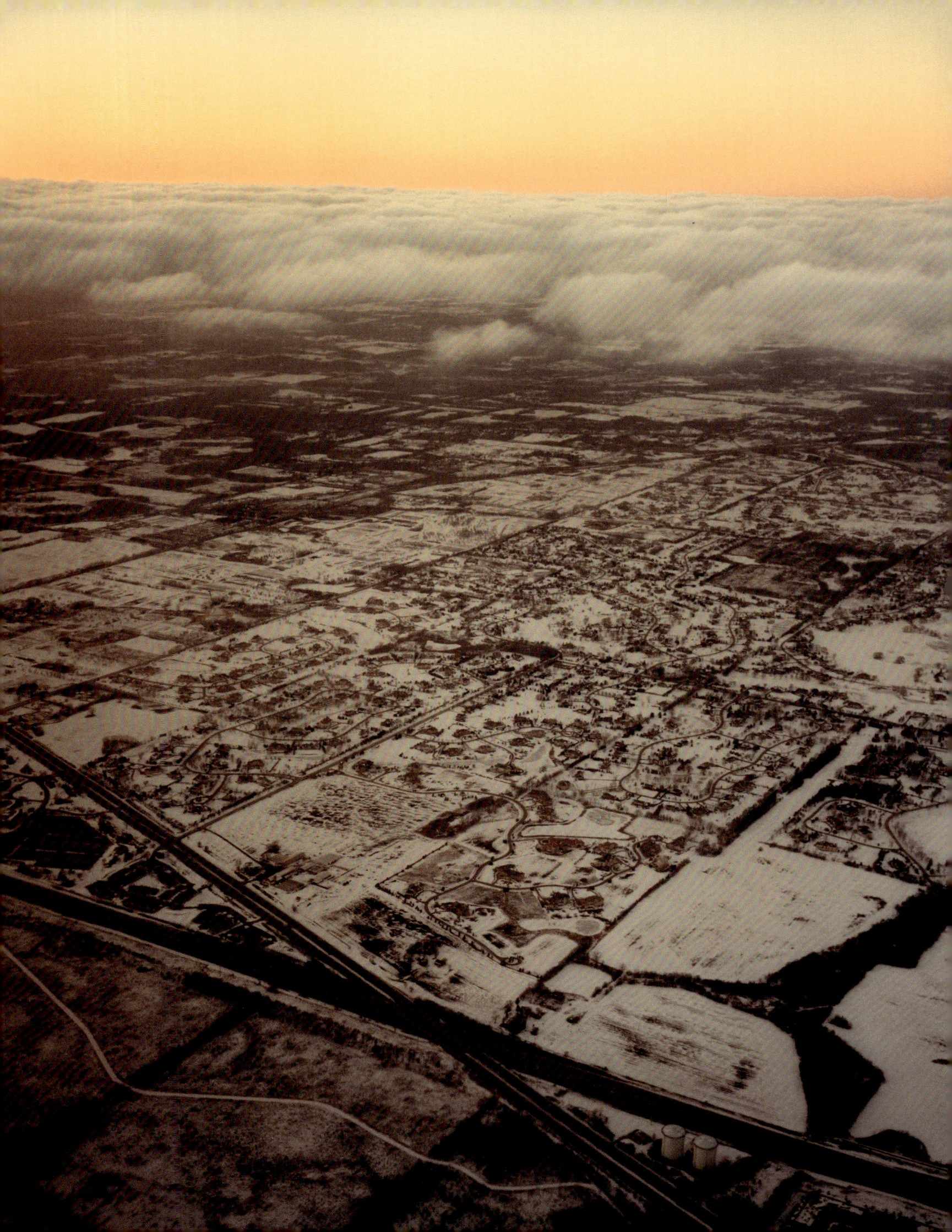

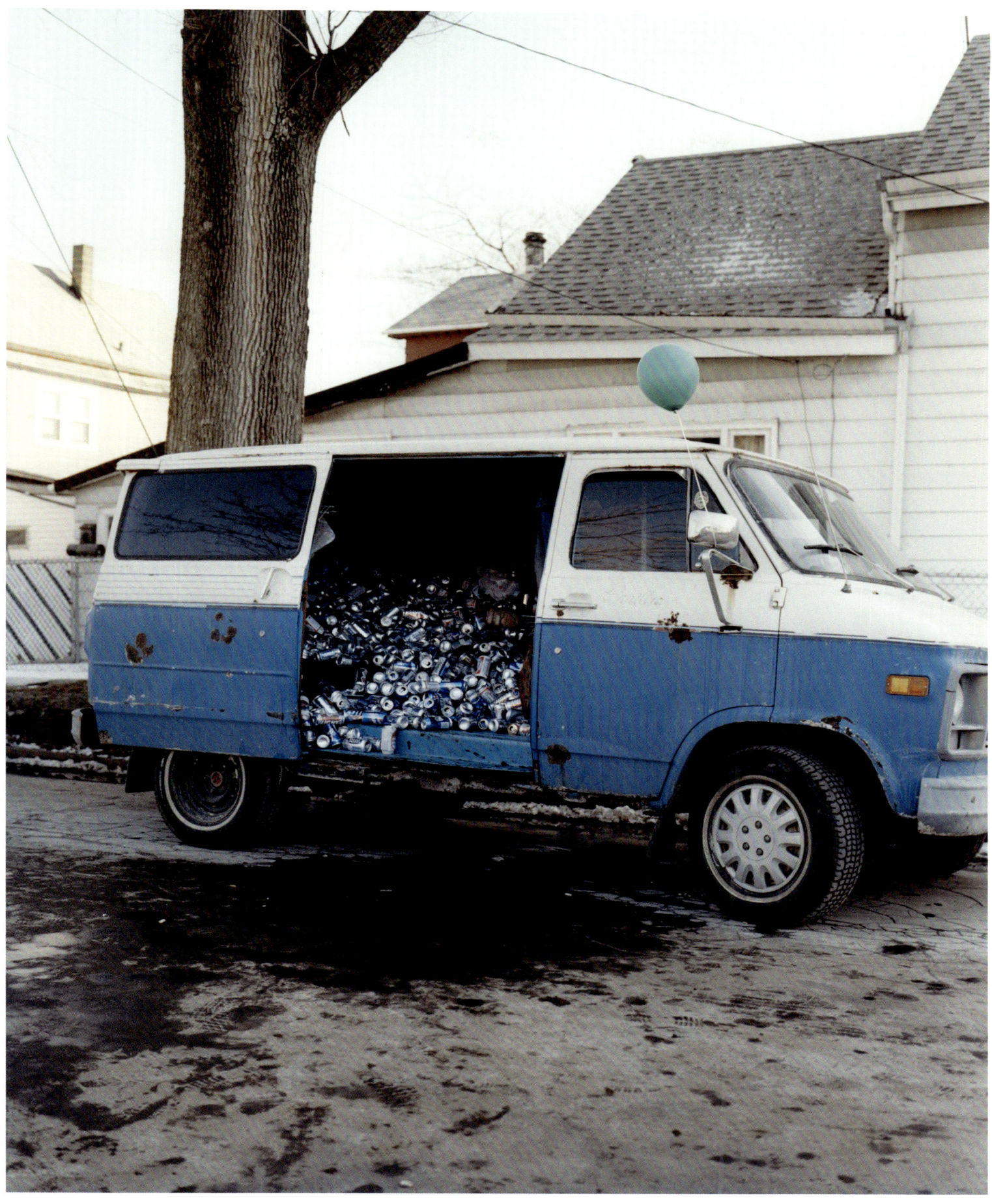

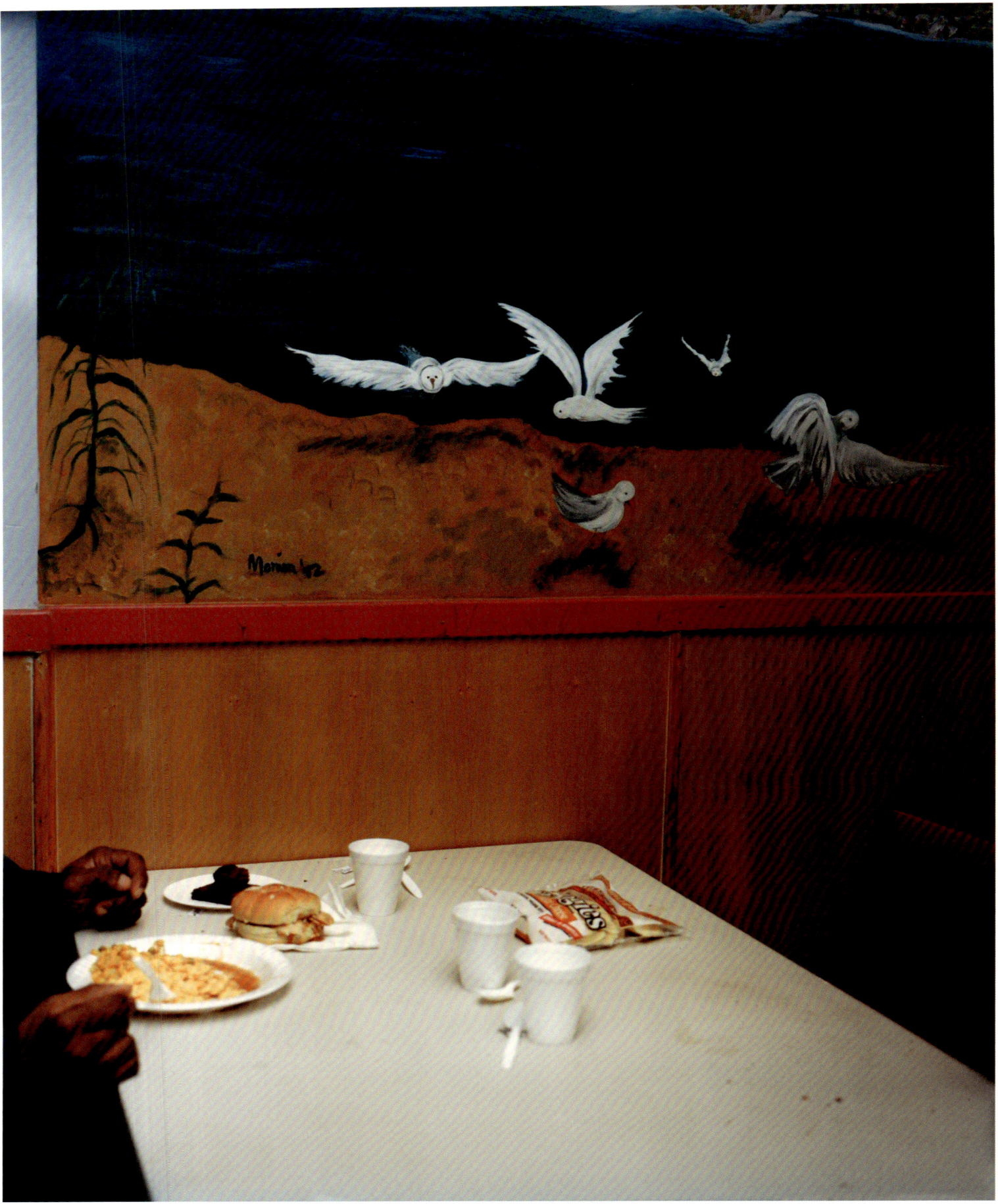

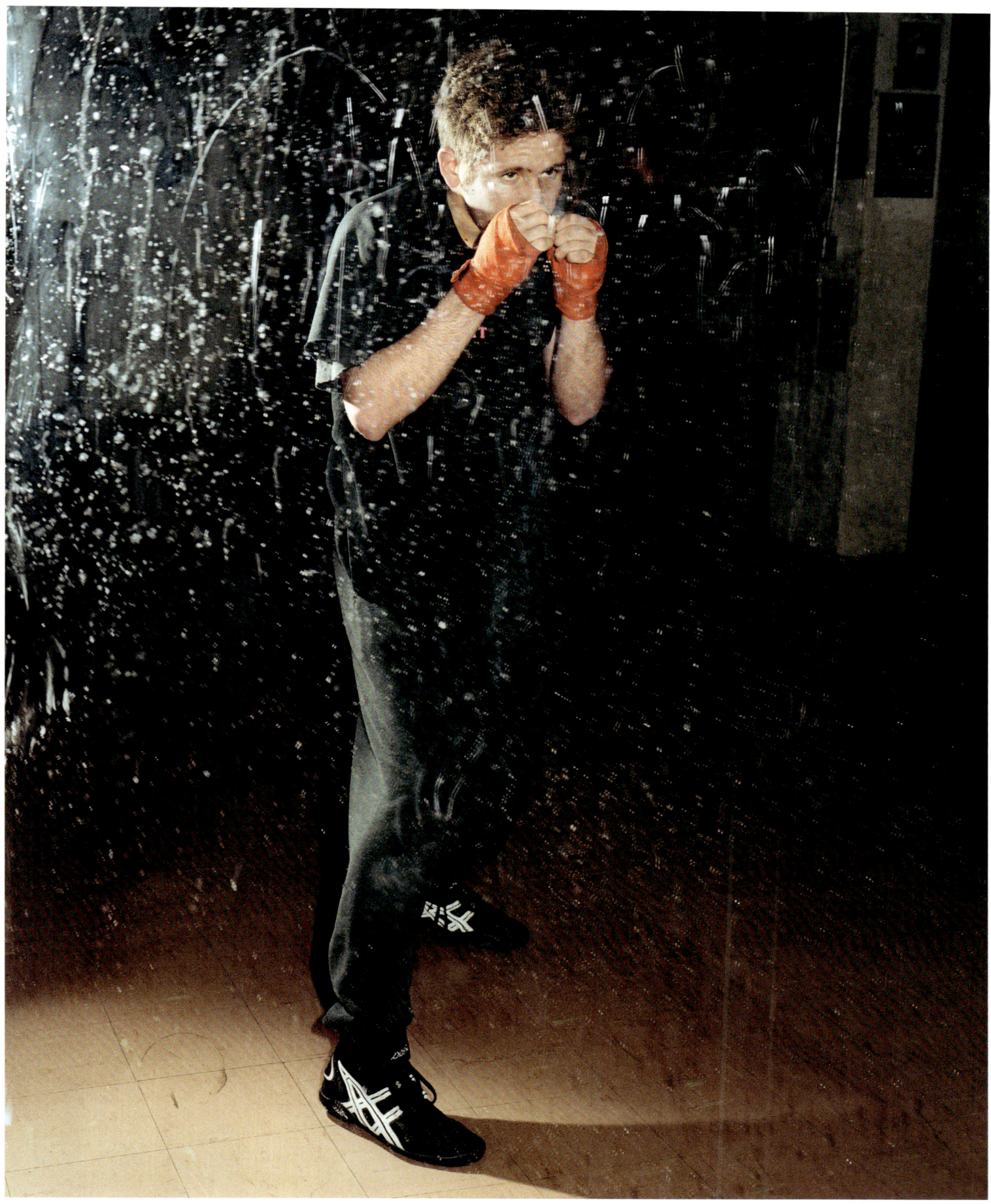

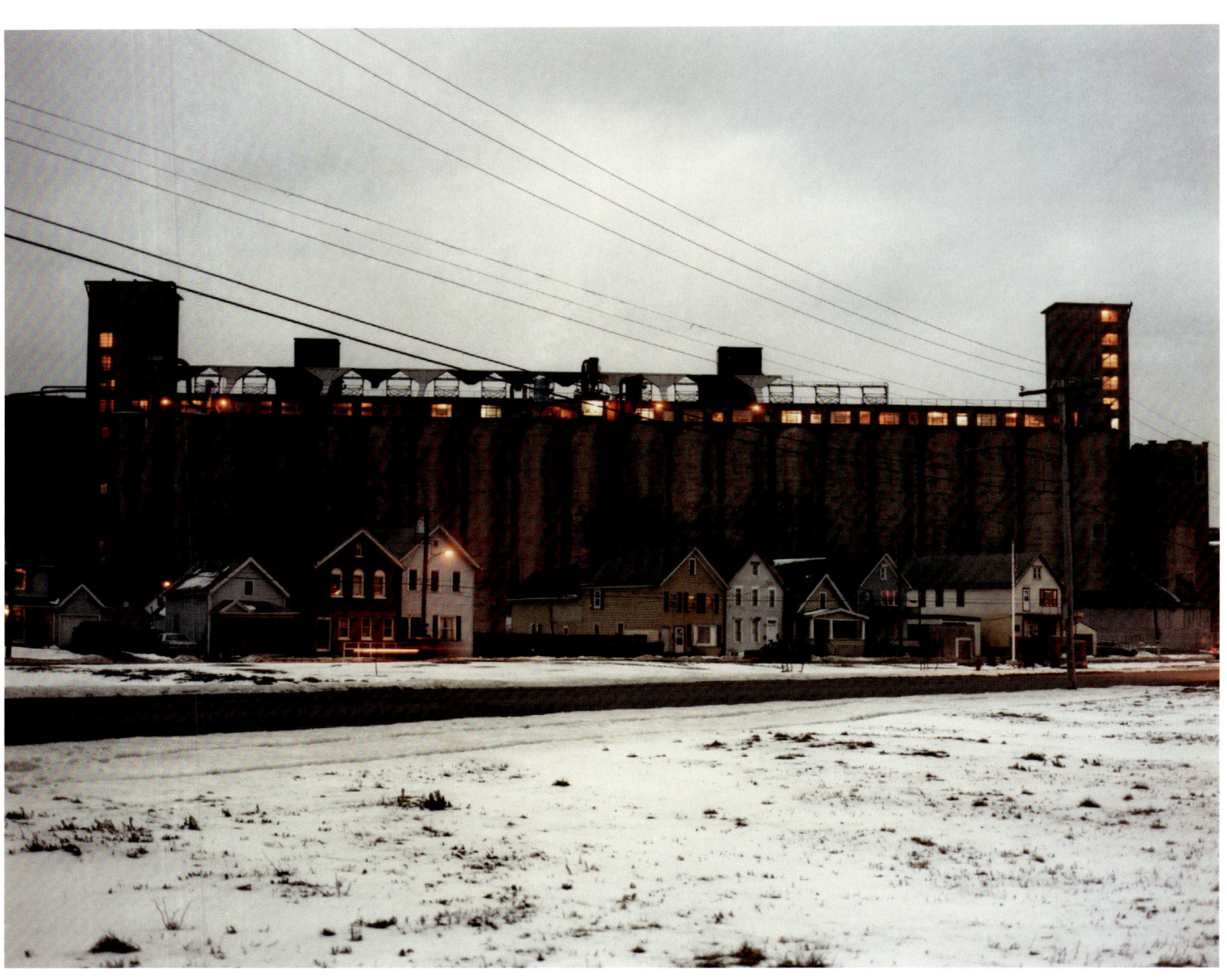

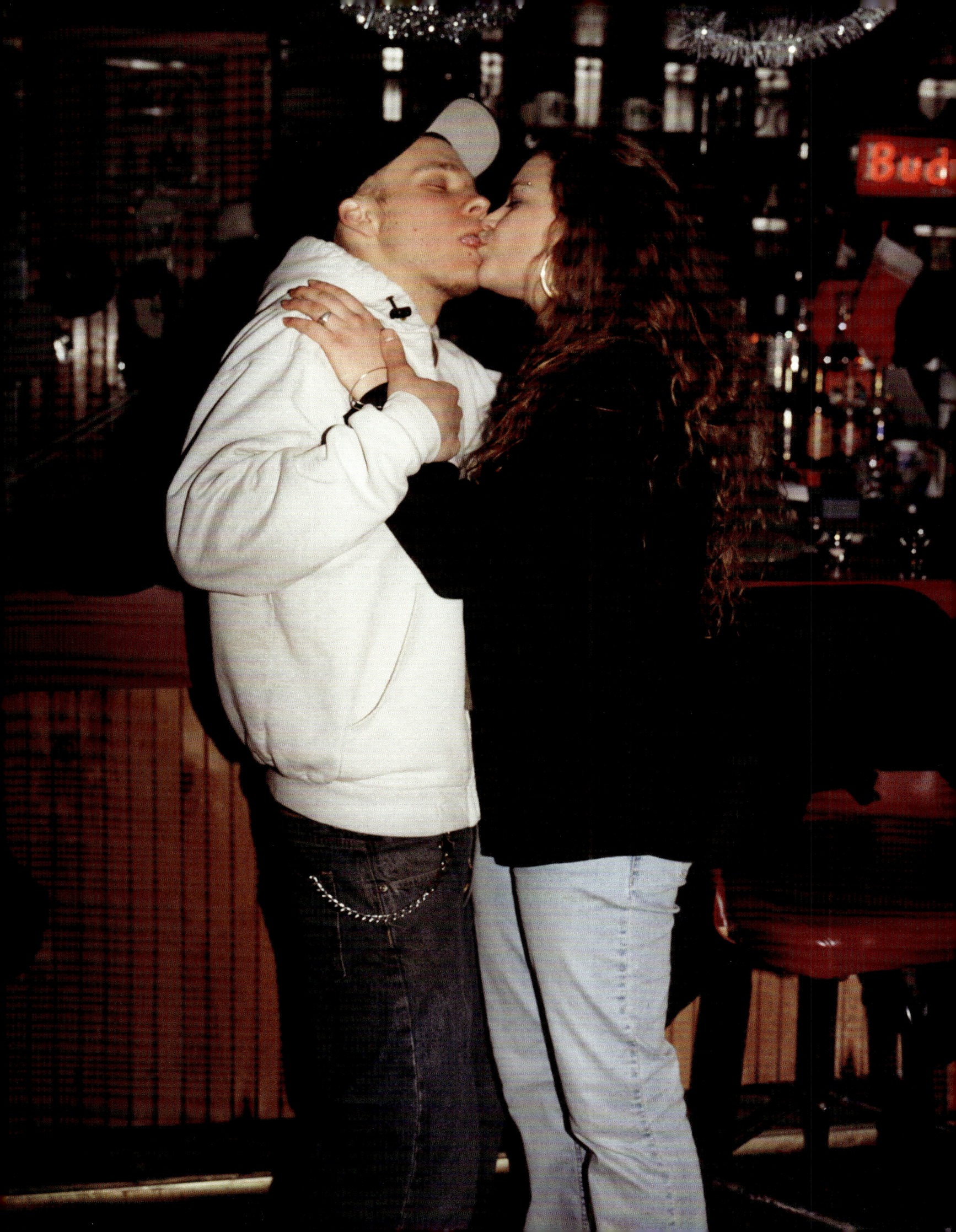

ALESSANDRA SANGUINETTI

Chris Jennings

BLACK RIVER FALLS

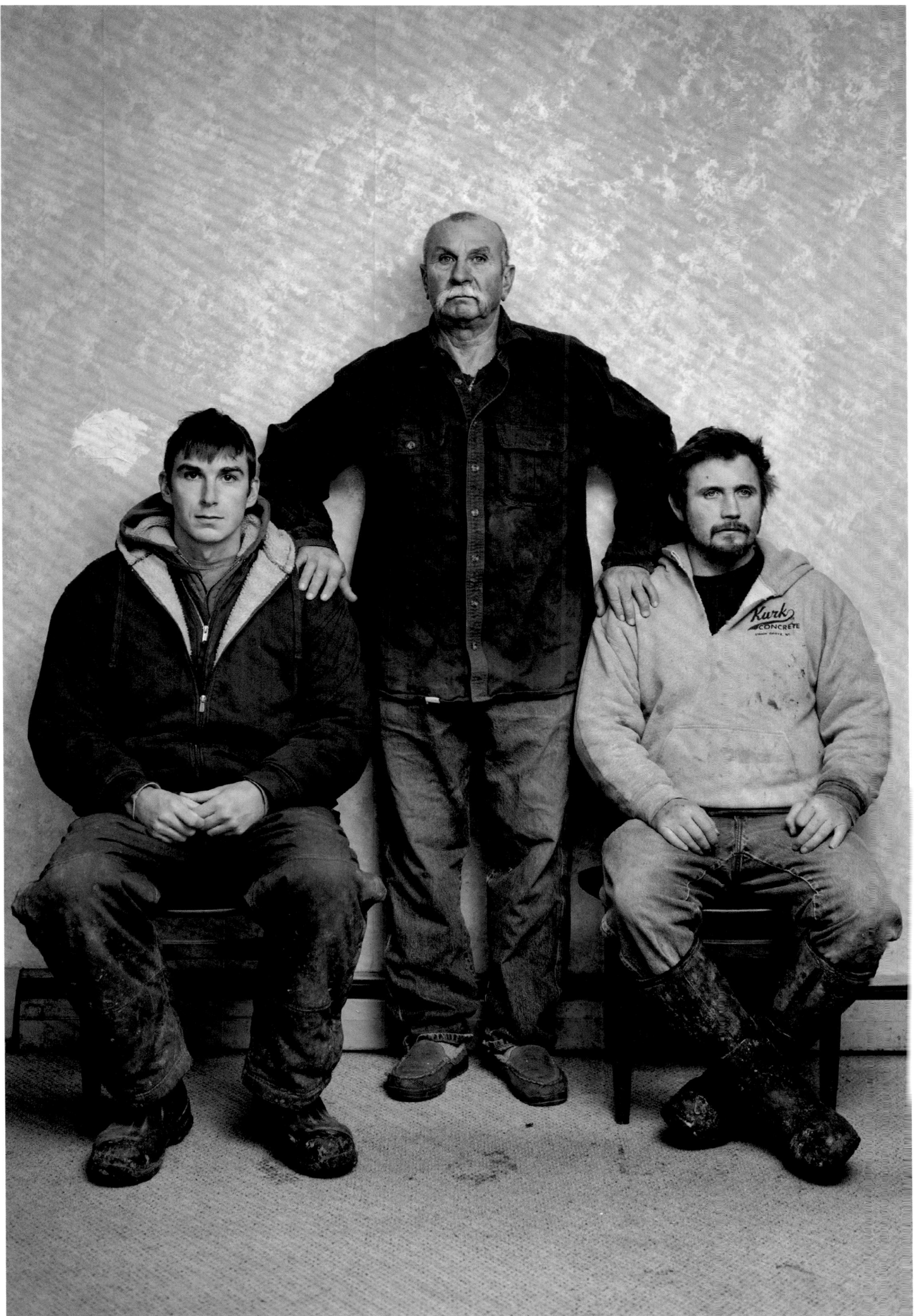

In the coldest part of 2014, the photographer Alessandra Sanguinetti went to Black River Falls, Wisconsin, for the first time. Using the local paper as her guide, Sanguinetti documented the rituals of small-town life in formal, black-and-white images. It snowed furiously. Her trip to Wisconsin, she now recalls, was like revisiting a place in her mind.

"The pictures you're about to see are of people who were once actually alive." That stark preamble—at once ominous and weirdly redundant—introduces *Wisconsin Death Trip* (1973), Michael Lesy's book-length montage of archival photographs and news clippings from Black River Falls at the end of the nineteenth century. The needless reminder that the people depicted in thousands of images by an uncelebrated local photographer named Charles Van Schaick were "once actually alive" somehow makes them all the more dead.

Lesy's book, with its punk title and Dada aesthetic, became something of a cult object in the 1970s. It was part of a small tide of art and writing intent on putting some blood and weirdness back into Americans' sense of their past—of traversing the gulf between *then* and *now* that straight history rarely spans. Somehow a copy landed on a coffee table in Argentina, which is where nine-year-old Alessandra Sanguinetti came upon it. "It sent me into a panic," she remembers. That surely had something to do with the dozens of images of grim young girls, some of them dead, others alive but unaccountably marked off from their schoolmates by black circles, as if preselected for the terrors enumerated on every page. "I suddenly realized I would die," Sanguinetti recalls. Her next thought was to ask for a camera.

Wisconsin Death Trip chronicles a community stalked by Old Testament levels of suffering and delusion. Cryptic headlines and juxtapositions subvert the usual narratives about rural America. Instead of a historian's account of the devastation experienced by farming communities during the financial depression of the 1890s, we encounter young Norwegian immigrants "deranged on the subject of religion" and driven to flamboyant suicide by dynamite and locomotive. Instead of Ken Burns's lonesome fiddle, we hear half-drunk oompah bands. Instead of Dorothea Lange's dusty saints, we get Mary Sweeney, the notorious "Wisconsin window smasher," bingeing on cocaine and destroying plate glass throughout the state. It would be hard to tally whether more lives in Black River Falls were claimed by diphtheria, arson, morphine overdose, or gunplay. This is not the frontier of myth. It is a town that both the frontier and the myth raced past, a place of diminishing prospects and long, frozen winters. Flipping the pages, something like a narrative gathers incrementally, depicting a grim slide from economic collapse to depression to lunacy.

The photographs Sanguinetti took in the winter of 2014, and on two subsequent visits, tell a far less gothic story. Black River Falls is doing better than it was in the 1890s. Yet many of the serious, quiet faces she captured would not be out of place on Van Schaick's glass-plate negatives. Familiar scenes of rural American life—a Catholic church choir, eccentric domestic clutter, a teenage boy wearing his sousaphone like an albatross— seem somehow mysterious, almost ancient or sacred. Nervous currents thrum beneath the surface. There may be madness and great reversals of fortune here, but the stronger impression is of uncertainty, stagnation, and the mollifying rhythms of tradition and the calendar. And of course, the beautiful deathly cold of winter remains unchanged.

Lesy's book lets the imagination run across a great abyss of time, animating the suffering and hysteria of a long-ago place in all of its strange ambiguity. Sanguinetti's photographs cover a different sort of distance. Black River Falls is the seat of Jackson County, which helped deliver the traditionally Democratic state of Wisconsin to Donald Trump. At a moment when half the country stands baffled and appalled at the moral and political impulses of the other half, these images offer an unusually intimate look across the divide.

Chris Jennings is the author of
*Paradise Now: The Story of American
Utopianism* (2016).

Previous page:
*Rich, Doug, and Andrew,
Spoerlein Never Rest
Farm. Salem, Wisconsin,*
2014

Opposite:
*June Velie. Black River
Falls, Wisconsin,* 2014

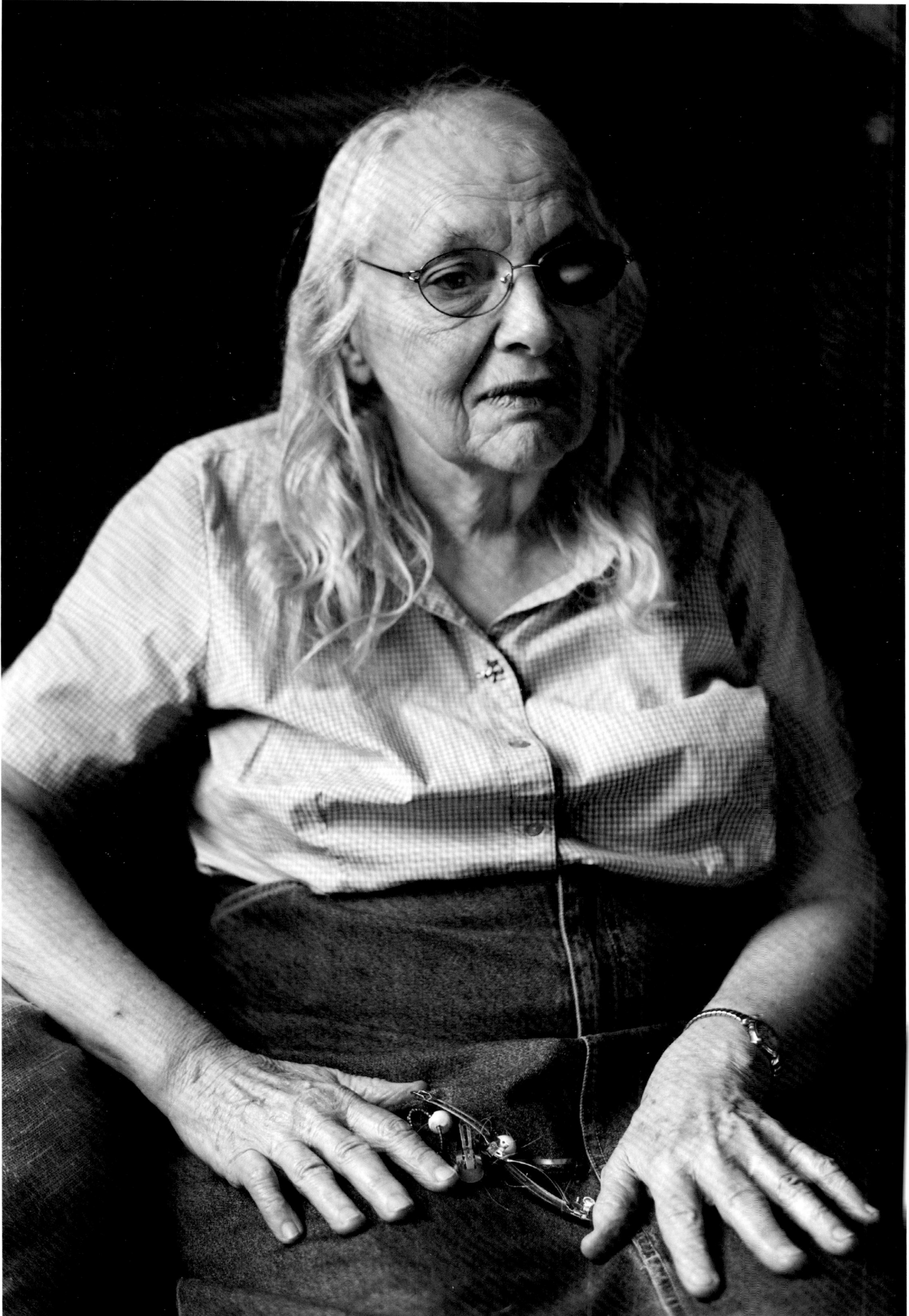

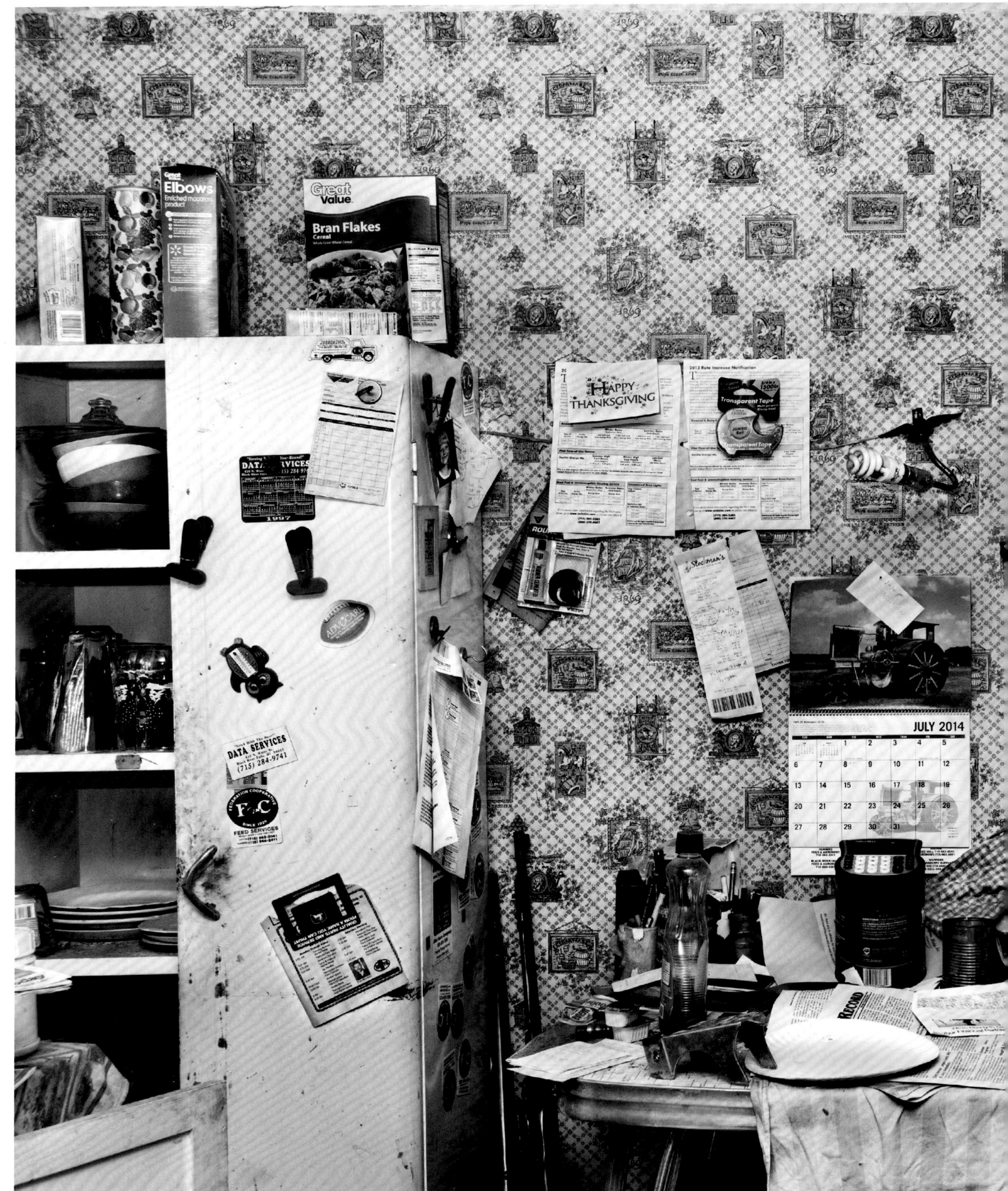

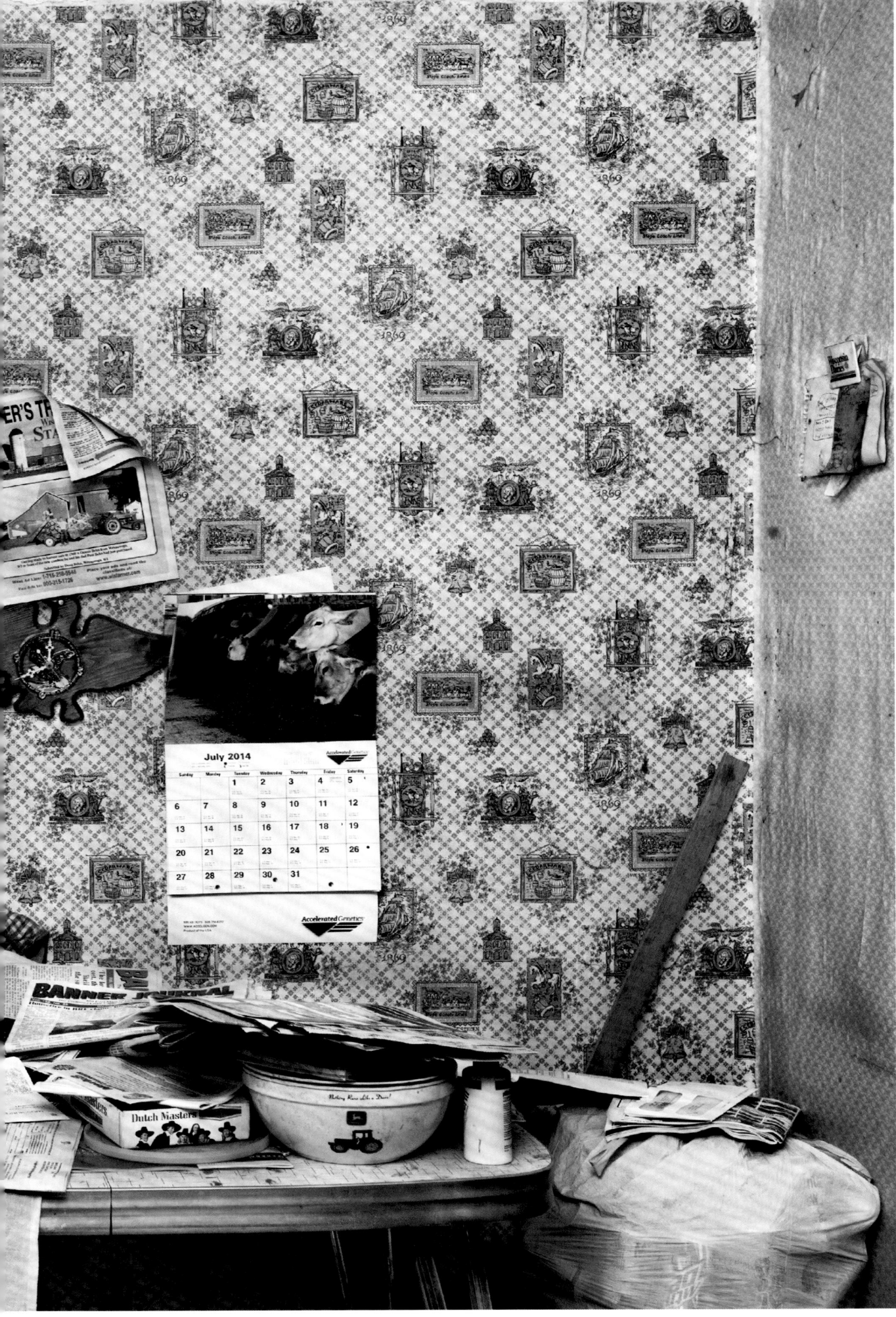

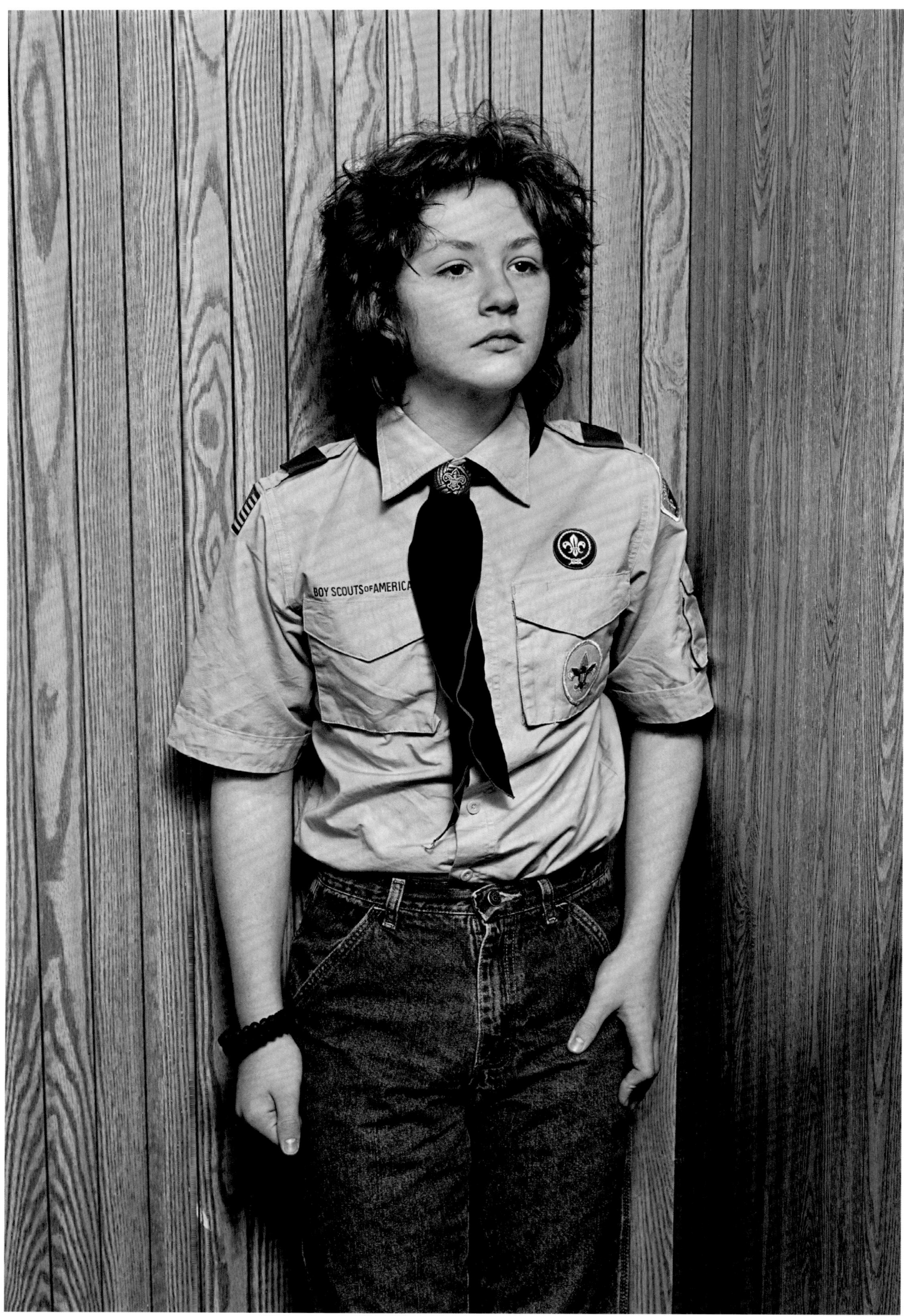

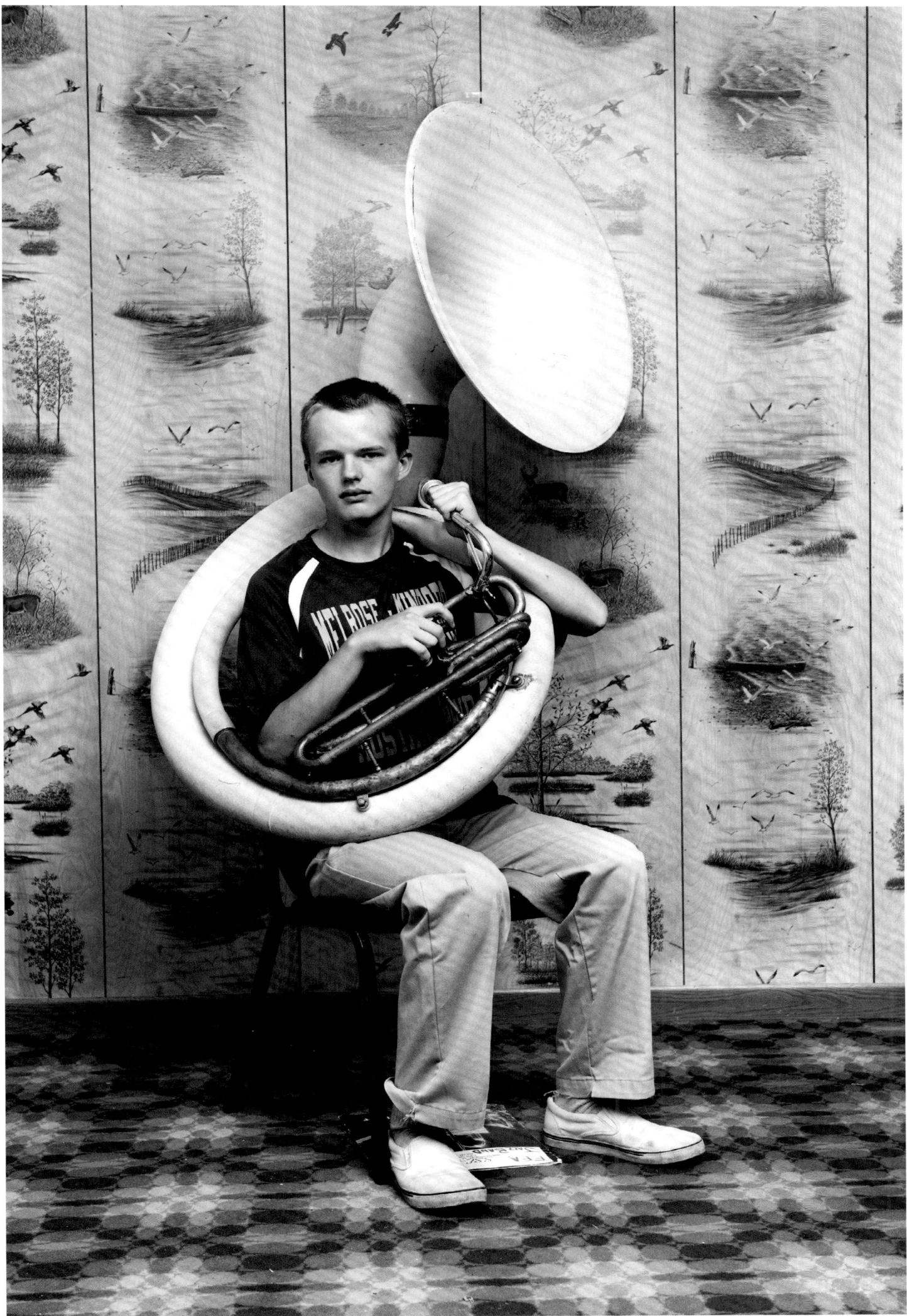

Page 44:
Eagle Scout. Hixton, Wisconsin, 2014

Previous page:
Fourth of July. Melrose, Wisconsin, 2014

This spread:
Sunday choir. Black River Falls, Wisconsin, 2014
All photographs courtesy the artist

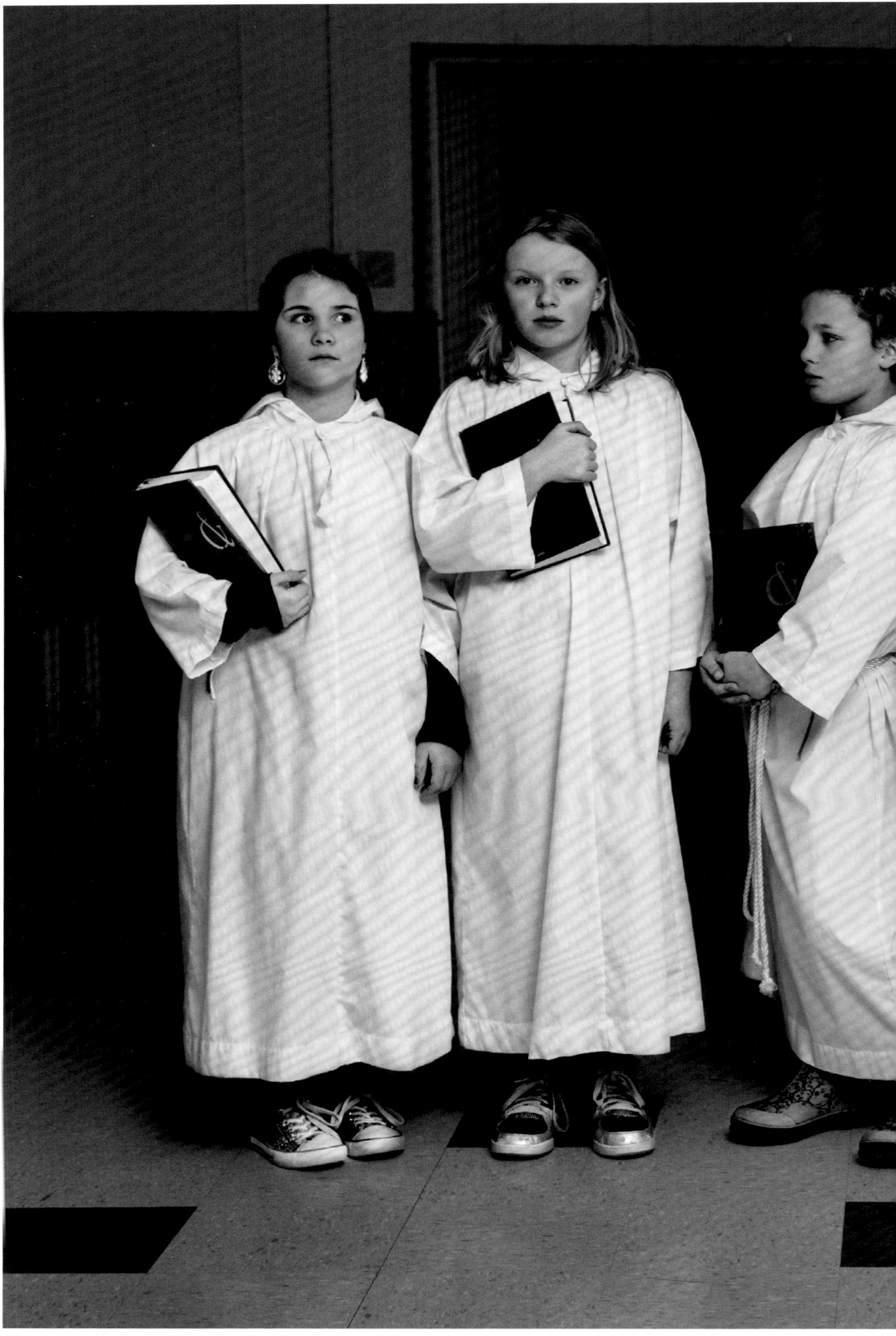

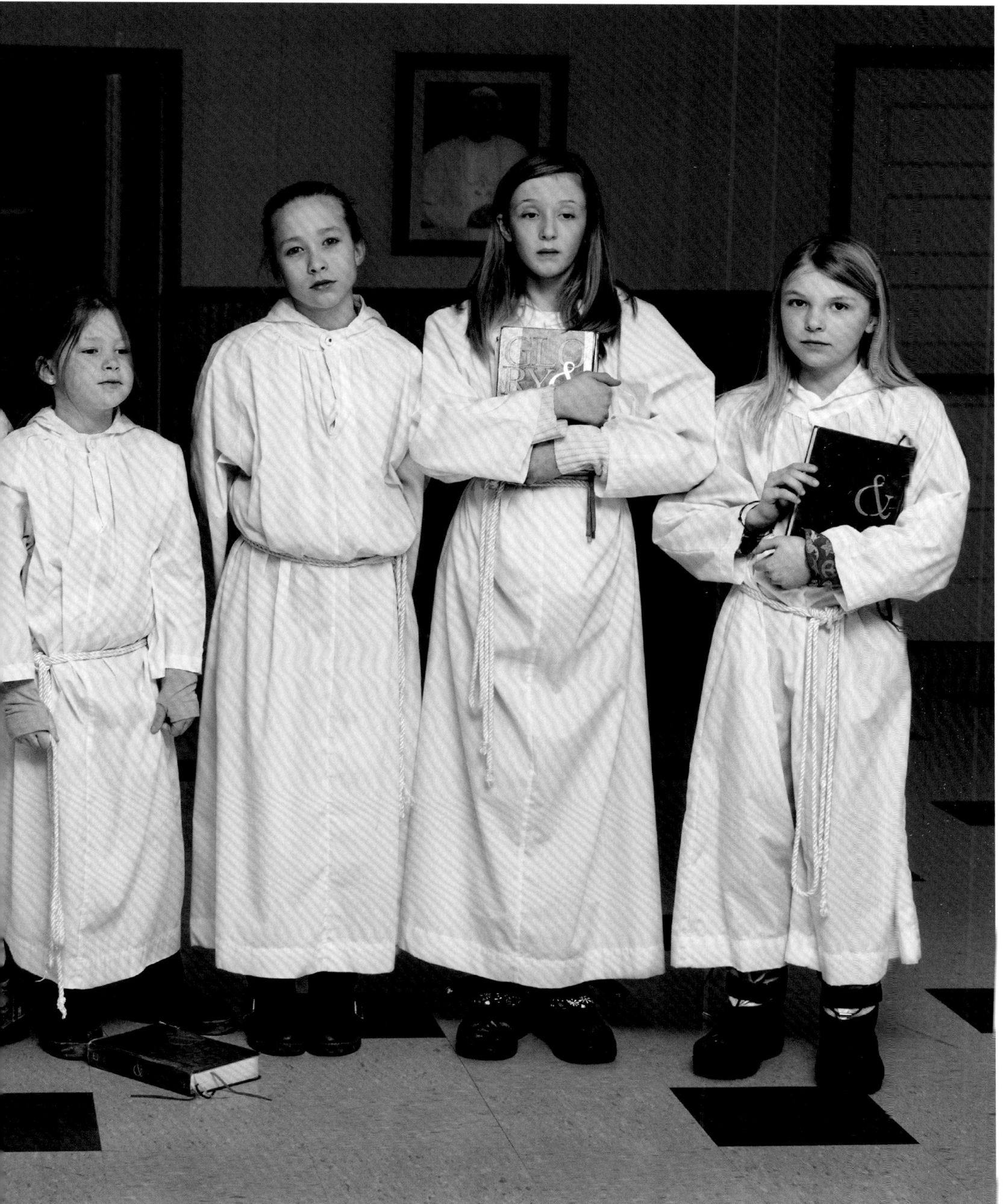

Carolyn Drake

Diary

Garnette Cadogan

Sometimes you need the eyes of an outsider to see your world afresh. The sustained focus of the newcomer; the quizzical glances of the passerby; the curiosity-filled wanderings of the traveler—they refresh our ideas of ourselves and help us rediscover the familiar. Indeed, they even render the invisible visible. Seeing alongside outsiders expands our scope—and, at its best, deepens our understanding and appreciation—by returning us to a childlike inquisitiveness. As the Polish poet Wisława Szymborska wrote, "there are no questions more urgent / than the naïve ones."

Carolyn Drake, who has photographed across the world (notably in western China and the Ukraine), where she benefited from the outsider's remove, returned in 2013, after seven years away, to her native United States and chose to pursue the naïve questions by adopting the stance of a stranger. In fact, she had become a stranger of sorts—much of her country felt foreign, as she had been "thinking about other places for a long time." But she was also too close to her country, and it too much a part of her, for her to see people and their environments as clearly as she desired. She needed to revisit her homeland with a new way of looking.

She decided to counter her disadvantage by traveling westward, using the nineteenth-century diary of an ancestor who, during a time of national expansion, went from Iowa to California. The diary is both guide and point of departure; Drake wanted to undertake a journey with a personal connection, and connect with those she encountered, not, as she said recently,

Kyle in Target parking lot,
Twin Falls, Idaho, 2016

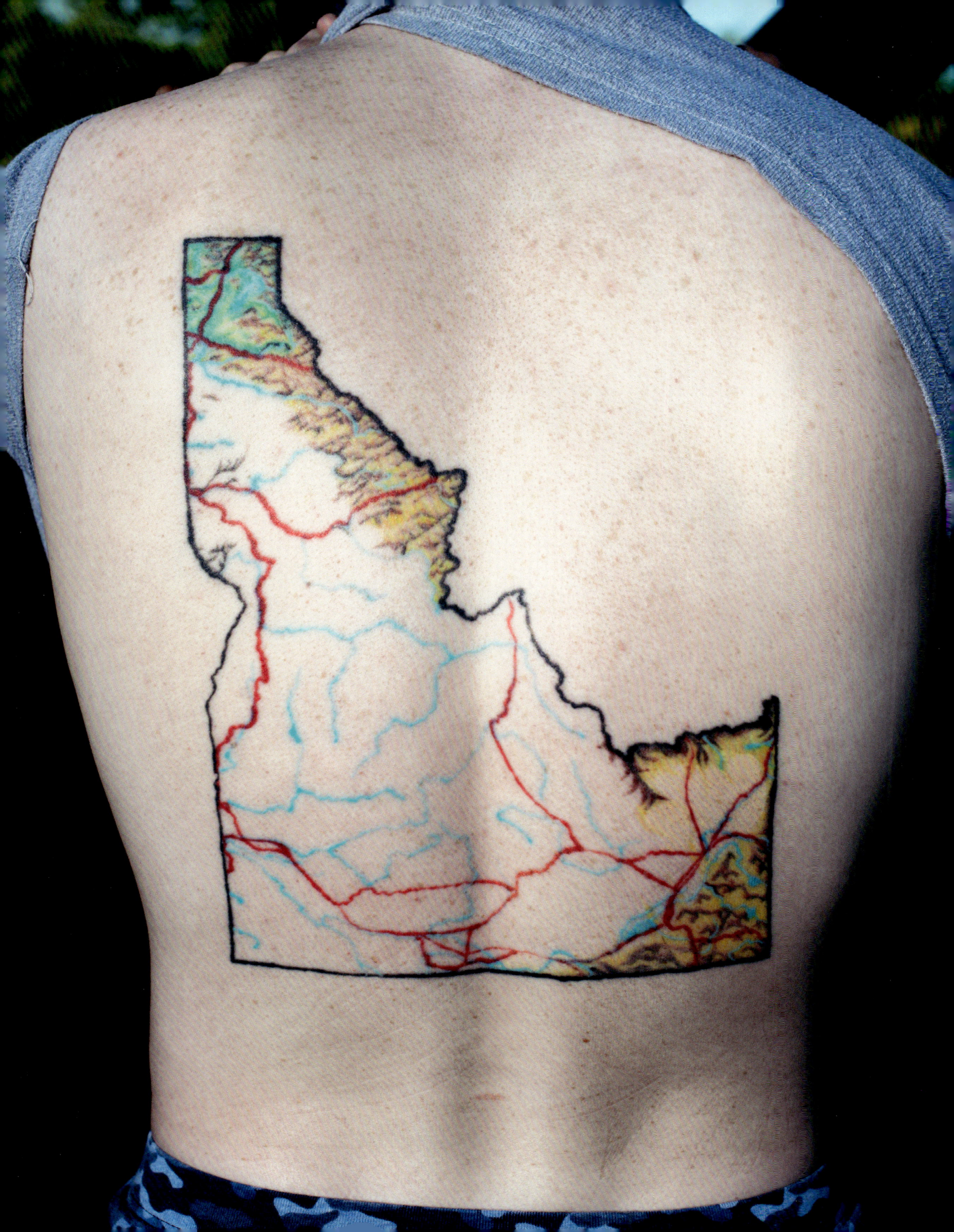

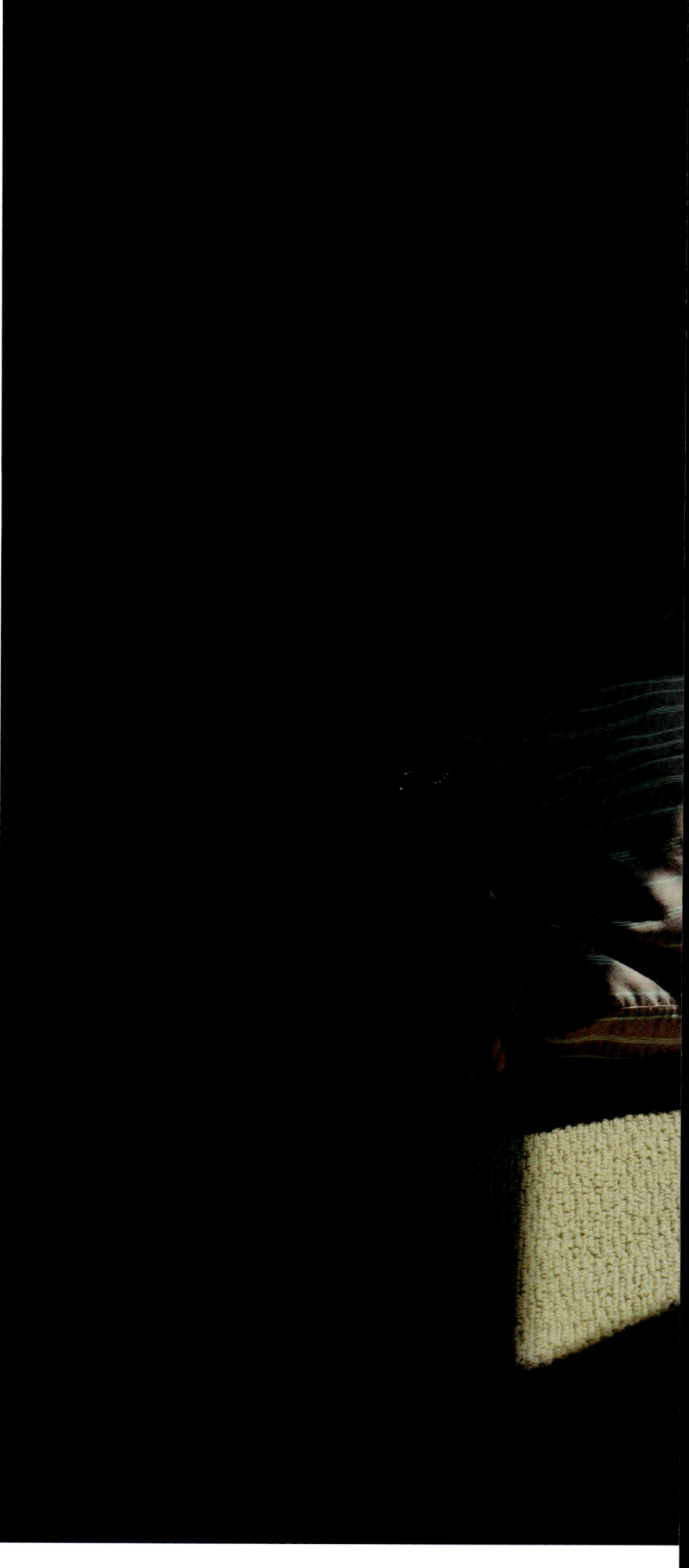

"re-enact the journey or reaffirm our national mythologies. Rather, I'm seeking out stories that subvert and confound the boilerplate Western narrative." She not only traversed the landscape, but also circled it, paying patient attention to those who sprung up from the soil and those new to it.

Abandoning the romantic myths of the frontier for the stories that animate those in pursuit of or left behind by—or even unconcerned with—the American Dream, Drake captures the worlds she encounters with warmth and lyricism. A family of African refugees traveling from Boise, Idaho, makes a pit stop at a gas station in Baker City, Oregon, to pray and refuel. We've seen this gas station before—a staple of American realist photography—but this scene feels fresh, different: friendly banter with a stranger illuminates the life often found in the societal interstices between those from here and those from elsewhere. The encounter resembles a delightful community gathering; perhaps we haven't seen this gas station before, after all.

Drake gives us people inscribing themselves on the landscape—which might mean inscribing the place on one's very self (a tattoo of the state of Idaho adorns a man's back, its vibrant colors at once badge and beauty), or asserting one's agency in a place where daily life threatens to be a rote cycle of quiet desperation. Her interplay between the roles of insider and outsider suffuses her photographs, and we meet people who are as beguiling as they are mysterious: her subjects (students, refugees, workers, the unemployed, to name a few from a very broad range) draw you in with arresting gazes, but a moody atmosphere—those warm colors—holds you at bay, searching. It's as if Drake invites us to see people's agency, then insists it not be denied them—the African refugees' smiles, expanding the photograph's frame, intermingle with their veils. In their mystery is their magic.

Drake is rediscovering—discovering, really—the United States as a native-made-newcomer, and as one tracing a path behind those whose footsteps reveal the wild, varying textures of a nation too often reduced to myths, stereotypes, and clichés. "What is America to me?" her work asks, pointing to the outsiders, the recent transplants, the strangers among us. Will they be strangers forever? Or will they eventually be welcomed as Americans, too? Carolyn Drake reminds us, to borrow Robert Frost's words, that "America is hard to see." We ought not to forget, then, that the meaning of America is bound up in the treatment and fate of those who see the way we don't.

Garnette Cadogan is a Visiting Fellow at the Institute for Advanced Studies in Culture at the University of Virginia.

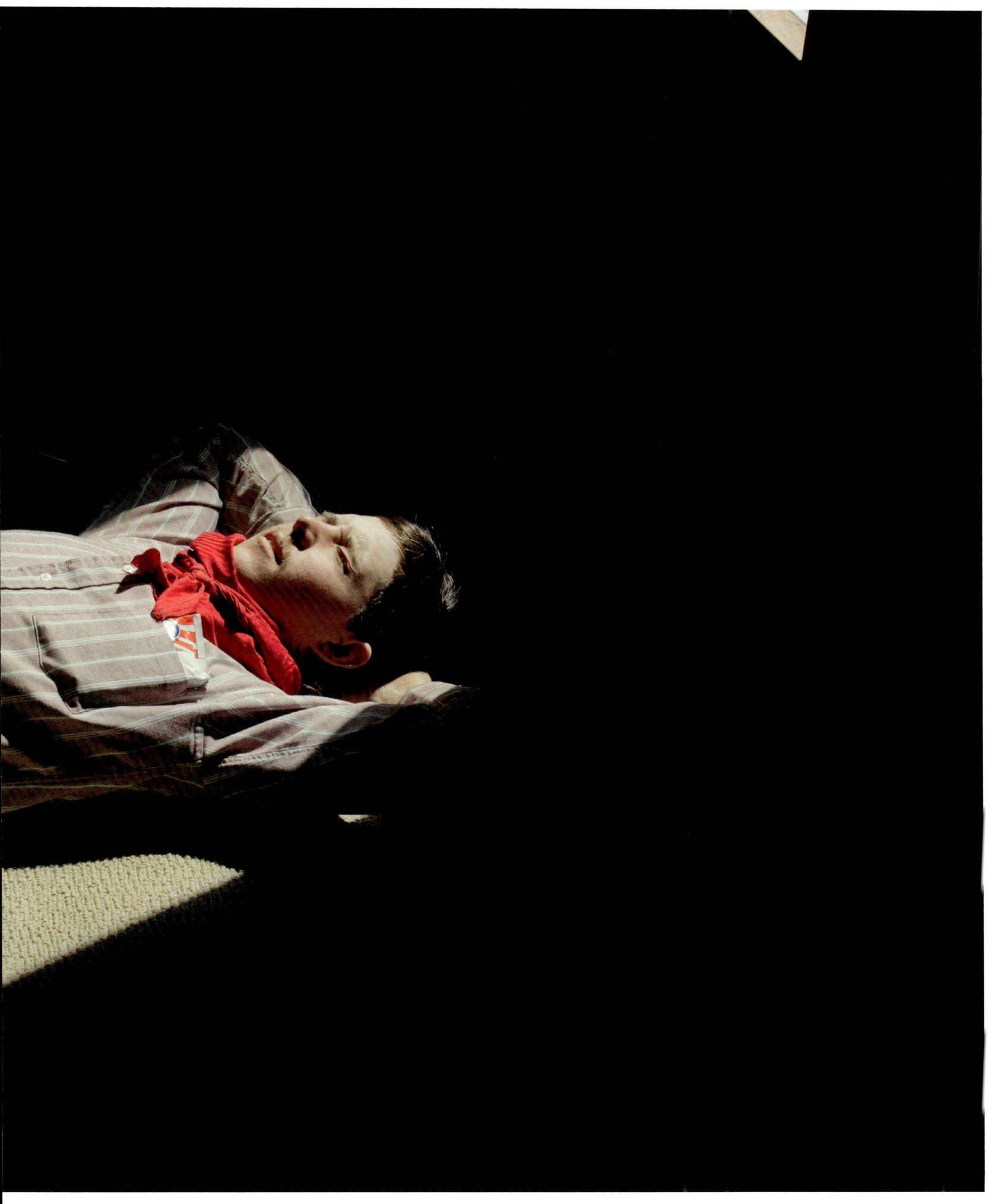

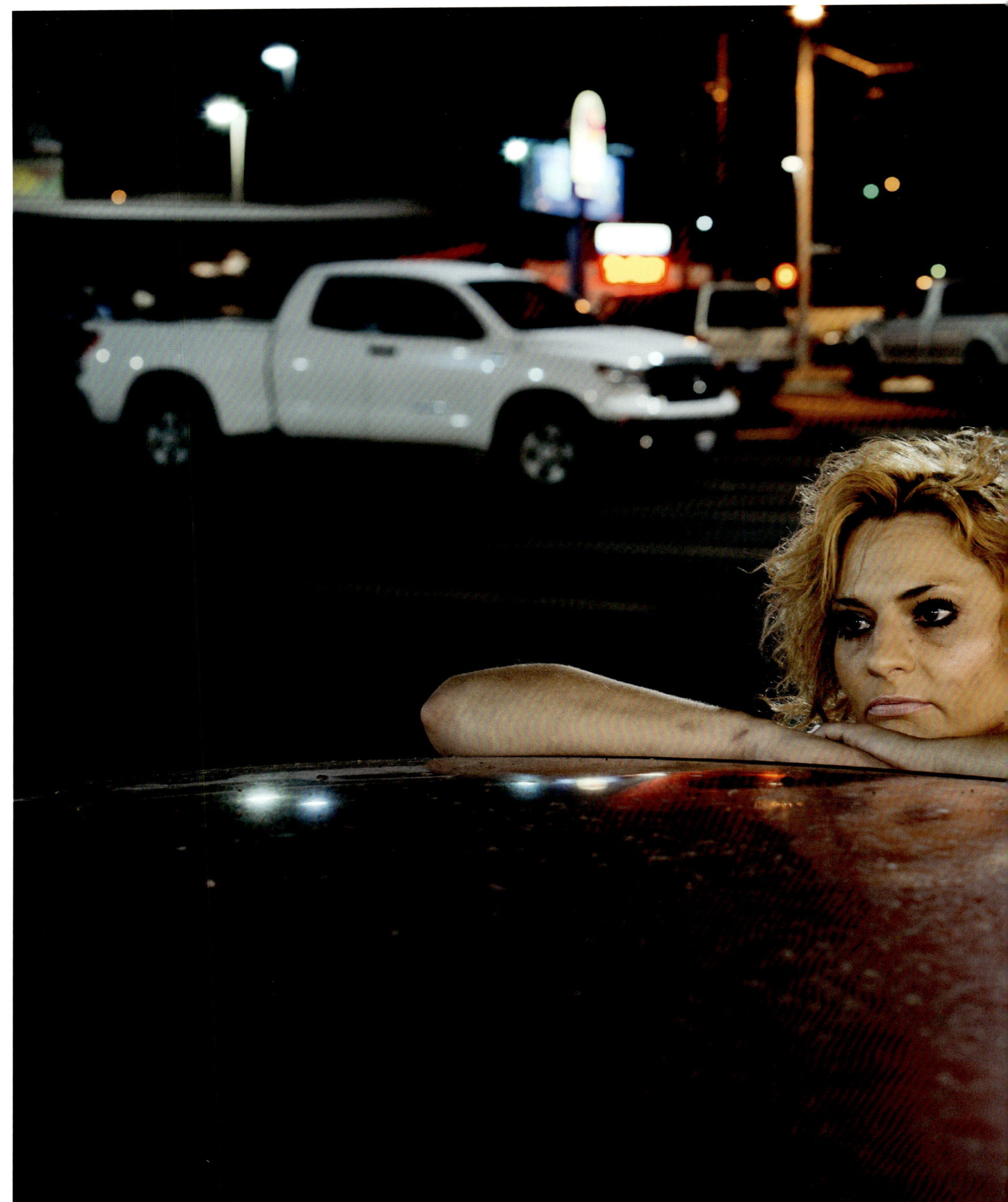

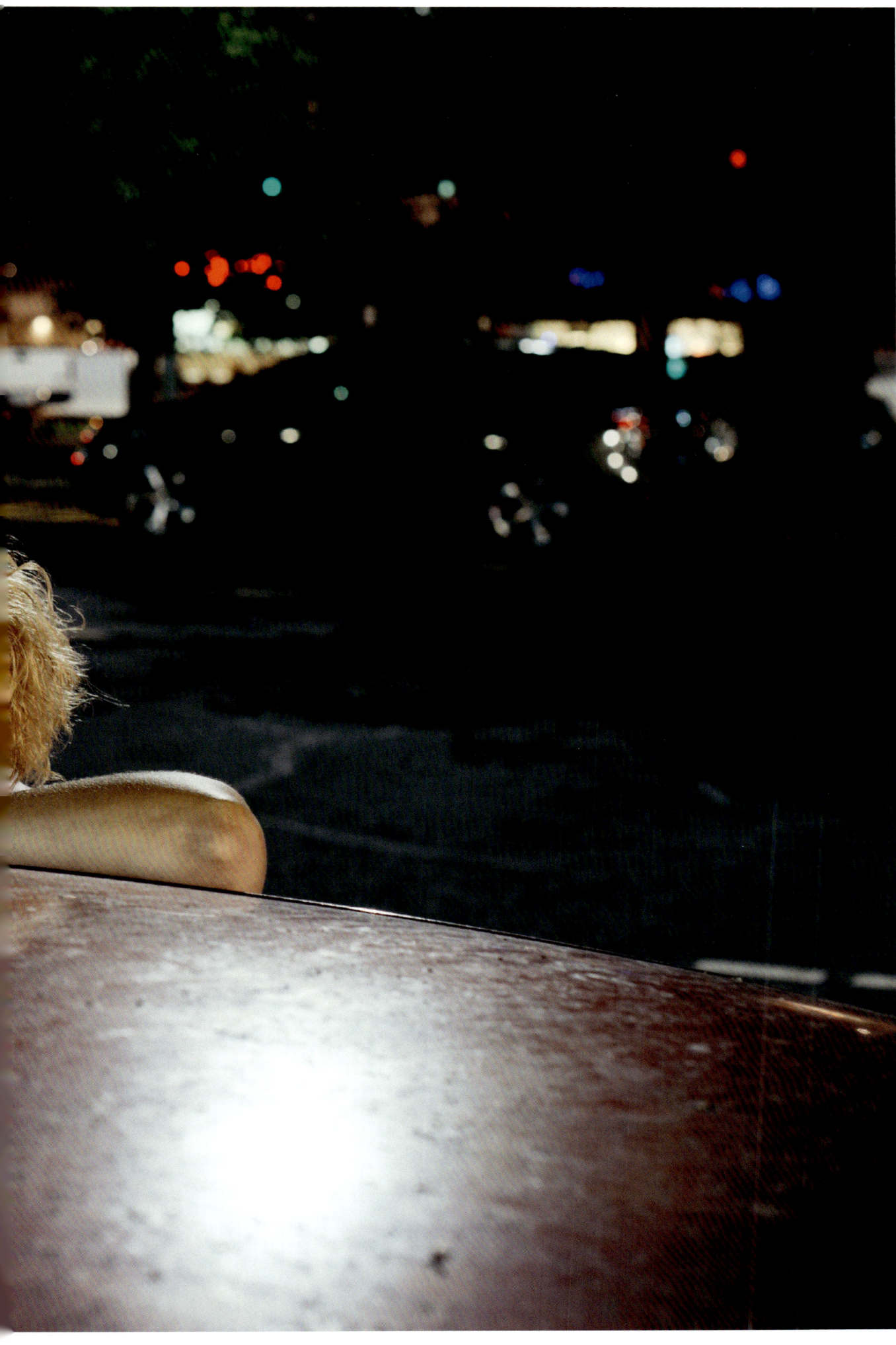

Previous spread:
Wyko McKee working on his friend Johnny Pavkov's ranch for the summer, Gooding, Idaho, 2016

This spread:
Lacy in Safeway parking lot, Pendleton, Oregon, 2015

Overleaf:
Road trip rest stop, Baker City, Oregon, 2015
All photographs © the artist/ Magnum Photos

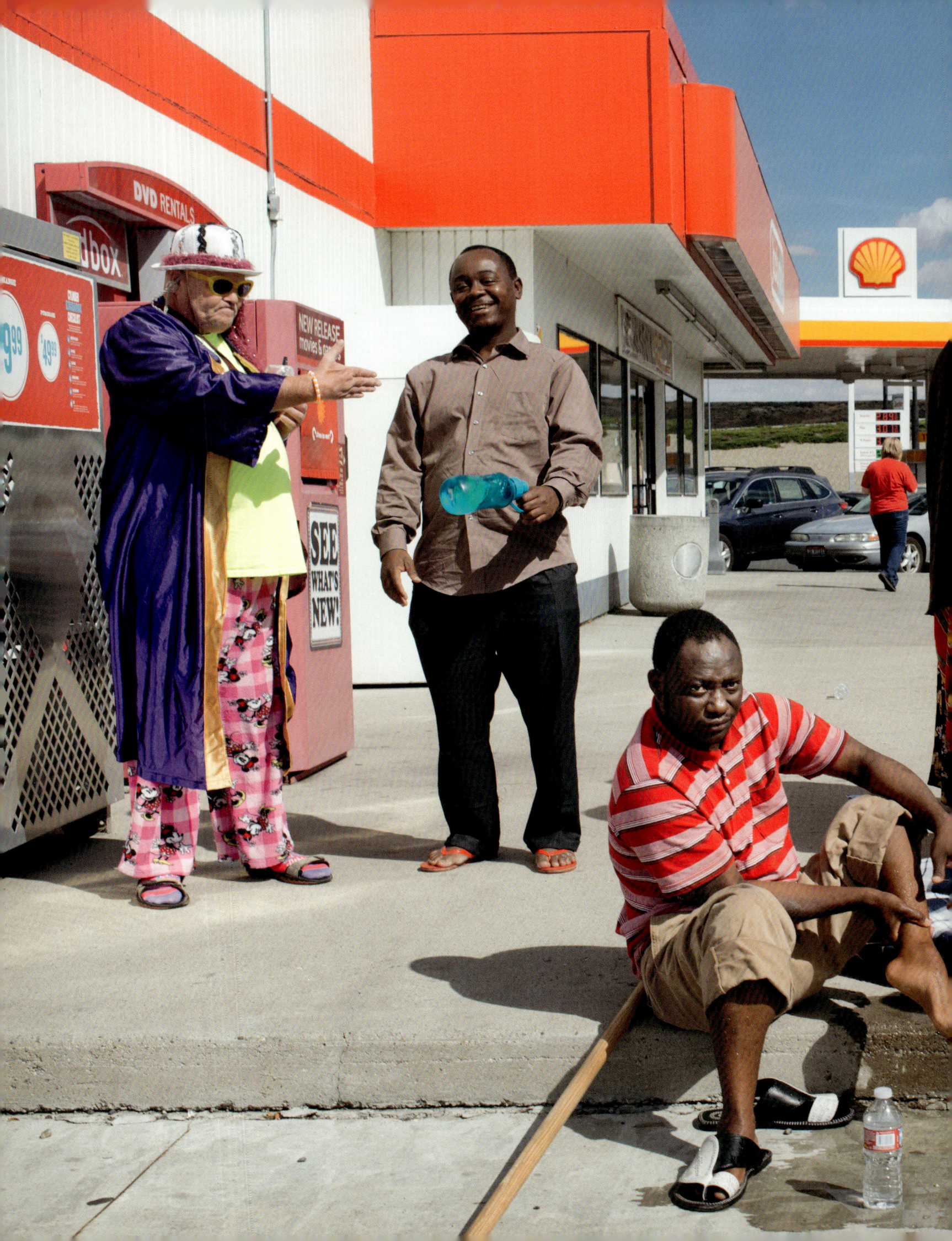

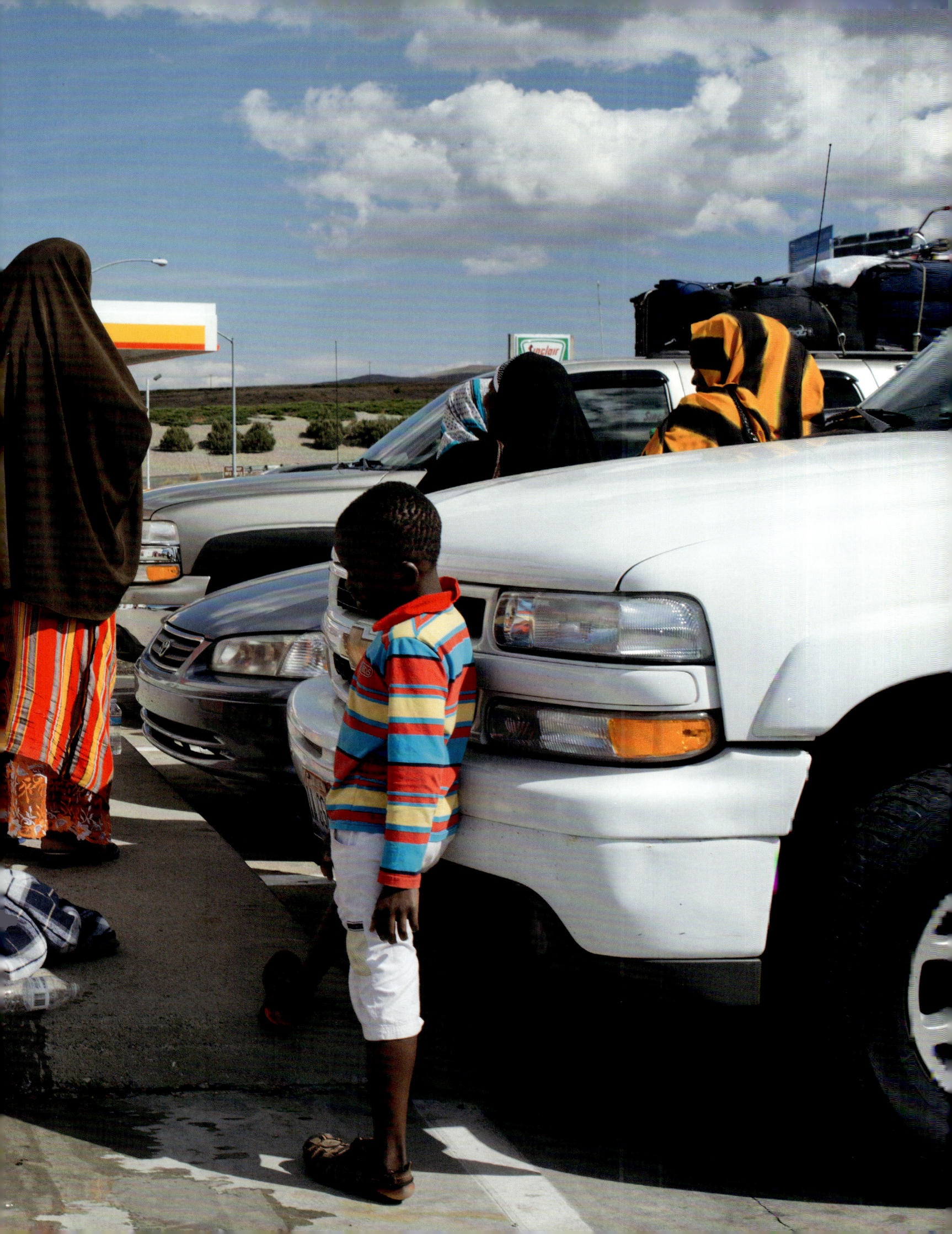

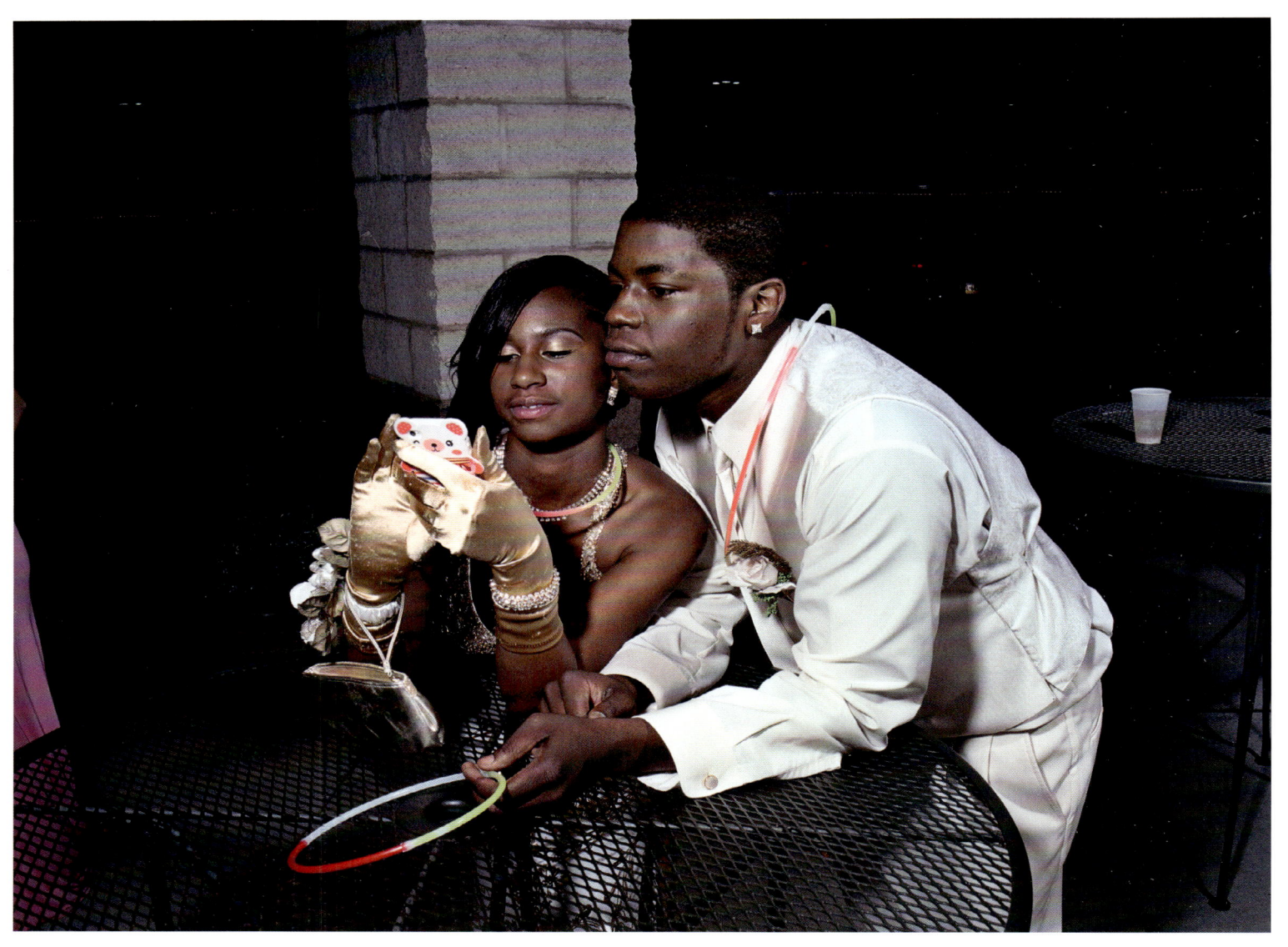

Mark Neville
Braddock/Sewickley

Stanley Wolukau-Wanambwa

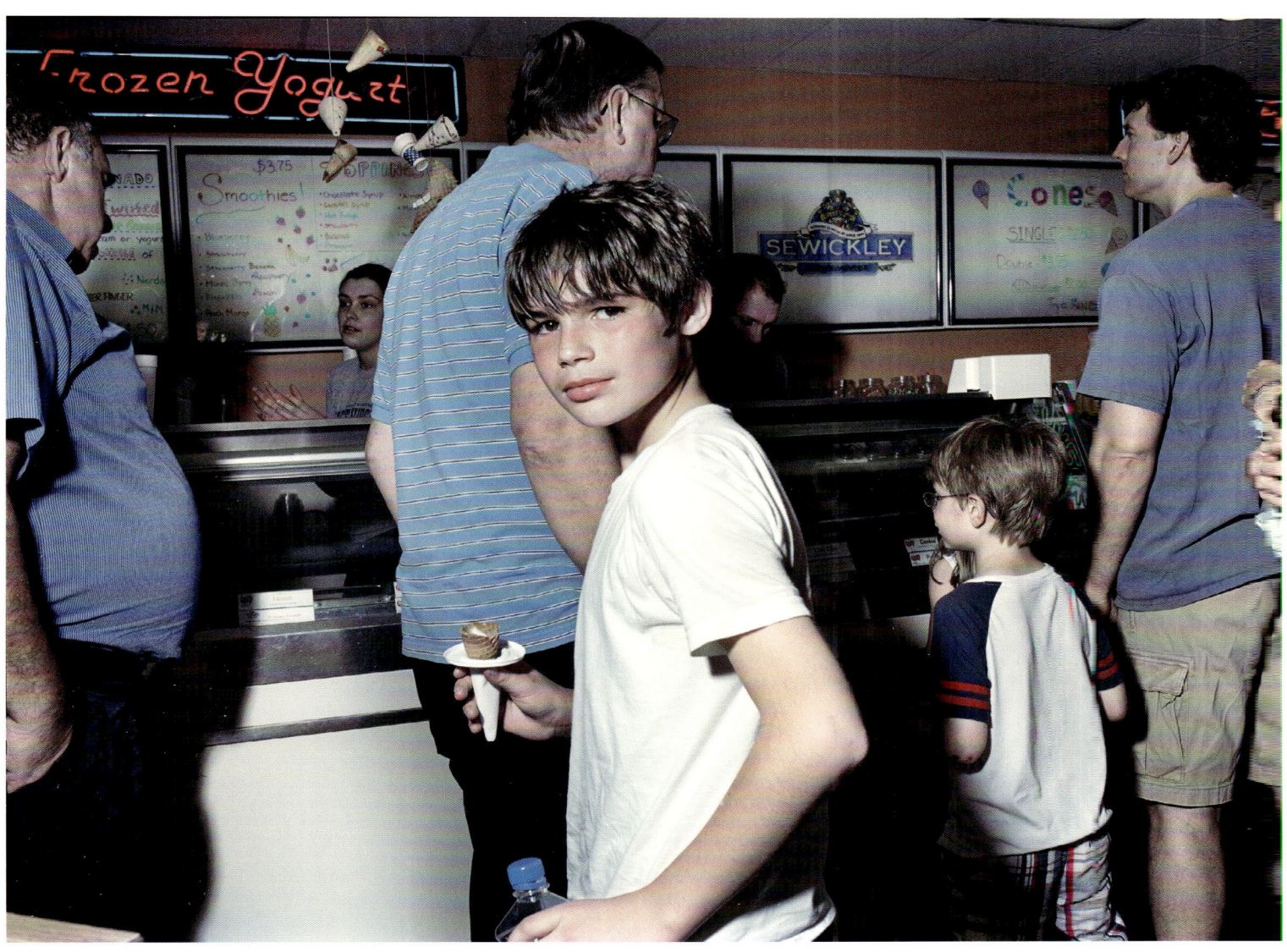

Opposite:
Sewickley Academy Prom,
2012

This page:
Sewickley Confectionery,
2012

British photographer Mark Neville typically undertakes long-term projects by living in unfamiliar communities and collaborating with local residents to portray people's bonds to place and to one another, a method of working he describes as intensely personal. In series like *The Port Glasgow Book Project* (2004–6), *Fancy Pictures* (2008), *Deeds Not Words* (2010–12), and *The Helmand Work* (2010–11), Neville investigates the articulation of power and class structure through prisms of war, deindustrialization, and environmental damage. The results of these projects—photobooks or exhibitions—are distributed either within the communities where the photographs were made, or to governmental and nongovernmental organizations directly involved in addressing the failing conditions depicted in the photographs. Neville conceives of his distribution strategy as a challenge to the convention of presenting social documentary photography in coffee-table books.

In 2012, Neville was commissioned by the Andy Warhol Museum, in Pittsburgh, to produce a body of work for the group exhibition *Factory Direct: Pittsburgh* (2012). He traveled for two months in Pennsylvania, first to Sewickley and then on to Braddock, exploring these distinct towns linked by their historical ties to steel production. The fortunes of Sewickley's and Braddock's residents devolve around the uneven inheritance of the gains from the region's industrial history; their separateness can be read not only in the stark disparity between wealth and poverty, but also along the quintessentially American dividing line of race.

Thus two double portraits—one in color, the other in black and white—show paired individuals, each symbiotically

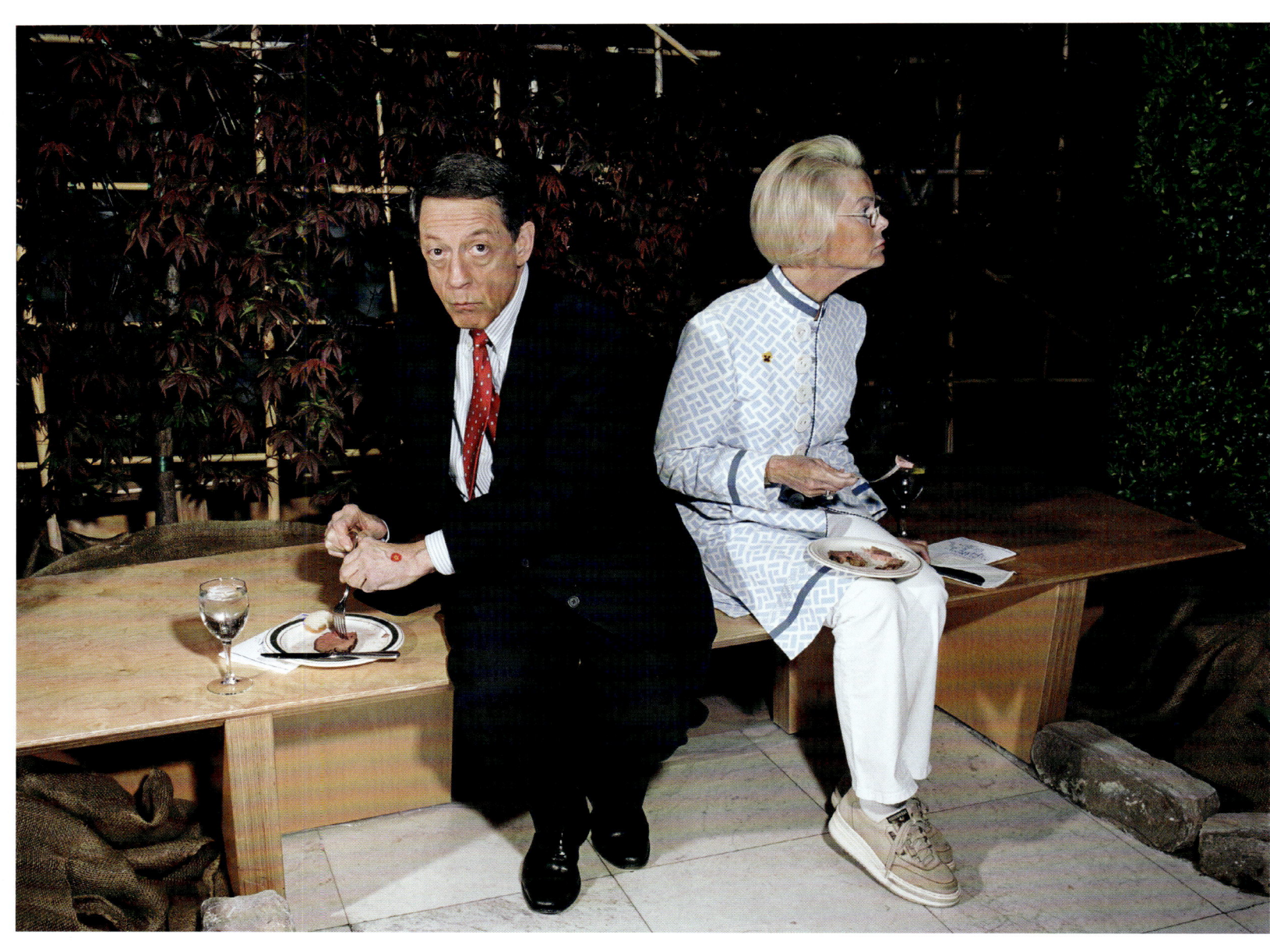

This page:
Art in Bloom Fundraiser, 2012

Opposite:
Braddock Farms, 2012

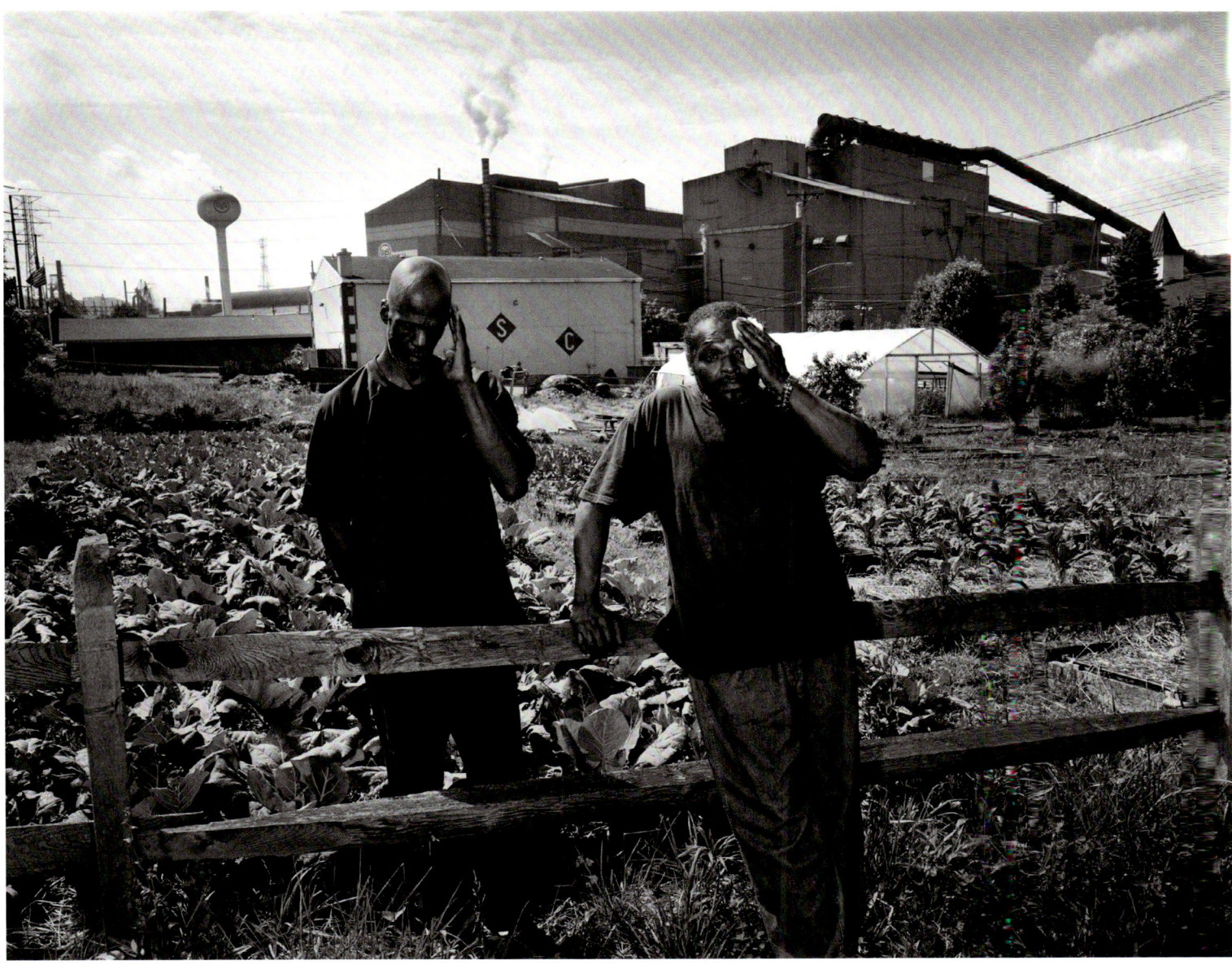

bonded to their partner by body or gesture. The Sewickley pair, a wealthy, middle-age couple, sit side-by-side at opposing angles as they eat slices of roast beef on a flash-lit patio. The Braddock pair, separated by a modest wooden fence, stand at the edge of an allotment framed by an enormous factory, each tenderly touching his brow in a moment of utter exhaustion. The photographs counterpose the labor of charity with the labor of sustenance, contrasting the comforts of leisure with a momentary reprieve. The pairings alert us to the hierarchical divisions of class according to which wealth is produced at one end of the economic spectrum, and degusted at the other.

Neville's work often attends to ritual and celebration as reflections of communal bonds and as willful expressions of freedom within the straitened circumstances of precarious employment and limited prospects. In Neville's series of candid photographs from the Woodland Hills and North Hills High School proms, it is alarming how segregated the groupings of students are by race. Neville's photographs question not only the distances and differences between Sewickley and Braddock, but also the umbilical ties that bind these two Americas together such that one may continue to feed so freely at the expense of the other. No dynamic seems more timely to consider in our effort to better grasp the racialized nature of capital in the postindustrial landscape of this new century.

Stanley Wolukau-Wanambwa is a photographer, writer, editor of The Great Leap Sideways, and a faculty member at Purchase College, SUNY.

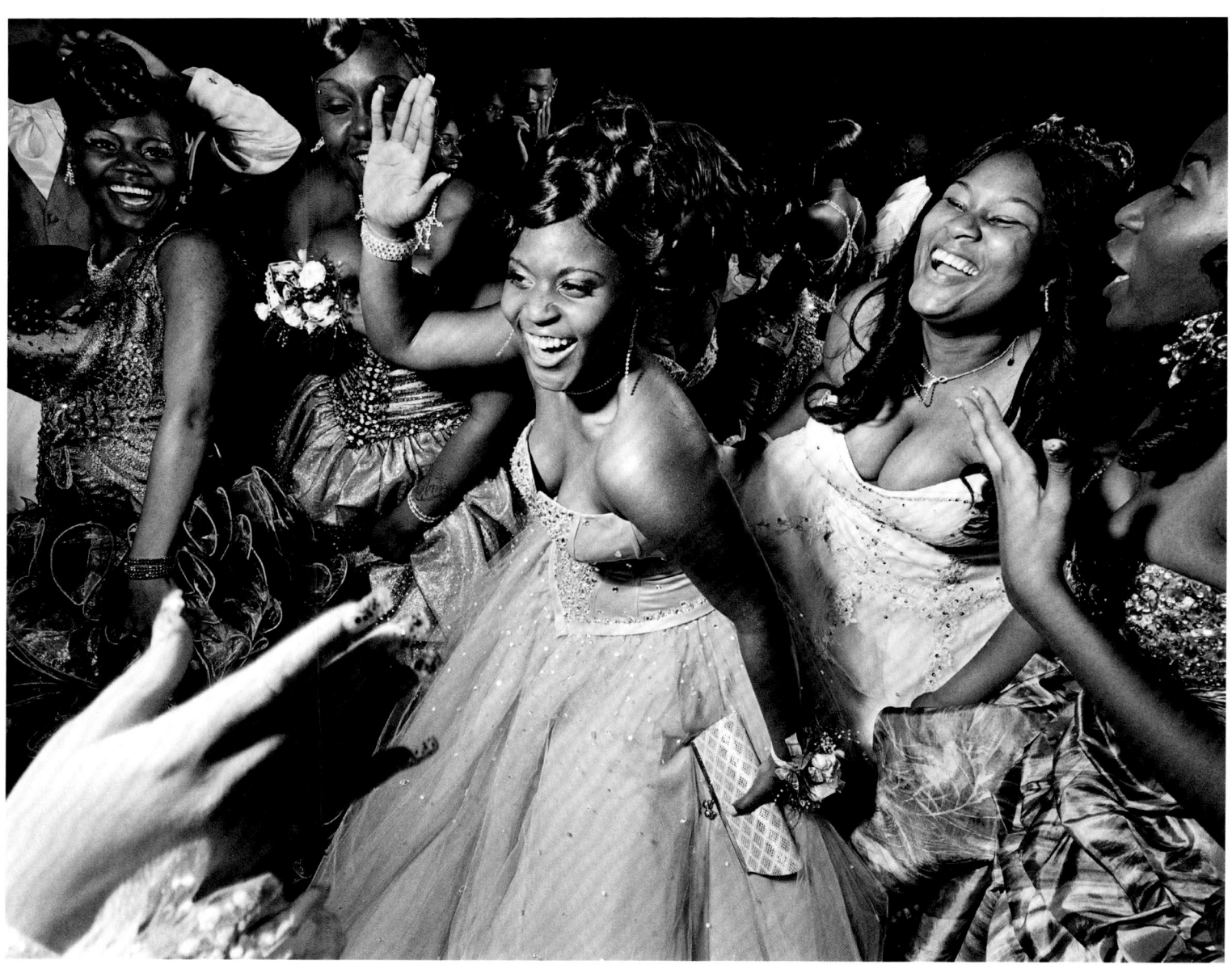

North Hills High School Prom, 3, 2012

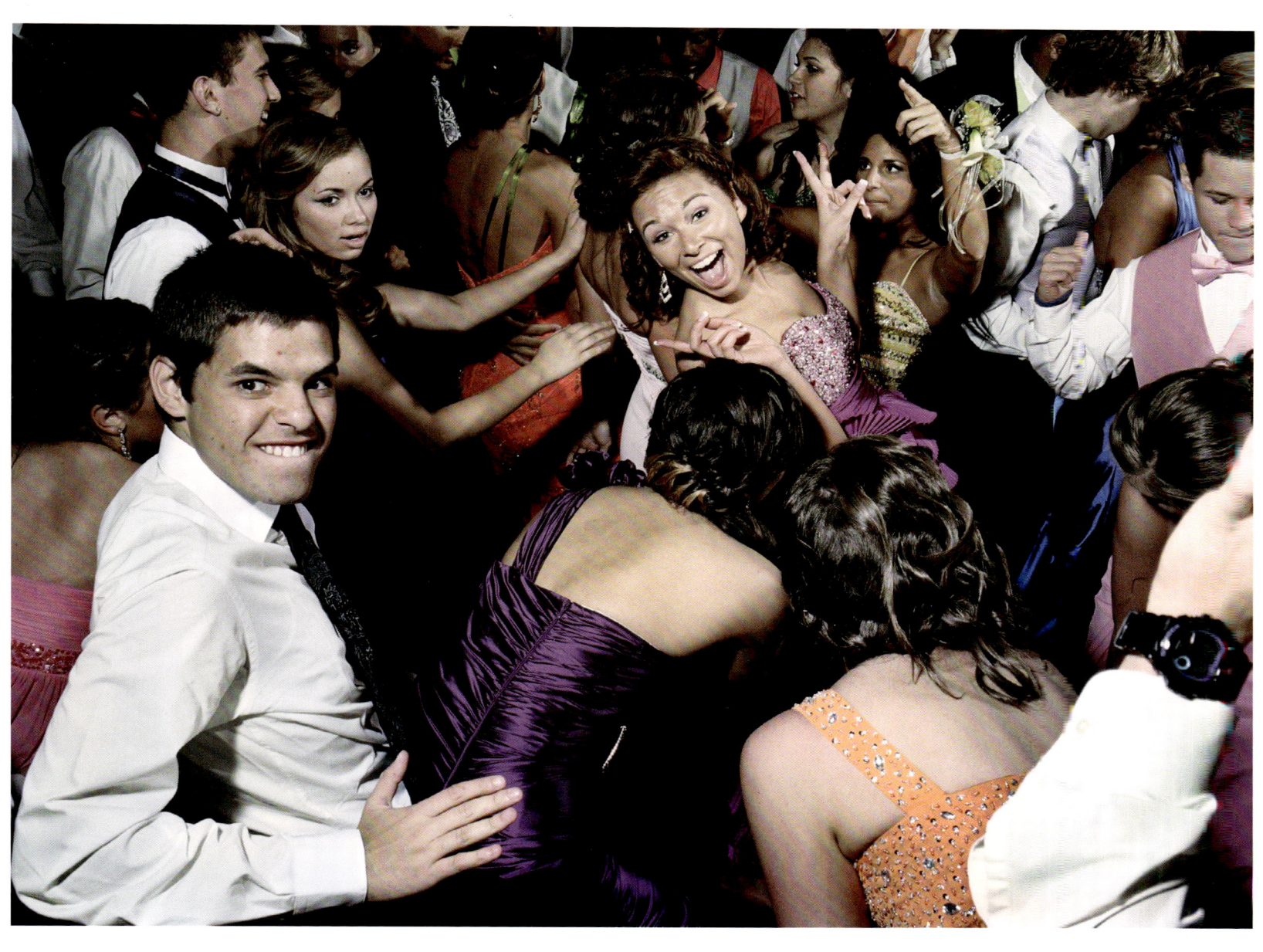

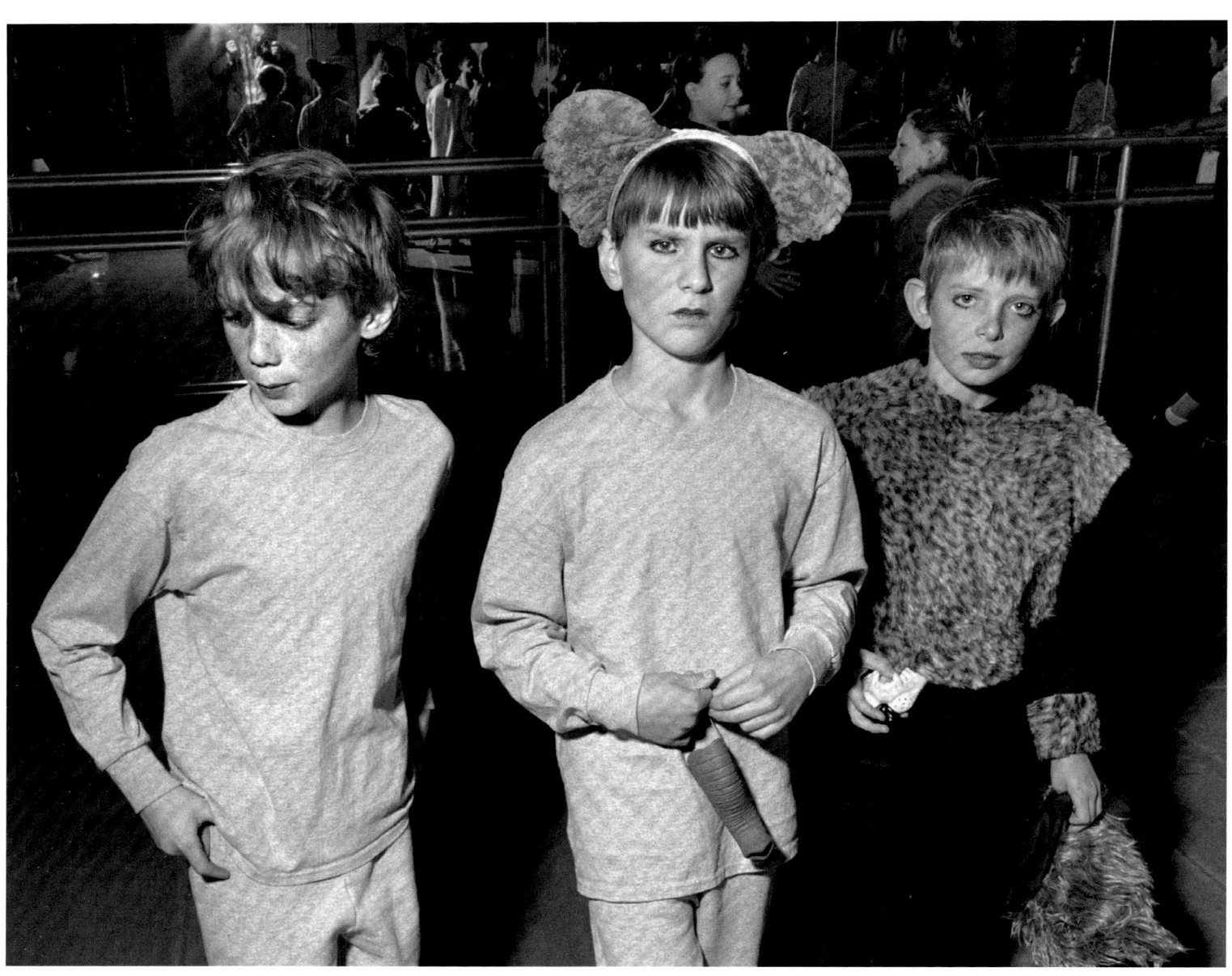

The Jungle Book Rehearsals, Sewickley Academy, 2012

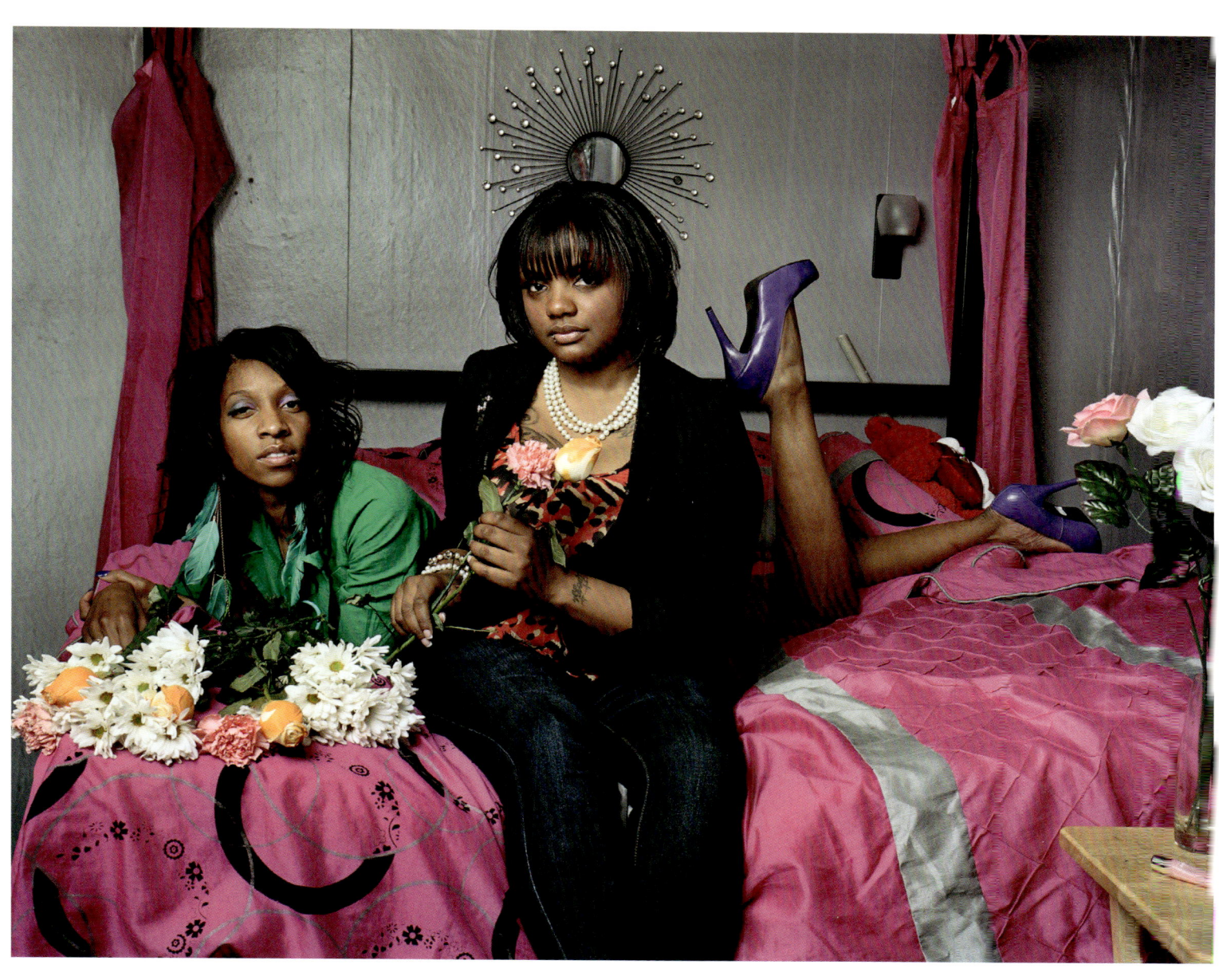

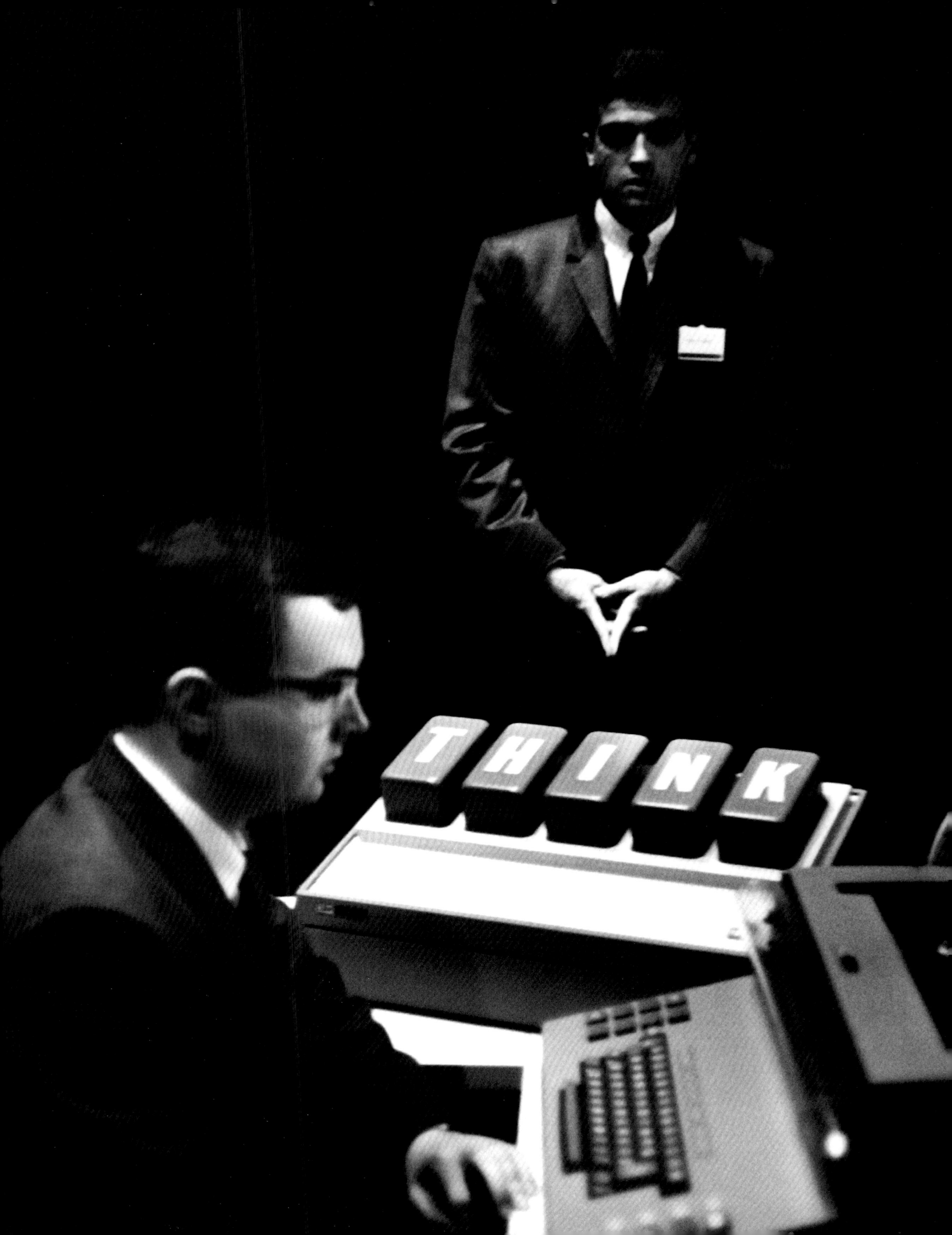

The Working Life

From the factory floor to the corner office, how do photographs describe the work we do?

David Campany

In 1899, Frances Benjamin Johnston was commissioned to photograph the working life of the Hampton Normal and Agricultural Institute, which had been founded in Hampton, Virginia, after the American Civil War to offer vocational education and practical training to freed slaves and Native Americans. Johnston's resulting photographs formed part of the American Negro Exhibit at the 1900 Exposition Universelle in Paris. The civil rights activist W. E. B. Du Bois, who helped organize the show, disliked separate education for African Americans, especially with its emphasis on manual labor, but he considered Johnston's work an "especially excellent series of photographs illustrating the Hampton idea of 'teaching by doing.'"

The Museum of Modern Art acquired an album of Johnston's Hampton prints in 1966, and the following year curator John Szarkowski discussed the work in his essay "Photography and the Mass Media." Illustrated with an image called *Stairway of the Treasurer's Residence: Students at Work*, the essay praises the formal and technical qualities of Johnston's platinum prints: "Miss Johnston demands and earns our attention. Having won it, she holds us by the richness and relevance of her description."

The graphic punch distilled in Hine's image dominated the depiction of American manual labor for decades.

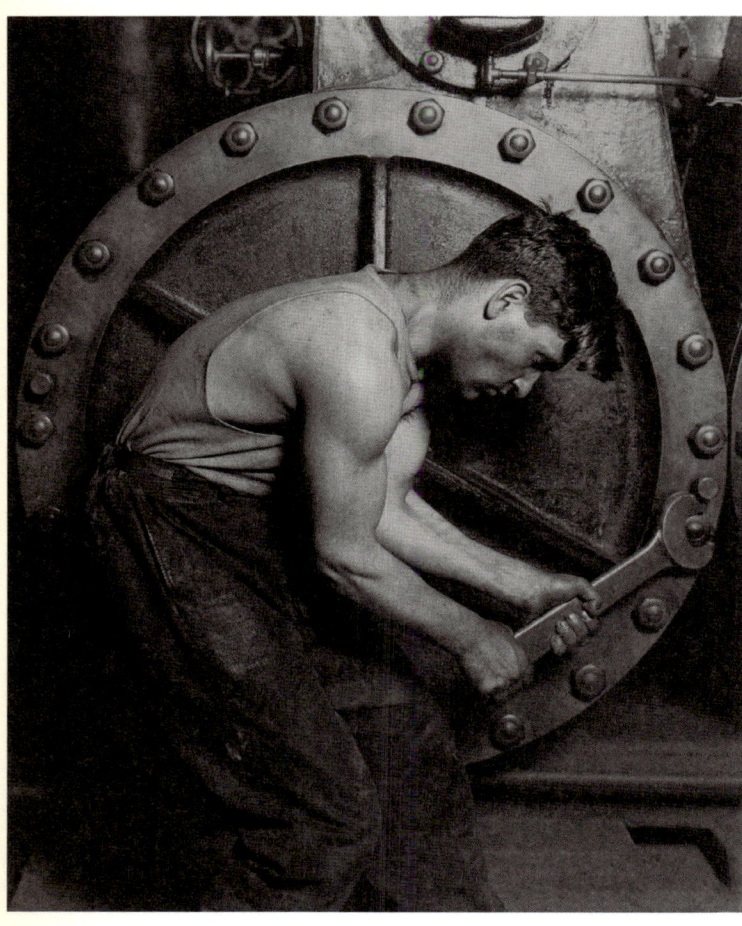

Lewis Hine, *Power house mechanic working on steam pump*, 1920
Courtesy the Getty's Open Content Program

But in 1982, this image of students at work reappeared in the artist Allan Sekula's essay "School is a Factory" with a very different reading. Sekula wrote that "the purpose of the Hampton album was promotional, serving as an aid to fund-raising. Thus the attitude of diligent and industrious servitude exhibited here might have been intended to impress white donors, like the steel manufacturer Andrew Carnegie, with the promise of converting a supposedly indolent and uneducated rural black population into disciplined, productive, and unrebellious proletarians."

We are in a moment when the idea—and image—of work is highly charged and politicized. In this circumstance, can an individual, or a nation, derive a self-image from the work it does? Johnston's choreographed scene, with posed working bodies interlocking, is an instructional photograph about instruction. A labored image of, and akin to, good carpentry. This doesn't stop it from being propaganda, but it doesn't make it propaganda, either. Photographs, particularly those depicting manual labor, are often the result of mixed intentions, practical hurdles, and aesthetic chances. While photography may *show*, it cannot *explain*. It is good at the "what" but not the "how" or the "why." Photographs visually describe labor, but cannot truly account for it.

At its beginning, the camera had such a close kinship with the cogs and levers of the Industrial Revolution that within decades a new "machine aesthetic" developed, peaking in the mid-twentieth century. But the camera found laboring human bodies to be equally photogenic, with their sweating skin, bold shapes, and furrowed brows. Lewis Hine's *Power house mechanic working on steam pump* (1920), an icon of American industrialism, is built on this duality. Does its formal unity suggest a utopian integration of man and machine, or is this an image of tension and alienation? Context can push the reading one way or the other, but the ambiguity is there.

The kind of graphic punch distilled in Hine's image dominated the depiction of American manual labor for many decades. It was partly a way to simplify the visual complexity of factories, workshops, and production lines, but there was also a rhetoric of heroic toil. This approach was pushed hard by *Fortune*, the nation's lavish magazine of business and industry, launched in 1930. Margaret Bourke-White's hyperbolic shots of factories and workers for the magazine have much in common with state photographs made in the Soviet Union at the same time. (Bourke-White was also keen to have *herself* depicted as the heroic working photographer for this can-do age.) But such extravagance always risked backfiring. In 1947 the media theorist Marshall McLuhan derided *Fortune* for its "managerial grand opera."

However, *Fortune*'s other key photographer was the antithesis of Bourke-White. Walker Evans photographed laborers throughout his career, but never actually while they labored. He preferred the less prescriptive arena of the street, at lunchtime or after hours. He also looked to common tools, or the workspace devoid of employees, shifting the camera's gaze away from the working body. Indeed, Evans sensed a much deeper consonance between photography and *unemployment*. "People out of work are not given to talking much about the one thing on their minds," he wrote in his photo-essay "People and Place in Trouble," published in *Fortune* in March 1961. "The plain non-artistic photograph may come closer to the matter, which is sheer personal distress." The static muteness of photography befits the silenced and stilled human. This profound insight went unnoticed, but Evans's circumspect attitude to picturing labor anticipated a great deal of the ensuing attempts to grapple with the challenge.

From the late 1950s to the early 2000s the German couple Bernd and Hilla Becher made extensive photographic surveys of industrial architecture across Europe and America. Their clear,

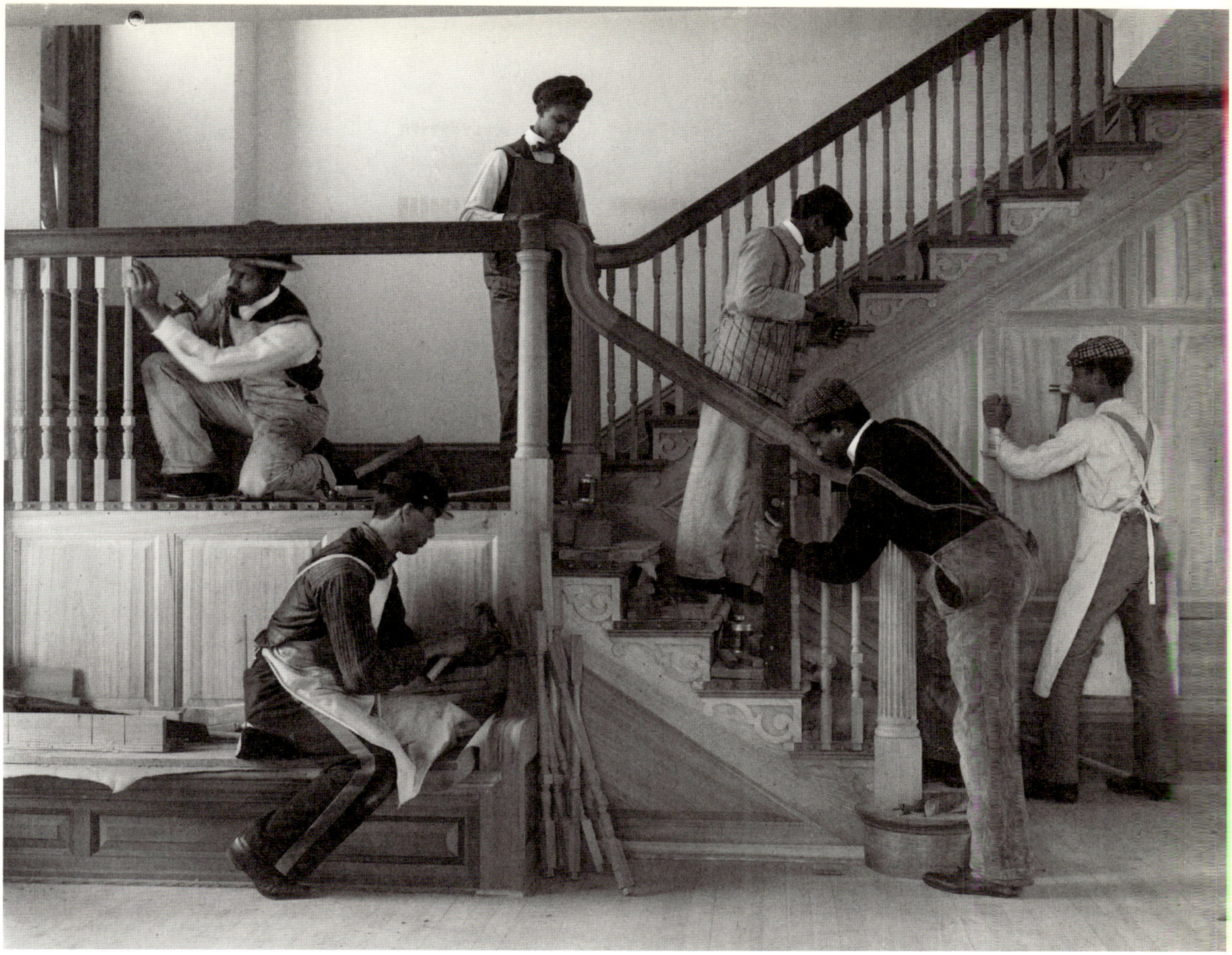

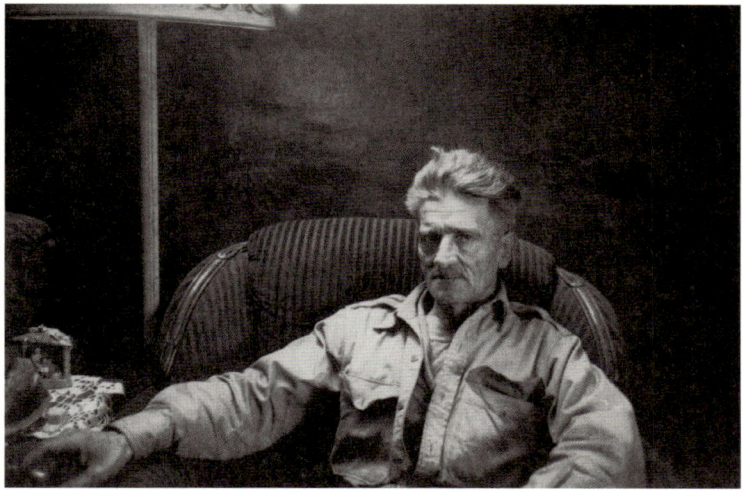

Top:
Frances Benjamin Johnston, *Stairway of the Treasurer's Residence: Students at Work,* **from the** *Hampton Album,* **1899–1900**
© The Museum of Modern Art/SCALA/Art Resource, New York

Bottom:
Walker Evans, *Unemployed Man,* **for** *Fortune* **magazine article "People and Places in Trouble," March 1961**
© Walker Evans Archive, The Metropolitan Museum of Art

frontal, and rectilinear images were taken with large-format cameras in the neutralized style of nineteenth-century architectural photography, and are almost always devoid of workers. The plain vision also masked the Bechers' own selfless labor. It is only when you see a grand survey exhibition of their prints, or consult their large books, that you can grasp the effort taken to build and operate these structures *and* the effort taken to document them. So while labor seems to be absent from the buildings and the photographs, it haunts from beyond the frame.

The Bechers restricted themselves to industrial forms that made sense to the eye, or, as they put it in their 1970 book *Anonymous Sculptures*, to "objects predominantly instrumental in character, whose shapes are the results of calculation and whose processes of development are optically evident." Mine shafts, lime kilns, and water towers, for example. They excluded nuclear power plants, because one cannot see from the outside how such facilities work.

In contrast, Lewis Baltz's now celebrated series *The New Industrial Parks Near Irvine, California* (1974) shows the exteriors of low-rise modular buildings that give no indication at all as to what is being made inside. "You don't know whether they are manufacturing pantyhose or megadeath," he once commented. He could have ventured in, as an investigative journalist, but there was something disarming about those exteriors. The uncertain status of labor in (and of) such images meant that at first the art world didn't know how to receive Baltz's work. When interest

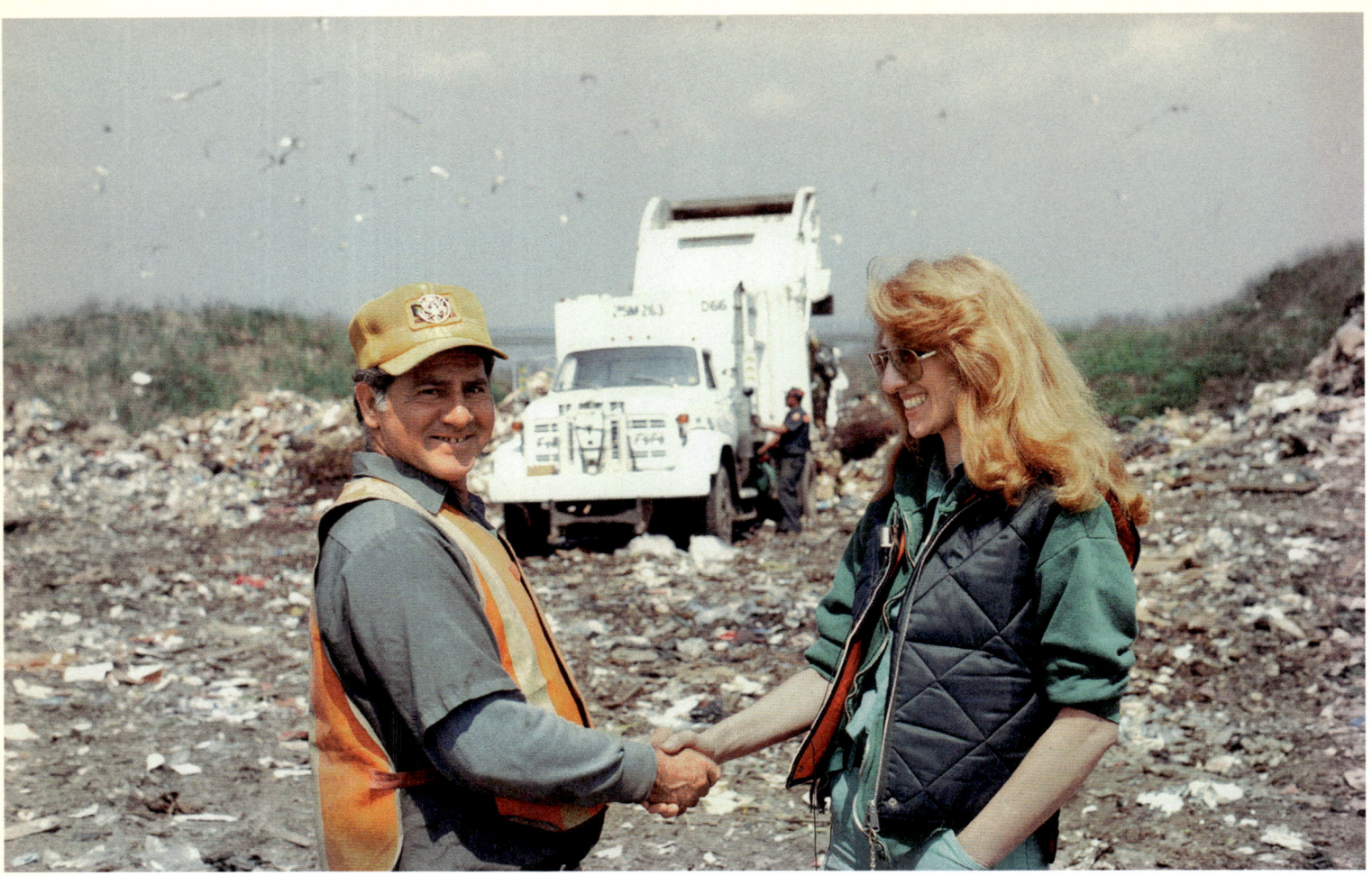

Mierle Laderman Ukeles,
Touch Sanitation
Performance, **1979–80**
Courtesy Ronald Feldman
Fine Arts, New York

did come it was in relation to minimalist sculpture and Conceptual art. For artists like Dan Flavin, a piece of sculpture could simply be an industrially standard form, like a fluorescent light tube. The conceptual turn in art happened for many reasons: the dead end of high modernism, new feminist voices, new political movements. In its downplaying of conspicuous craft, Conceptual art paralleled both the growing shift toward cheap mass manufacturing overseas and the great expansion of the service and leisure industries that continue to this day in so many "postindustrial" nations.

In this light, art practices coming out of the conceptual turn to directly address labor bring up particularly complicated strategies. Mierle Laderman Ukeles's *Touch Sanitation Performance* (1979–80) involved the artist literally "reaching out" to shake hands with New York City's 8,500 sanitation workers. We can certainly see this as a symbolic act of unity, and all those handshakes could be considered a lot of work in themselves, if not quite as arduous as clearing trash daily. Shaking so many hands isn't an everyday activity, but does it close the gap between art and everyday work? Or does it make the distance all the more palpable? For the people doing the handshaking it may close the gap, but what is a viewer's response? Are we to be inspired to do like the artist? To become a sanitation worker (if we're not one already)?

The gap between art and life can never really be closed, and there's a strong argument that it is key to art's potential to keep open a space of free thought and contemplation. But there are moments when the gap feels awkward. Photographing work and looking at photographs of work are often among those moments. This is partly because of the medium's equivocal status as labor, and the equally equivocal status of the photographer as laborer. Sure, photography can be very hard work, but it can also be no work at all; the earliest metaphors for the medium—"pencil of nature," "mirror with a memory"—emphasized ease and erased any sense of labor, or even intention. Any photographer who has been asked

Is the boss as trapped in formulaic behavior as the worker who disappoints him? Wall's tableau feels like a nightmarish karaoke of frustration.

to shoot a factory production line will be aware of how different their own labor is, and how differently they fit into the economy.

In Jeff Wall's *Outburst* (1989), the boss or floor manager of a garment sweatshop harangues a startled worker. The poses suggest sudden reaction but are stiff and caricatured. Is Wall's dramaturgy just plain awkward, or is he getting at the way labor relations often frustrate true expression and limit people to empty gestures that bypass true feelings? Is the boss as trapped in formulaic behavior as the worker who disappoints him? Wall's tableau feels like a nightmarish karaoke of frustration. Indeed, he first filmed his players in rehearsal, and then chose gestures from the footage to reenact before his camera. It's not a direct representation of labor, and it certainly doesn't attempt to dissolve art into life. Instead the representation of work and the work of representation rub against each other.

While art practices have been examining all of these representational strategies since the 1970s, the mass media depictions of American manual labor have dwindled, and far faster than the manufacturing base itself. It is rarely pictured in the news. As companies became increasingly image conscious and wary of bad press, photographers have found access more difficult. When the spaces of work *do* get photographed it's often by invitation, and with the restrictions that might imply. For decades, Magnum Photos has taken commissions to shoot for corporate annual reports. In 1969 the computer company IBM commissioned a book from Henri Cartier-Bresson, but the company itself was barely present in the results. Instead, the resulting book, *Man and Machine* (1969), cherry-picks from the photographer's back catalog of images, from horse-drawn ploughs to high-tech industry. While it is far

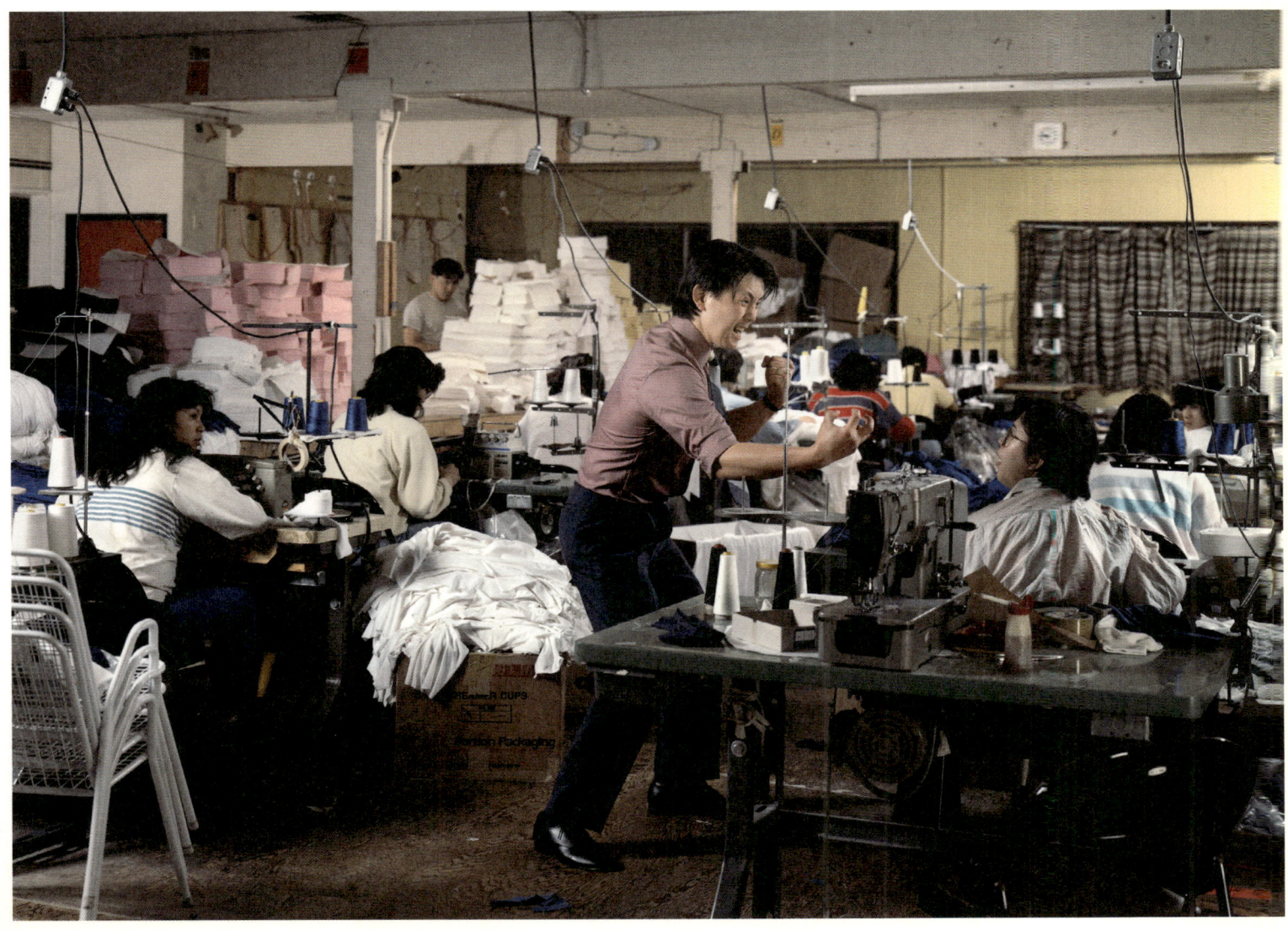

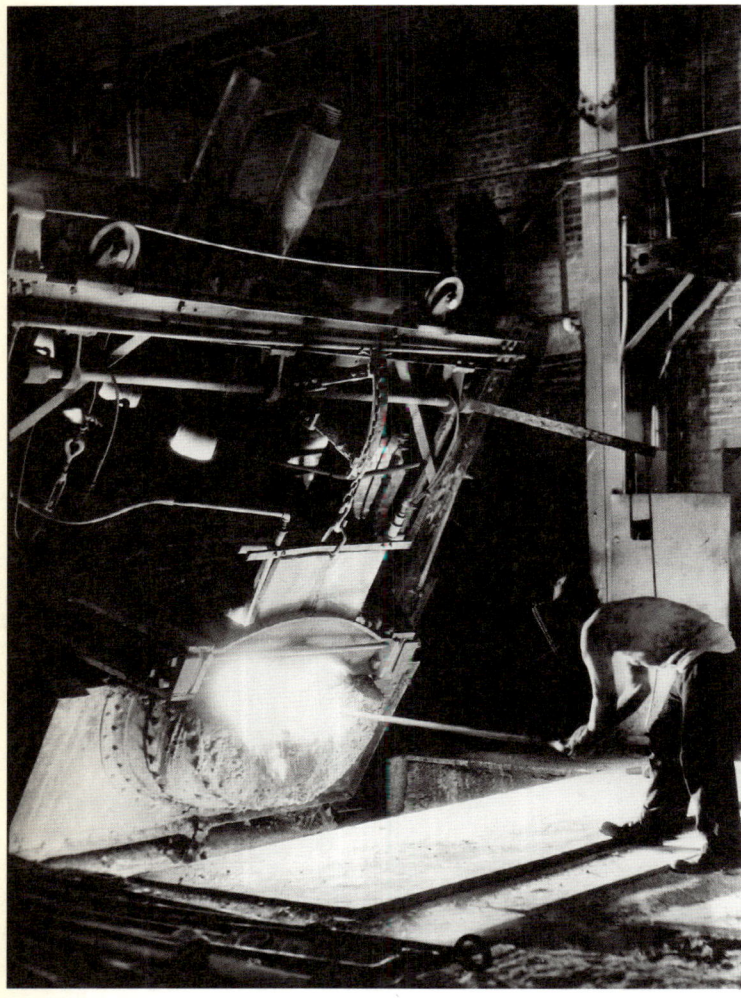

from Cartier-Bresson's finest publication, there's something revelatory about seeing dirty cogs and levers replaced by clean electronics while sensing the photographer's struggle to find ways of picturing the change.

Perhaps the most remarkable and extensive documentation of American labor has come from the photographer Lee Friedlander. Over decades and through several very different projects, all commissioned, he has built up a singularly compelling portrait of the nation at work. *Factory Valleys* (1979–80), a study of heavy and light industry in Ohio and Pennsylvania, was made at the invitation of the Akron Art Institute; in 1985 the Massachusetts Institute of Technology Museum commissioned photographs of workers seated at computers in and around Boston; in 1986 Cray Research of Chippewa Falls, Wisconsin, asked for a photobook of its supercomputer production, to be given directly to all its employees; in 1992 the Dreyfus Corporation in New York City asked for images of workers in its offices and trading floor; in 1995 the Gund Foundation commissioned pictures of manufacturing in Cleveland for its annual report; in 1995 *The New York Times Magazine* commissioned portraits of telemarketers at work in Omaha, Nebraska; and then, in 2007, *The New York Times Magazine* asked Friedlander to shoot backstage at New York Fashion Week.

The list sounds institutional, but in each case the commission came from a person within the company who understood Friedlander's vision and his way of photographing workers as individuals. Yes, they are often pictured in the seriocomic chaos of tubing, cable, or cloth, and at times it's difficult to see where limbs end and tools begin. But humans change the world of work, and work changes humans. These aren't corny attempts to pierce the soul of each person, nor to turn people into emblems of "work in general." There's no condescension or idolizing either, just complex pictures of complex people doing complex things.

What comes through is Friedlander's affection for his fellow human beings and their varied circumstances of toil. The photographer working his machine strives to make a picture of another person working theirs. And as always, Friedlandler makes his own labor look easy, wearing so lightly his years of honed and hard-won technique. Pictures from most of these projects were published in a 2002 book with the brilliantly double-edged title *Lee Friedlander at Work*. It was prefaced with a simple dedication: "To the memory of my uncle Neil Norme, who through his example taught me the honor and pleasure of work. He was a calm and purposeful man. Steady."

Honor and pleasure. Those are not words one often hears in relation to today's world of work, nor the depictions of it. It's unlikely that work will ever be pleasurable for everyone, which is all the more reason to regard it as honorable.

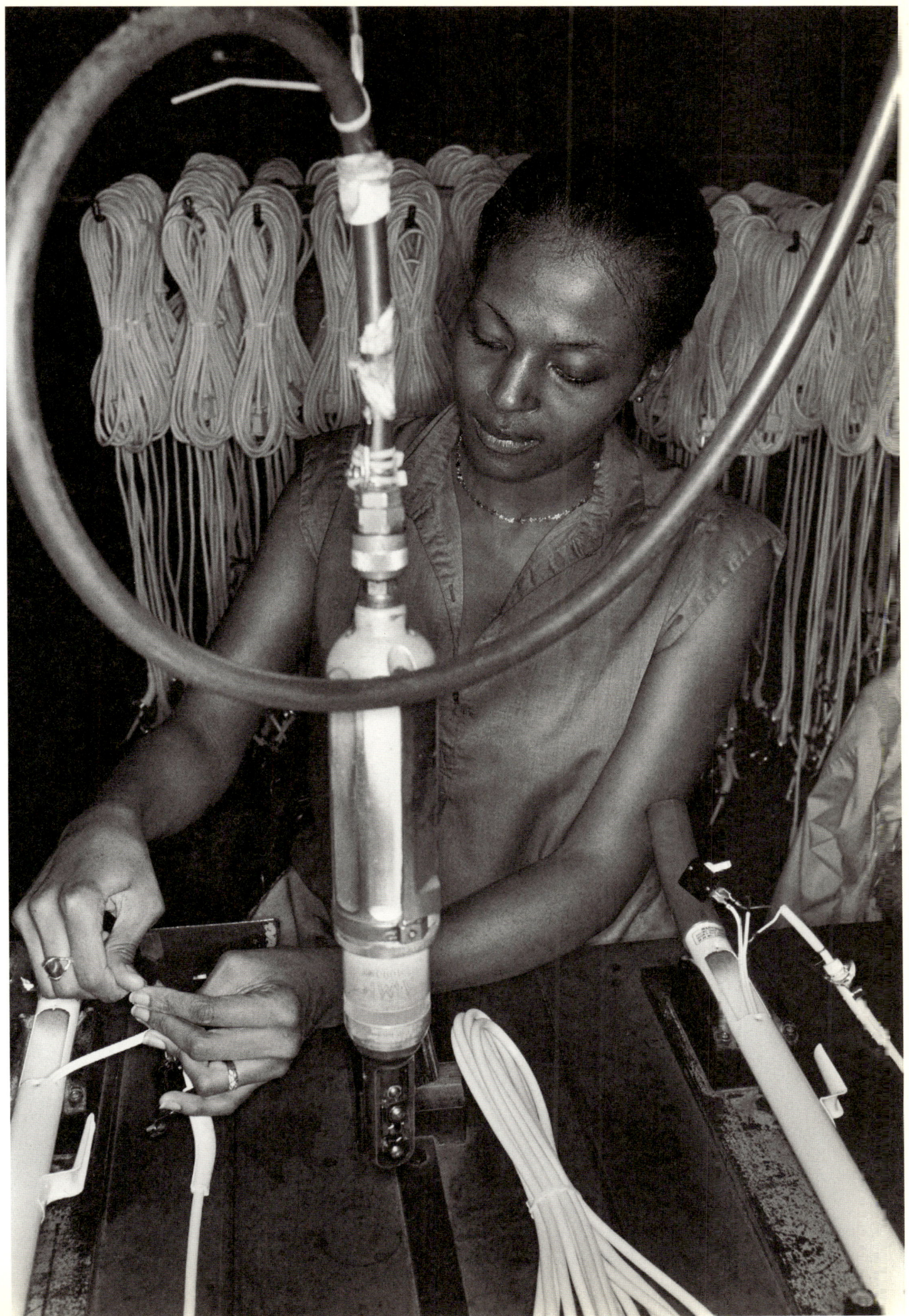

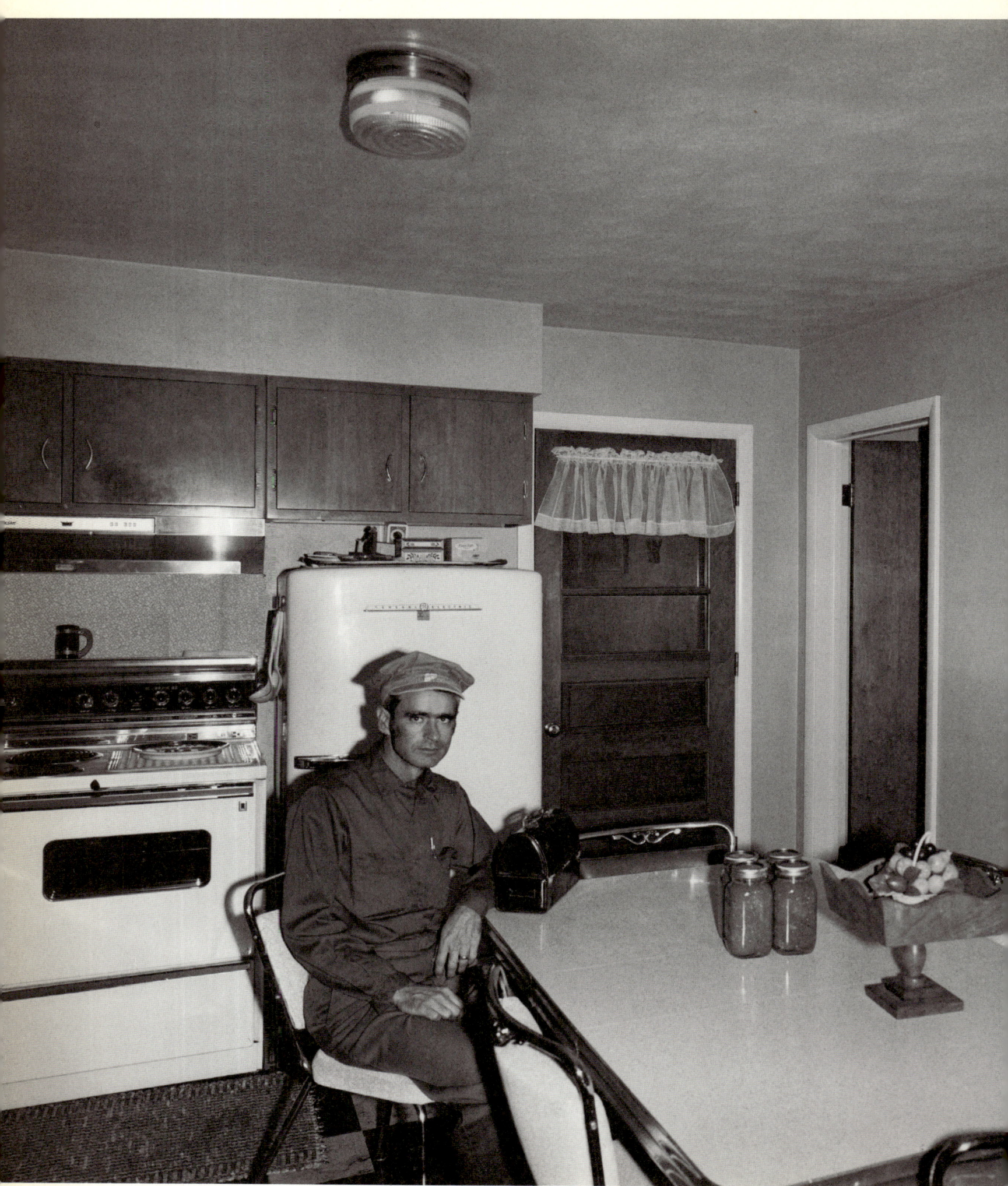

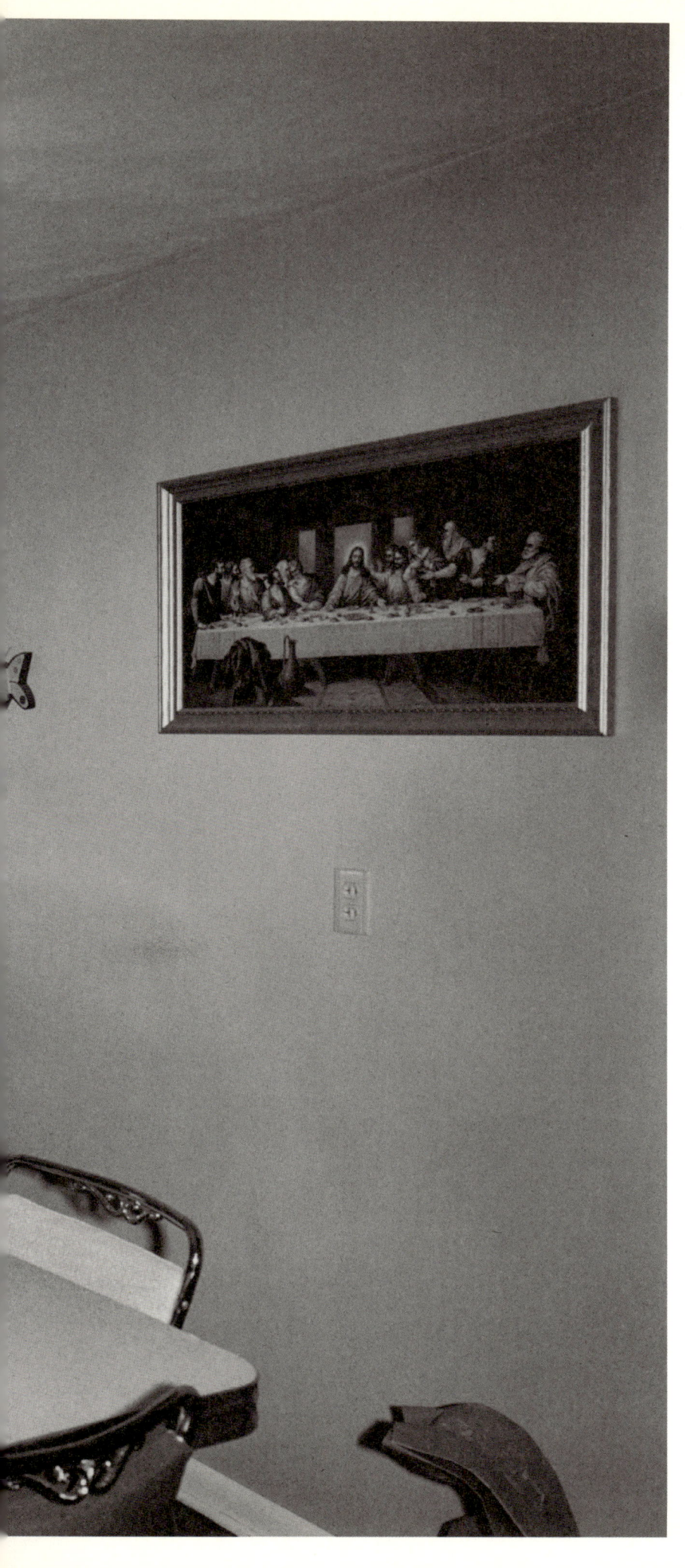

Chauncey Hare's Protest

An accomplished photographer—
and former Standard Oil
engineer—becomes an advocate
for the working class

Rebecca Bengal

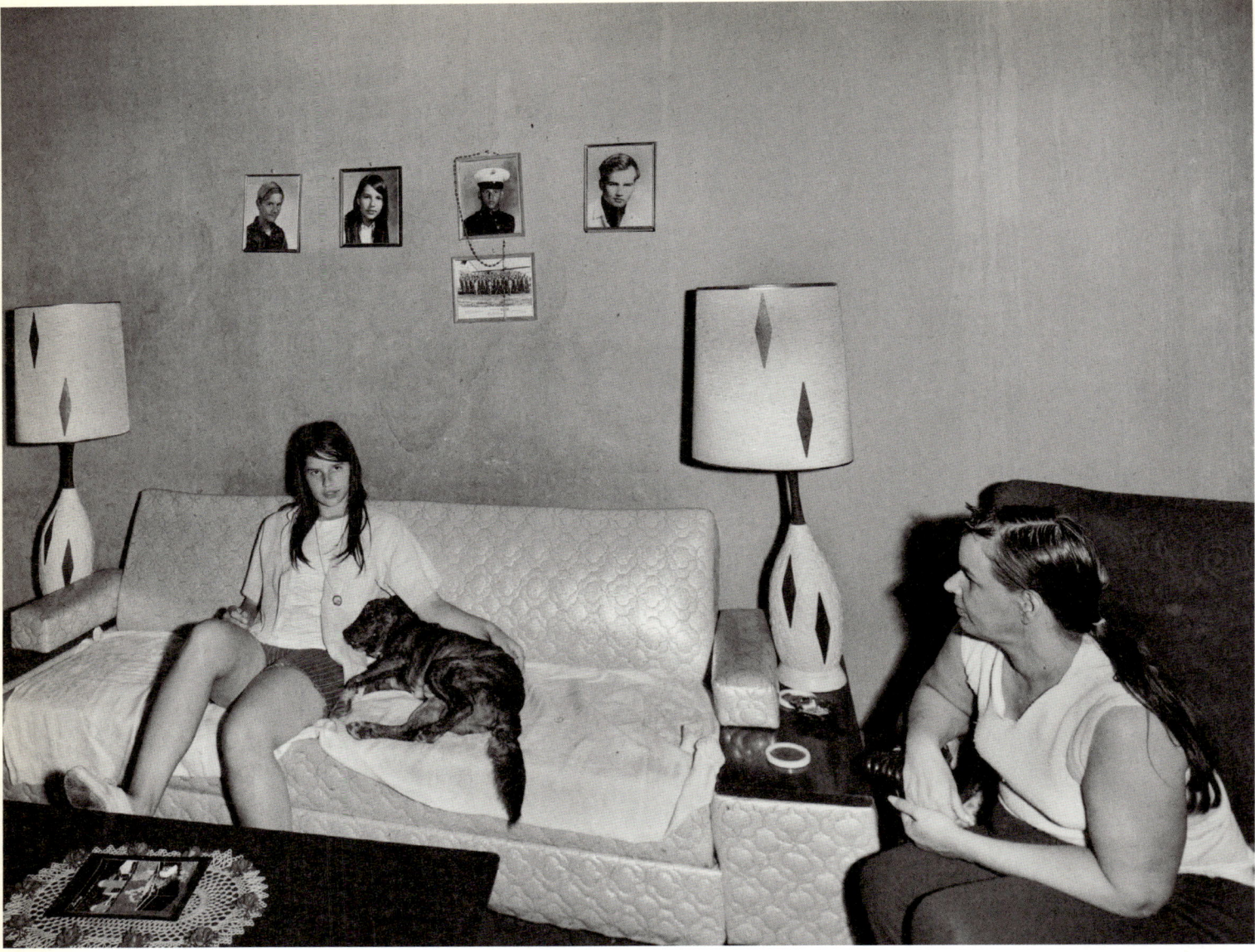

This page:
Cincinnati, Ohio,
1971

Opposite:
Oakland, California
1968-69

"These photographs were made by Chauncey Hare to protest and warn against the growing domination of working people by multi-national corporations and their elite owners and managers."

In the summer of 1979, as long lines queued up outside the San Francisco Museum of Modern Art for the highly anticipated arrival of *Mirrors and Windows: American Photography since 1960*, a John Szarkowski–curated exhibition, one man walked in the opposite direction. The show carried with it the electric buzz of a star curator redefining photography for a new age and anointing a current generation of photographers. Szarkowski divided them into two camps. There were the "mirrors," photographers he categorized as "romantic" and "expressionist," Robert Rauschenberg, Duane Michals, and Andy Warhol among them. Those in Szarkowski's "windows" group, whose work he called "realist" ("because no other word was better"), included Garry Winogrand, Diane Arbus, Lee Friedlander, Helen Levitt, William Eggleston, and Stephen Shore, as well as a rather intense-looking individual pressing fliers into the hands of passersby, demanding the removal of his own photograph and urging a boycott of the exhibition altogether. The flier called for outrage at the show's corporate sponsorship by tobacco giant Philip Morris.

On that day in June, Chauncey Hare was at the pinnacle of his photographic career. Two years earlier he had flown to New York for the opening of *The Effects of Technology on the Individual: Photographs by Chauncey Hare*, his solo show at the Museum

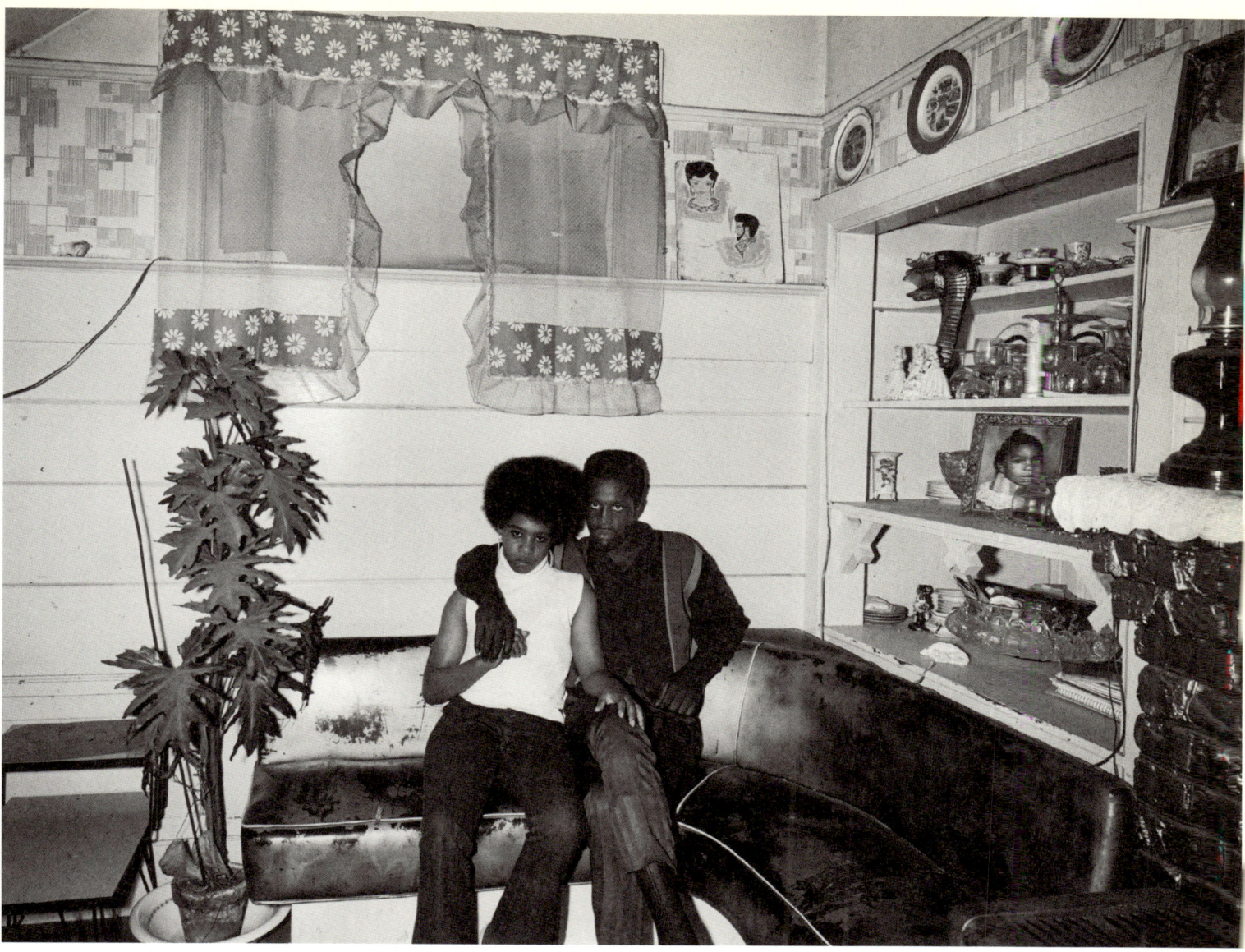

of Modern Art, curated by Szarkowski. "I heard later that no one expected to see a short, knapsack-carrying, sandal wearing, ex-corporate engineer playing the role of a three-time Guggenheim Fellow photographer," Hare wrote of his Manhattan experience. He stayed at the West Side Y but was taken to lavish "expense account meals" with Aperture, who published his first book of photographs, *Interior America*, in 1978. Two months after Hare picketed *Mirrors and Windows*, Janet Malcolm reviewed *Interior America* alongside *Walker Evans: First and Last* (1978) and a 1978 reprint of Robert Frank's *The Americans* (1959), calling Hare's pictures of working people in their homes and workplaces and towns "devastating." "He shows us to ourselves," Malcolm wrote in *The New Yorker*, her review brilliantly titled "Slouching Towards Bethlehem, Pa.," "as perhaps no other documentary photographer has ever done."

"We all thought he was crazy," Jack von Euw recently recalled of the day he met Chauncey Hare. He was speaking from his office at the Bancroft Library at the University of California, Berkeley, where he is curator of the pictorial collection, home to Hare's archives. "At that time I was an aspiring photographer and most of us would have given our left arm to be in that show. John was the kingmaker."

When von Euw visited *Mirrors and Windows* in 1979, he found himself unsettled by the message delivered by Hare and also unable to ignore the presence of Philip Morris, whose name was boldly lettered on the gallery walls. "What did it mean that such a large corporation and one that merchandised cancer as a by-product

should sponsor an art exhibition?" von Euw wrote decades later in the afterword to *Protest Photographs* (2009), Hare's third book. What seemed an act of self-sabotage in 1979 did not end Hare's photographic career—he would do that on his own terms—but it did illuminate the current of protest that rises from the core of his pictures. Von Euw tucked Hare's flier in his pocket and kept it for many years.

Rare is the photographer who desires a mention of personal stories to frame the work; rarer still is the photographer who insists on it absolutely. But in all three books of photographs Hare published, he contributed a substantial and distinct autobiographical essay. His resistance to *Mirrors and Windows* is the defining moment of his life as a photographer: his awakening, though occurred more than a decade prior, in March 1968, in Point Richmond, California. Point Richmond is under an hour's drive from Berkeley and the Haight, but a biopic of the turning point of Hare's life in the late '60s would not cue Jefferson Airplane or stock footage of flower children on acid. Chauncey Hare later wrote of meeting Orville England, who would become not only his most pivotal photographic subject but a close friend, "I was reminded of fairy tale gnomes who ask questions that may determine your fate." England, a stocky, genial man, approached Hare and asked if he wanted to buy a little plastic camera. How could this stranger have known, Hare wondered, that he had a Leica concealed in his jacket? He accompanied England and his wife Helen home.

Hare, an engineer at the Standard Oil Company, typically roamed the streets, camera in coat, on his lunch break. He had taken

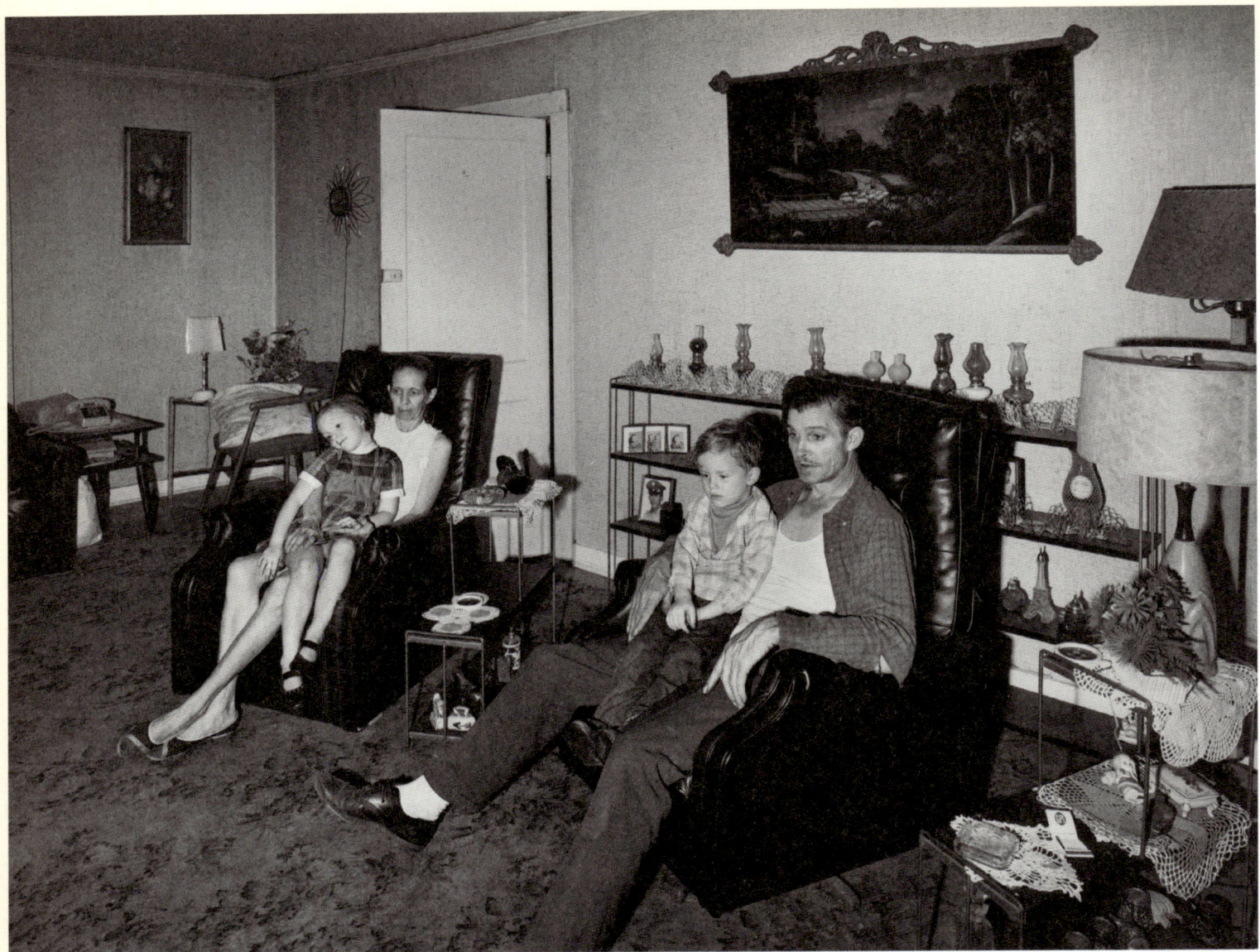

up photography much in the way he had taken up fishing, except in a few years' time he had gone from shyly shooting landscapes and developing his film in a closet darkroom to making pictures not only with his Leica but also with a large-format view camera. He eventually learned that England, a refinery worker, had become disabled after being exposed to asbestos on the job. Hare's own grandfather had lost the use of a leg while working at Pittsburgh Steel. Objects and ephemera of England's home, which Hare returned to photograph the next day, evoked the concrete, household details Hare remembered from summers at his grandparents' house in Pennsylvania. If Hare was to eventually become the kind of photographer Szarkowski called a "window," Orville England was the mirror he needed, the reflection of his own life and the omen that would propel it forward. The photograph he made upon his return, of England sitting in his kitchen, was Hare's first real look into interior America.

Reproductions of Leonardo da Vinci's *The Last Supper* and paintings of horses and kittens and streams fill the rooms that Hare came to photograph in Pennsylvania, West Virginia, Ohio, the Sierra foothills, the San Francisco Bay Area, and places in between. Lamps, kettles, coffee cans, telephones, water heaters, blank televisions, and wall mirrors amplify the harrowing effect of his images. He rarely took more than one or two photographs at a time; he arrived bearing letters of recommendation from the Guggenheim Foundation and the Smithsonian, and came to experience what he called "magic"—"people expecting me when I had not met them before."

And yet, even when they are in a room together, Hare's subjects are revealed as utterly alone. In Wheeling, West Virginia, a husband and wife sit in separate armchairs, a child on each lap, like a pair of isolated islands adrift in a room crammed with doilies, plastic flowers, a collection of lanterns, and cheap art. The husband and wife wear television expressions, slack-jawed and stunned. "I've also discovered that by evening most of masculine Interior America is a little bit drunk," Hare wrote.

In his writings, Hare acknowledges the "deception" of using a wide-angle lens. Some subjects were not even aware they would appear in the frame, and definitely not imagining that certain details would creep into the picture: electric cords, dirty surfaces, windows and doors that opened onto other, dingier spaces. Sometimes Hare's camera is pitched to such a capacious angle that the apparent vastness of the room is terrifying. In other pictures, the camera's position lends itself to claustrophobic effect: floors recede into walls or wallpaper seems to swallow the carpet whole.

If there is a literary analogue, Hare's photographs might be a short story by Raymond Carver or Lucia Berlin. Hare discovers his decisive moment in the things no one wants him to see. "If anyone tries to keep me from looking somewhere, say, an upstairs bedroom," he wrote, "that's where I know I need to go." There might be an infant alone in a room. Or a man stalking through a boardinghouse, glaring at the camera. "You sonofabitch," he said to Hare. A telephone cord unwinds across the length of a living room, corralling the various family members. Janet Malcolm observed

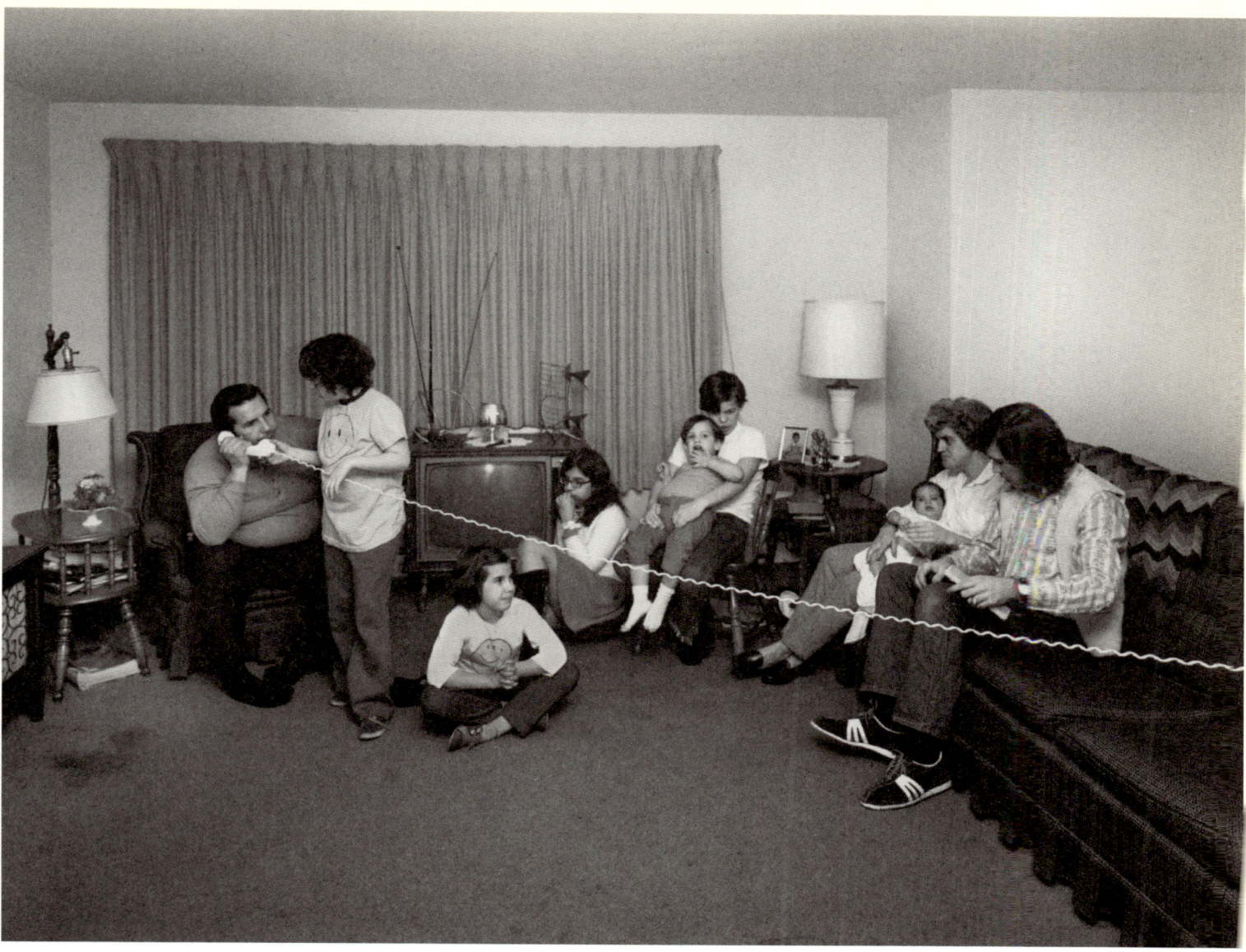

Opposite:
Wheeling, West Virginia,
1972

This page:
West Chester,
Pennsylvania, 1972

Hare enters the homes that Robert Frank sped past when taking the pictures for *The Americans.*

that with *Interior America*, Hare enters the homes that Frank sped past when taking the pictures for *The Americans*.

The spiritless worlds he discovered within reflected his own life. Hare is descended from his paternal steelworker grandfather and a maternal grandfather who worked for the Shredded Wheat factory in Niagara Falls, New York. His mother, chronically depressed, spent days locked in her room. His father was an engineer who took pride in having an employee who washed his car for him. Hare's life proceeded in seemingly inevitable fashion: He went to engineering school at Columbia University without thinking much about it. He married his first wife, an Austrian waitress named Gertrude, without bothering to fall in love. He got his first job at Standard Oil (which became Chevron) in California without much trouble. A good recruiter, he noted in *Protest Photographs*, would have been suspicious of a company man who studied short stories at night.

At Chevron, Hare once worked with a team whose response to the nitrogen dioxide emanating from the refinery stacks was to recommend a way to render the gas colorless so that it would go undetected. Years in, his own invisible fears and unhappiness manifested in chronic nausea and vomiting. When he began photographing in the '60s, the symptoms disappeared. In 1950, Hare was granted leave from his job to travel the country in an Econoline van and photograph with his Guggenheim money. With subsequent Guggenheim grants, Hare earned permission to bring his camera into his own workplace, as well as into interiors of other corporations. "He took on the hardest subject there was,"

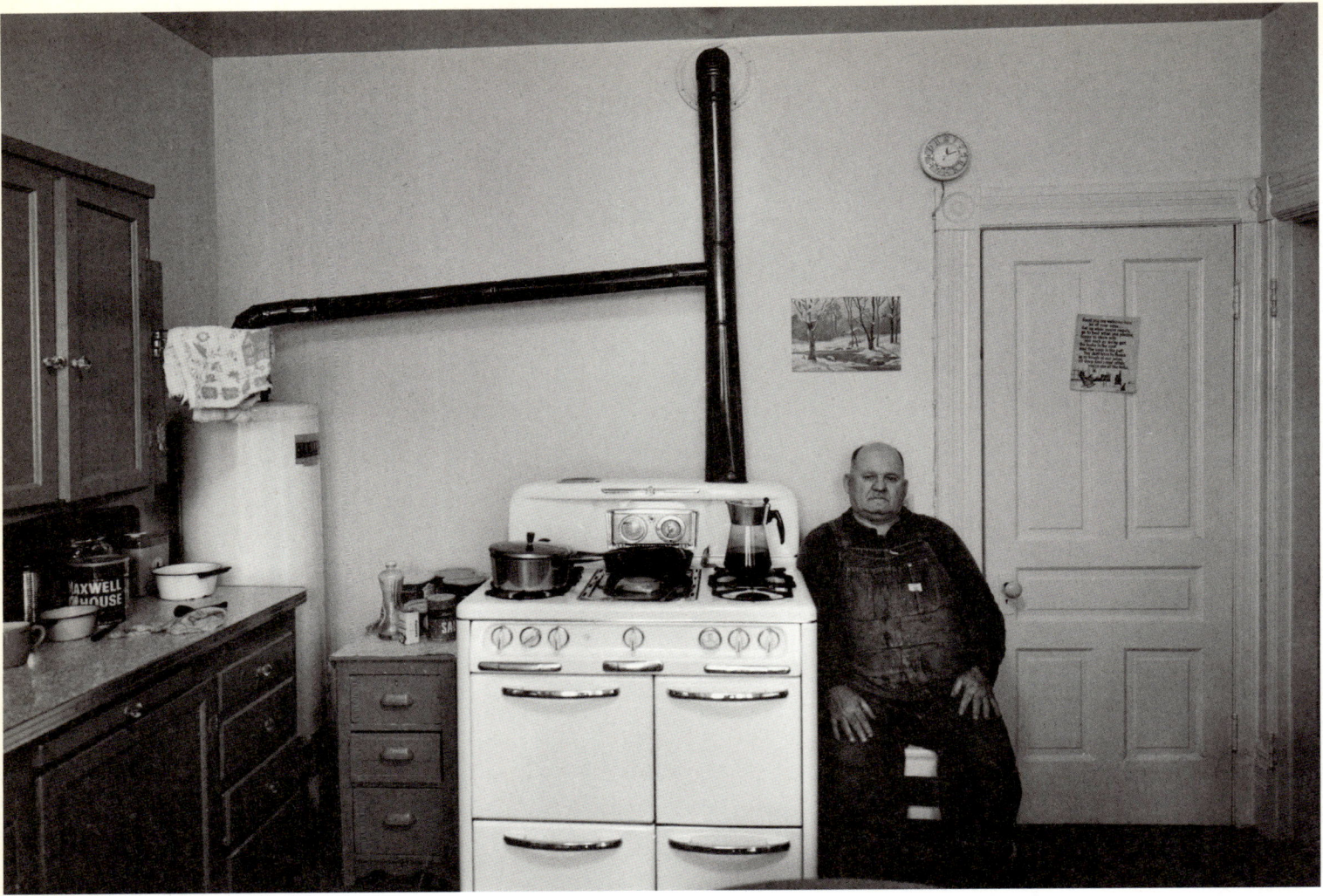

This page:
Orville England, Richmond, California, 1968

Opposite:
Standard Oil Company of California, Richmond, California, 1976–77
All photographs ©
The Bancroft Library,
University of California,
Berkeley

If the Bancroft Library didn't agree to Hare's conditions, Chauncey Hare's entire photographic record was destined for a bonfire.

recalls Bill Owens, who was then making the pictures that would become *Suburbia* (1973). "Ordinary people doing ordinary work in ordinary offices."

Hare's fight to publish *This Was Corporate America* in 1984 triggered a period that he describes as cutting ties with the photography and art world. "Each photograph had become a record of promise I had taken on," he wrote, and to sell those records, or to show them as purely aesthetic images, he believed, would have been tantamount to selling the people.

Ken Light, who was making photographs of industrial workers when he first met Hare in the early 1980s, corresponded with him for years. "He felt a complete responsibility to the people he photographed, and wanting to change the world or change their status and I think that's why he gave it up," Light said recently. "With *Interior America*, people thought he was the new Walker Evans. But Evans was very disconnected from the people he photographed. He was interested in the image, the actual object. And Chauncey was this wonderful photographer for whom the photograph wasn't enough. He cared about the people."

After divorcing Gertrude, and giving up custody of their son, Victor, Hare eventually moved in with Orville and Helen, caring for them until Orville's death. He immersed himself in the life of one of the prostitutes he photographed, and tried to help her beat a heroin addiction. He began attending what he described as "meet-members-of-the-opposite-sex" parties on Saturday nights and "newspaper dating." Mostly he went out with psychotherapists and psychologists; he baked them apple pies. When Judy Wyatt, a therapist, answered a personal ad in the *San Francisco Bay Guardian*, she found herself meeting a "wiry man, compact, handsome in a falcon-like way, wearing light-blue corduroy bell-bottoms and a

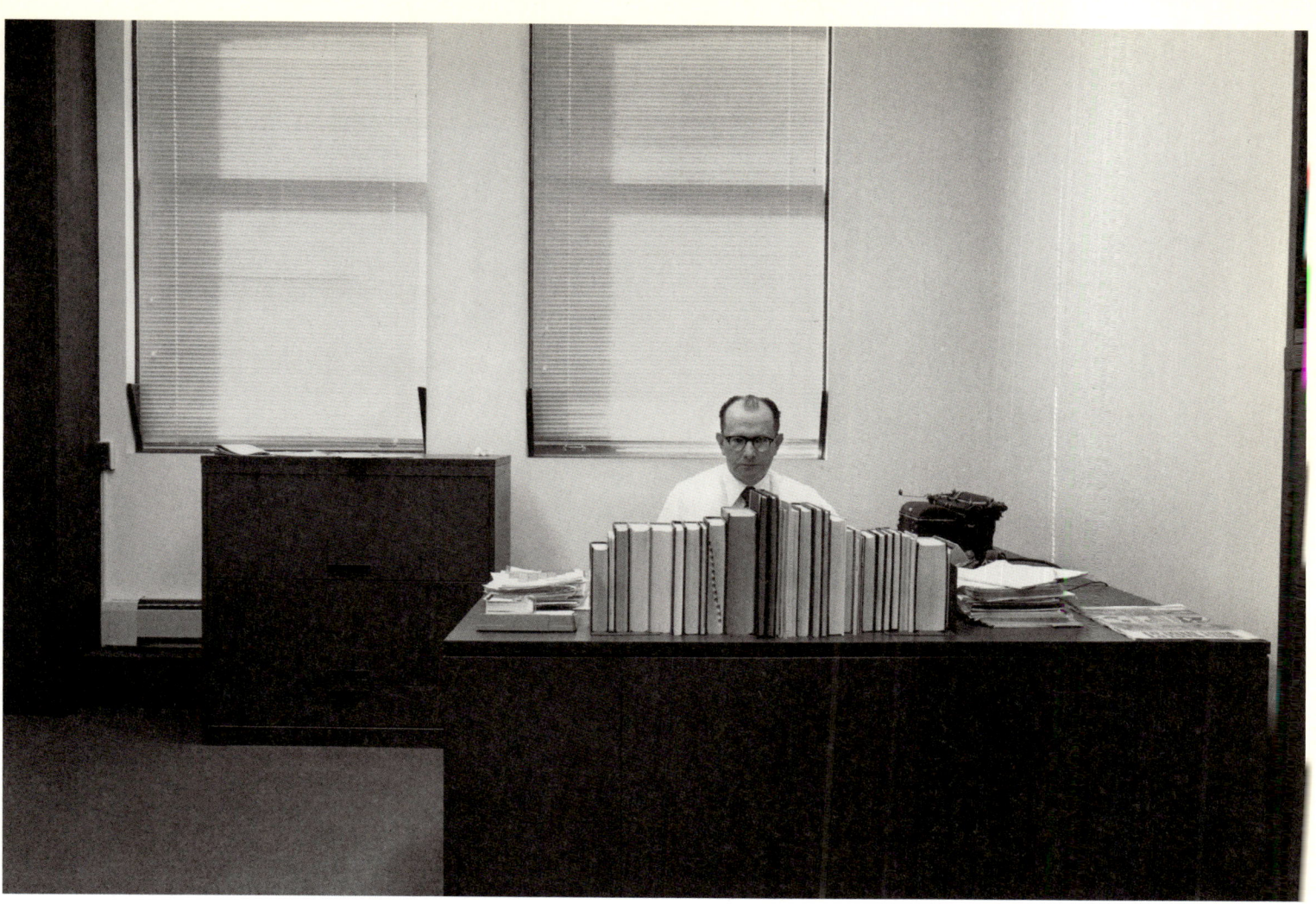

jacket. There was a tense, imploded energy running stiff through him—a little frightening." And yet, there was an instant spark between them. The next day, Hare called Wyatt and told her, "You are the one." "Our values were a perfect match," he later wrote. They fell in love, and into lifelong collaboration.

After they were married, Hare got a series of degrees—an MFA from the San Francisco Art Institute, and an MA in organizational development from Pepperdine University, completing his thesis on employee morale at the U.S. Environmental Protection Agency, where he was then working. Several months into the job, an EPA worker who had been hired at the same time as Hare leapt from a nearby building to his death. Hare was eventually fired when the agency got wind of his morale survey. During one of their vacations to Yosemite, Wyatt coined the term "work abuse," and she and Hare, who became a licensed therapist himself, began dedicating their professional lives to counseling people traumatized by their jobs. They published a book, *Work Abuse: How to Recognize and Survive It* (1997), and they maintain a private practice in San Francisco, where they still live.

One day in 1999, Jack von Euw picked up his phone and heard at the other end of the line the man he'd seen picketing his own art exhibition twenty years before. "It was as if I had received a ransom call," von Euw wrote. Hare was looking to donate his photographs, but on very specific terms. The work could not be sold; the work could not leave the library; the work could not be shown out of context—hence the statement that accompanies the photographs published in this issue. If the Bancroft Library didn't agree to Hare's conditions, well, von Euw was certain that Chauncey Hare's entire photographic record was destined for a bonfire. He agreed to meet Hare at a warehouse in Oakland with a flashlight, old clothes, and a large screwdriver. What he found was astounding: a massive

collection of prints, negatives, books, accumulations of everything that represented Hare's life as a photographer. "In my view his work is unparalleled," von Euw recounted. "You'd have to go back to the days of the Farm Security Administration. Chauncey is a writer, but he writes with his camera. I can't think of another photographer who is as closely related to writing as he is except maybe Eugene Smith. And his photographs have never been more relevant than they are now."

Hare was able to get up close to the riders on their BART commutes, he once said, simply because he was fueled by rage, an emotion that, along with severe anxiety, is what continually motivated his work. The aim was always something that lay beyond the offices and kitchens of the lives he encountered: "My photographs," he wrote, "demand a spiritual awakening."

Rebecca Bengal is a writer based in New York.

KATY GRANNAN

A Conversation with Sarah M. Miller

CENTRAL VALLEY

California's vaunted highways and bridges make it possible to drive through the state's vast Central Valley without seeing, or feeling, much of anything. Beneath that infrastructure, nature and humanity are frequently neglected, left to go wild and to improvise. Katy Grannan's 2016 film *The Nine* stops to take a long, slow look at a community in one such liminal zone: South Ninth Street in the town of Modesto. Called the Nine by its denizens, it's a ragtag stretch of residential motels populated by hustlers, addicts, and outcasts. The area abuts the soaring South Ninth Street Bridge, which crosses the majestic Tuolumne River. Underneath is a lush but littered riverbank. Some visit the river to wash off the day; others live there, devising new families; some die there as Jane Does. The people of the Nine are profoundly invisible.

Grannan spent five years on and off with her subjects, coming to count them as friends and creative collaborators. Her film portrait of the Nine's shifting communities is a companion project to *The 99*, Grannan's photographic series of people in hardscrabble towns along Highway 99, a main artery of the Central Valley. Those portraits make aggressive use of California's blinding sunlight in a counterpoise of monumentality and anonymity. The film, by contrast, is intimate and tragic. Closely observed moments of grace give way to anger, stories of abuse give way to glimmers of humor and hope, claustrophobic hotel rooms are intercut with instances of beauty among the river-world beneath the bridge. In *The Nine*, the survival mechanism of storytelling forms the common thread, as Grannan permits her subjects more distance, more darkness, more vulnerability. Last November, in the days immediately following the presidential election, writer Sarah M. Miller spoke with Grannan about her engagement with the American landscape, visibility, and inequality.

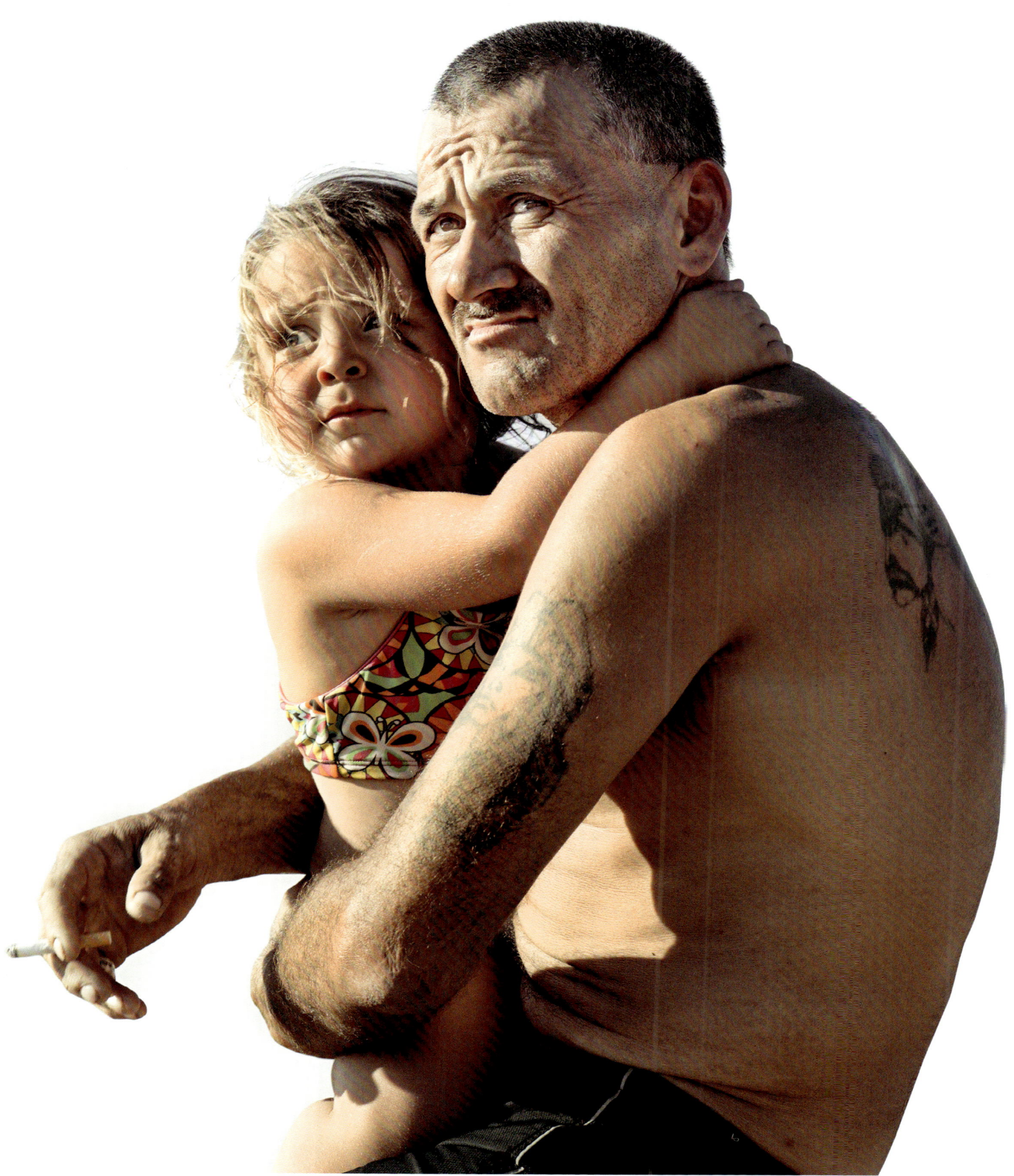

Sarah M. Miller: **Why did you decide to explore the extreme marginalization in the Central Valley? I know you've also photographed in San Francisco and Los Angeles. But clearly, the work found its ideal form for you in the Central Valley and became deeply affecting there.**

Katy Grannan: The Central Valley is a place to pass through. There's a real arrogance on the coast about the region. The psychology of the landscape really drew me in—you have to contend with yourself when there is so much space, with the feeling that almost nothing is happening. In contrast to much of California, the Central Valley seems to be utterly without delusion.

That led me to wandering the 99, where migrants arrived during the Great Depression, and the American Dream kind of stopped right there. A lot hasn't changed, frankly. It has a slightly different face. It's the twenty-first century. But there's so much of that region that looks like a third-world country.

Around the time I met my friends on the Nine, and some of the other people I was photographing throughout the Central Valley,

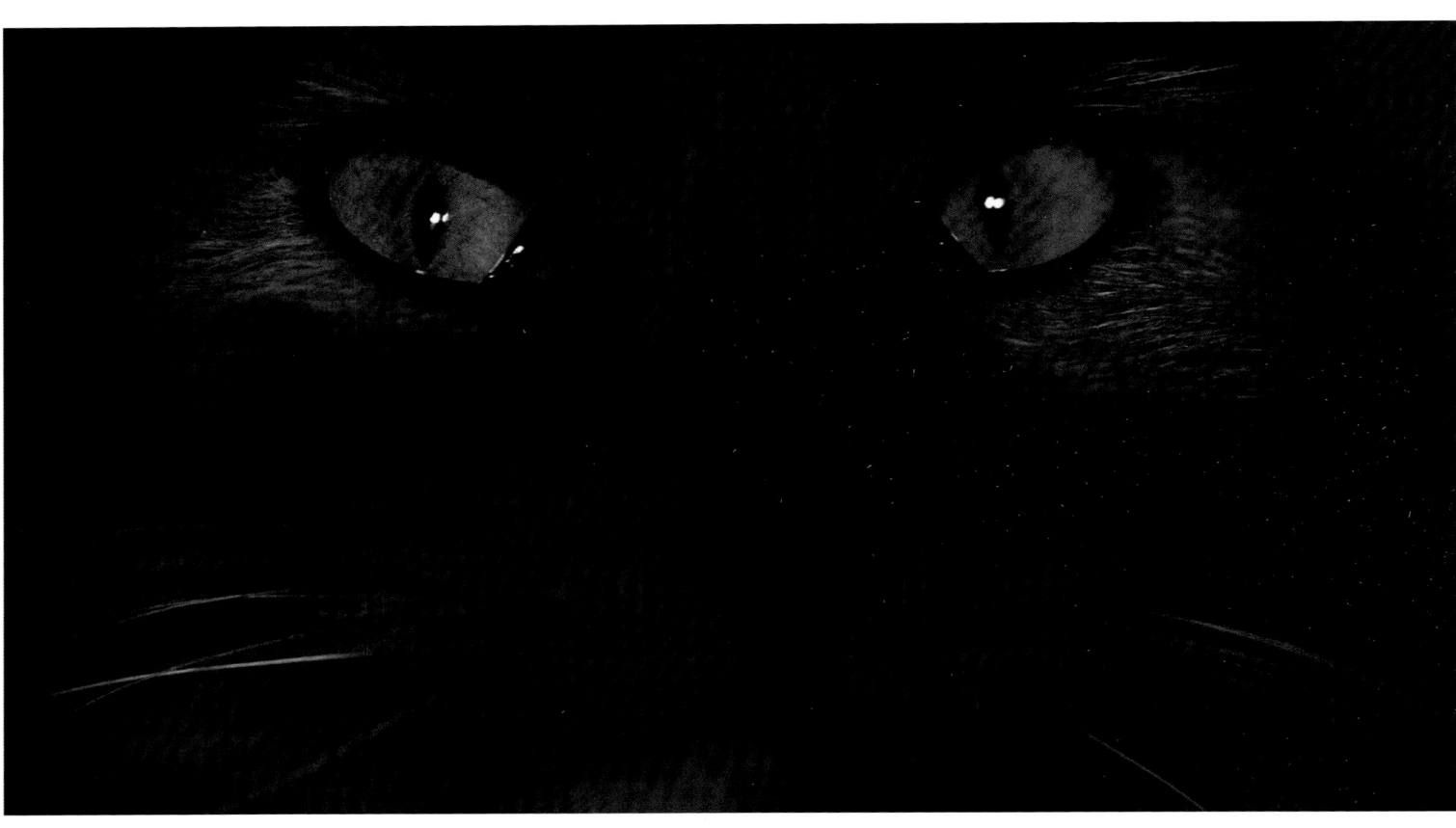

Film Still No. 4 (Cleo),
from *The Nine,* 2016

my oldest childhood friend was dying. We lived next door to each other in Massachusetts all of our lives until we both left home. At some point, she took a left turn, and things spiraled out of control. She ended up on the street, a heroin addict, a prostitute—it was incredibly sad. My cousin was on the street with her, so I always knew what was going on, but there was nothing I could do about it. I used to walk around Boston with her photograph—"Have you seen this woman?"

That experience made me want to spend more time with women like Heather, people who are regarded as Jane Does, throwaways. The women on the Nine were sort of surrogates for Heather, and I wanted to share their stories.

SM: **I ask, because I think for urban East Coasters—I'm one too—the landscape of California can be disorienting. It takes so long to see how disparity and suffering are arrayed geographically or take visual form here.**

KG: And yet, we're fooling ourselves, East Coast, West Coast, wherever, in-between—we tell ourselves stories about who we are as Americans, when the facts just don't add up. Because the truth is, we're not all born into the same conditions and we don't have equal opportunities.

So moving to the West Coast, I actually felt a sense of relief—you cannot avoid reality, because the sun is shining, illuminating everything, including the failure, the delusion, all of it. I want to look right at it, and to reach beyond what I know.

SM: I was struck by how impressionistic and nonnarrative *The Nine* is. It's really a photographer's film, where you let quiet moments of observation linger and linger, and they convey so much. You've resisted the impulse to explain or to narrate the community you're exploring, and whose pain you're expressing. I'm curious, especially in the context of talking about art as political: Why resist argument? Why resist narrative?

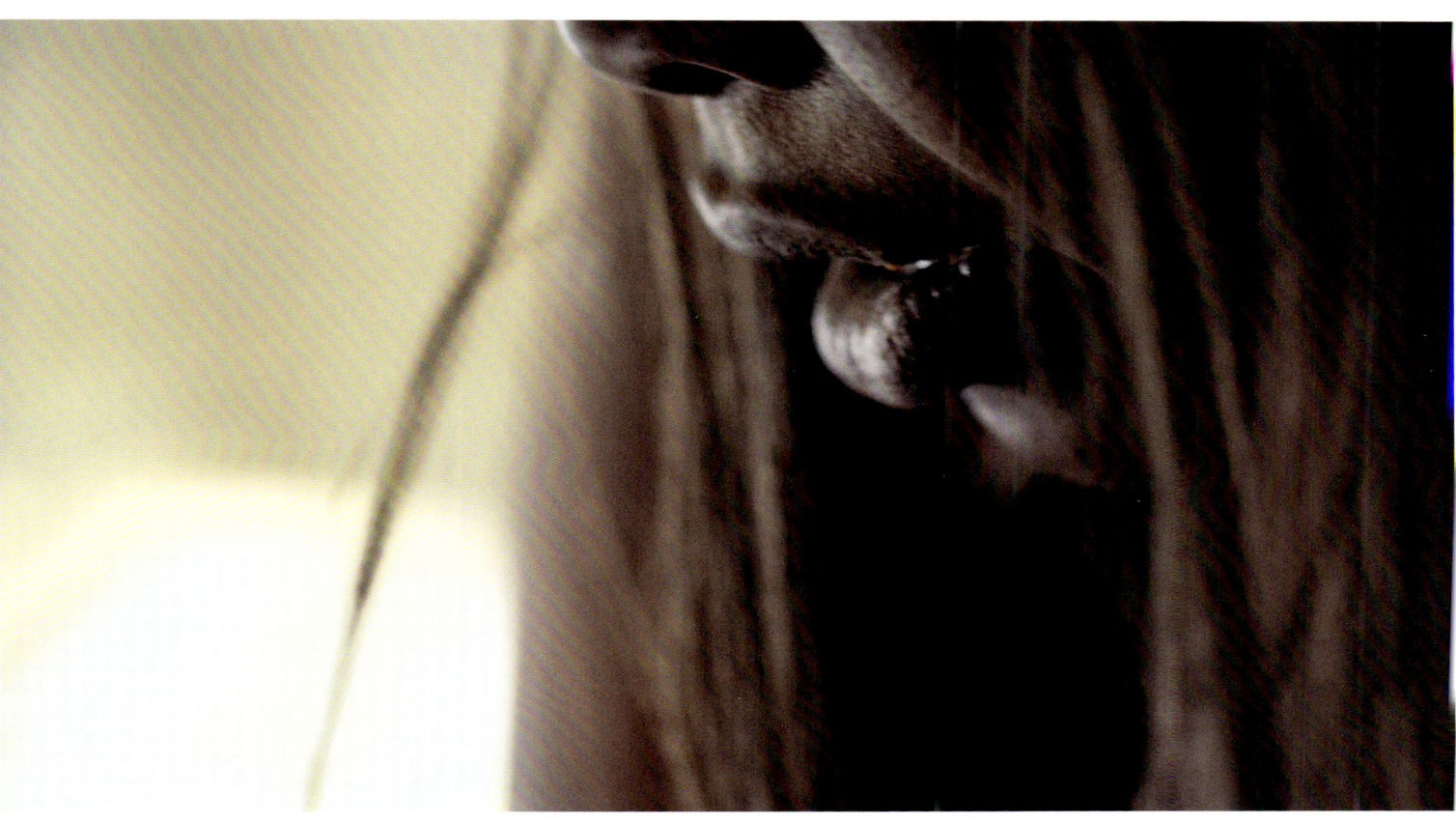

Film Still No. 6 (Lips),
from *The Nine*, 2016

KG: I didn't want to just provide information or shove an issue down anyone's throat. I'm not interested in illustration. I think that mystery is absolutely essential in both still photography and cinema. I didn't want to sensationalize or focus too much on the drama of the Nine. Because 90 percent of the time it doesn't look like that at all. So what do the mundane, ordinary moments look like? These are women who have children. They miss their kids, they miss their families, and they have a lot of regrets. That's what they're talking about most of the time. They're also gossiping and hanging out by the river, like anyone might hang out by a river on a sunny day. This approach to storytelling lets the audience have their own experience, to really sit with these people and this landscape. I don't need to raise my fist in protest—the experience of the film speaks for itself.

SM: You have a lot of respect for the participants' efforts to tell stories about their lives, even when those stories become disconnected and delusional, or aspirational in a way that the

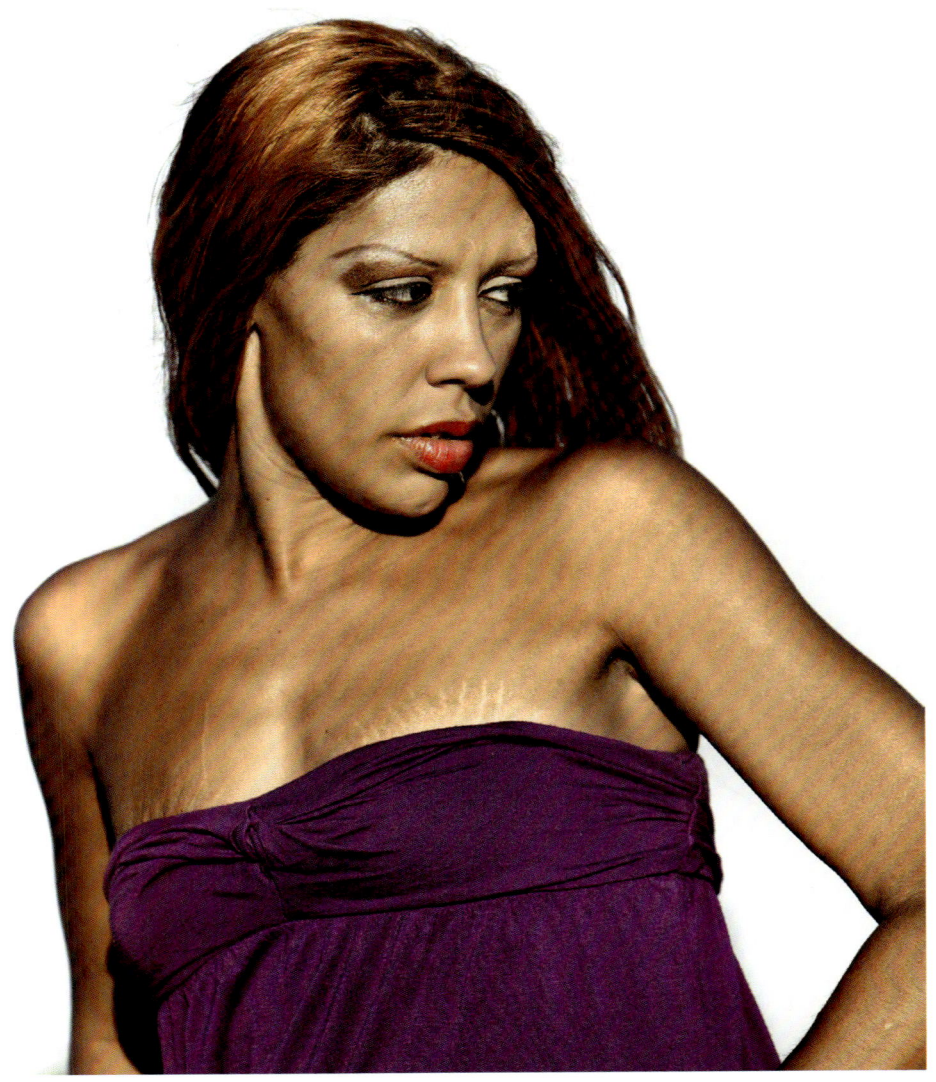

audience will see as delusional. The film is very moving, because you pay so much attention to the ways in which they try to structure their experience by explaining what happened to them, and fantasizing about what's going to happen to them.

KG: We all do that, we reinvent history all the time. We choose specific memories to create a new narrative in our minds. We're very selective. I've always thought that the family album is really a fiction. This was my first realization that photographs lie. Obviously, social media does the same thing; we're creating new and improved stories.

SM: **People have compared your work to Dorothea Lange's trajectory quite a few times. You live in Berkeley. You've traveled the 99 looking for the dispossessed of your generation. But there has also been discomfort expressed about your photographs. They are seen as harsh. They're harsh in their lighting and isolation of the subjects, in their monumental size, in the way that you allow the light to illuminate the ravages of time and drugs and abuse on bodies.**
      Did you ever feel like you were following Lange's footsteps on purpose? And if so, were you also trying to make a

statement about what kind of approach is viable now? Is there a reason to reinvent the aesthetic of illuminating people who are not seen?

KG: I was conscious of the fact, obviously, that Lange worked in that region, but I never intentionally followed in her footsteps. People love those talking points, I guess. I'm not sure if I'm reinventing the aesthetic of seeing the unseen—but I know this is still a pervasive fact of our lives. Despite all the pictures in the world, there is so much that's unseen—people, landscapes, entire regions, small gestures, overlooked details. I don't think the goal should ever be reinvention, or novelty for its own sake—it's about communicating your particular way of seeing and perceiving. People who think this work is harsh must be living in rarefied air. I never feel like I'm sensationalizing anything or anyone at all. I'm very conscious of what it means to be seen, what a photograph of a person represents.

SM: **I wonder if people find your work difficult because what they really don't want to see is your subject, whereas they would not be at all appalled to see a brightly lit, monumentally sized portrait of a Hollywood actress.**

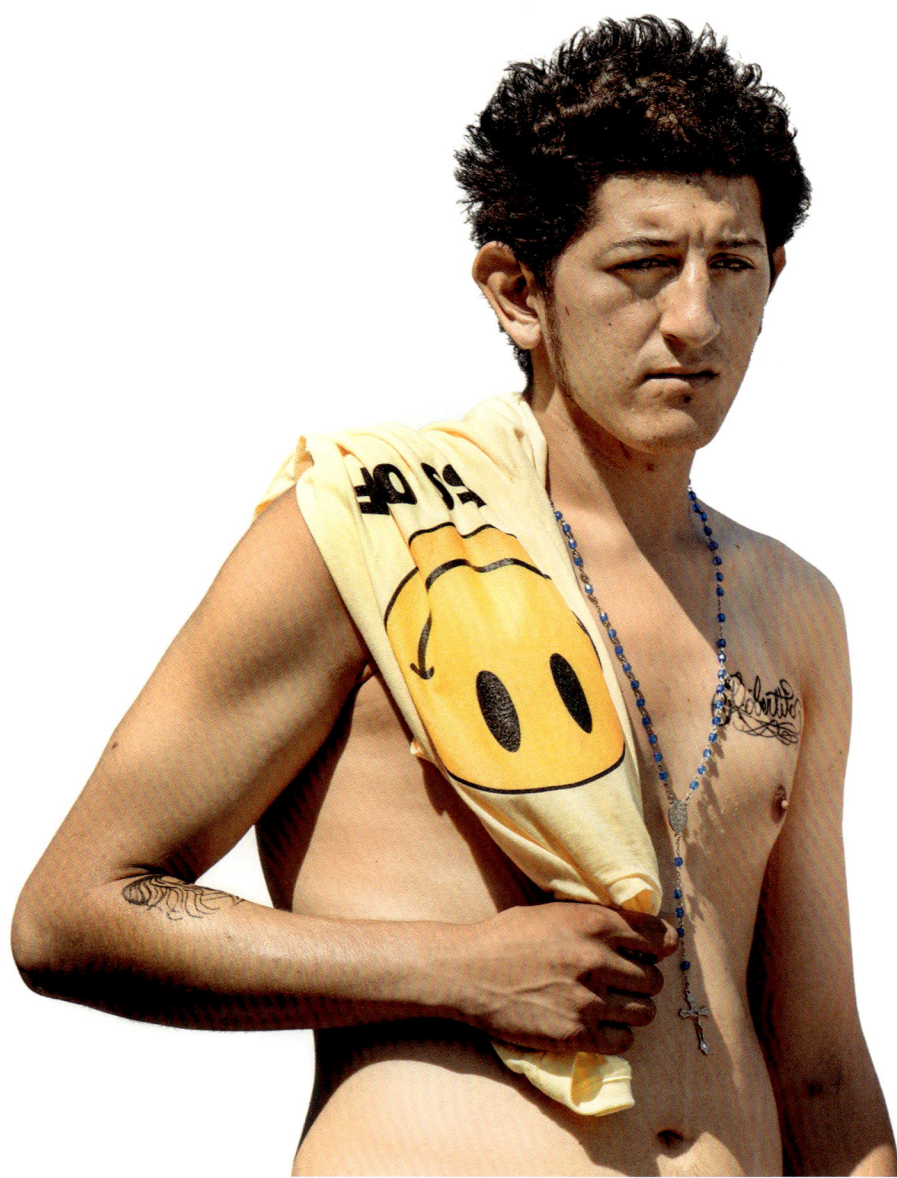

KG: Yes, no question. Or a beautiful piece of abstraction. Something pleasing to the eye, that could easily hang on the living room wall. That's fine, I get it, but I'm more interested in going to a river in Bakersfield or Modesto, photographing a regular guy and his daughter enjoying a sunny day together.

SM: Also, you see those people in their ongoing context, as they live their lives. Was that an impetus for making the film? It gives a storytelling platform and a slow, oblique introduction to your subjects in their environment. They're like two opposite forms of representation, the photographs and the film, and it's interesting how together they provide a kind of nuance to each other.

KG: Making a film is a very different kind of portrait. There are so many elements to play with; the soundscape is another character, and editing is like sculpture. People are seen and heard. They can speak for themselves. Kiki, who is really the heart of the film, had a particularly keen awareness and sensitivity about our collaboration. She directly addresses the main ethical dilemma: "Are you going to leave me once you get what you want?"

SM: That was heartbreaking.

KG: I thought, Well, she just addressed the elephant in the room with my work, with anyone whose work involves other human beings. Photographers, writers, filmmakers—we've all been accused of exploiting people. With my work, sometimes there's an assumption that the person being photographed isn't capable of making their own choice, when, in fact, the process is collaborative and consensual, and I rely completely on their generosity and openness. I try to respect that, but most importantly, I need to respect the integrity of the work. In the end, Kiki decided that she not only wanted to make the film, but that she also gained self-respect through it. We hear her come to this realization. And I love the fact that twice, she told me to stop talking so she could finish her thought. With a still photograph, you don't see the negotiations, the pushback, or the fact that people are smart enough to understand exactly what's happening. I get accused of making harsh pictures, and yet on the Nine, everybody I've photographed has their picture hanging on the wall.

SM: And they're attuned to transactions. They're very aware of how much of survival is transactional.

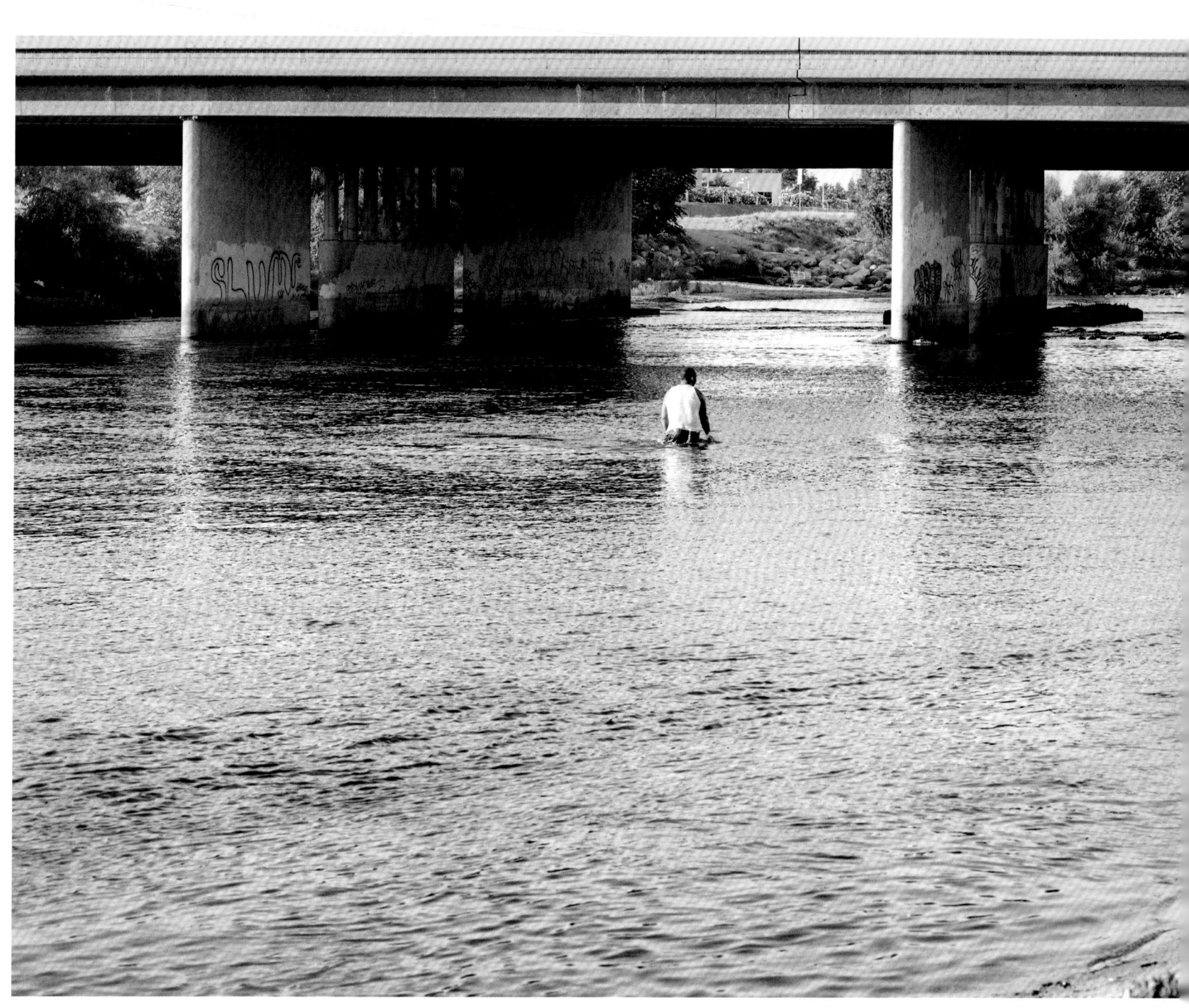

Procession on the
Kern River, Bakersfield,
California, 2011

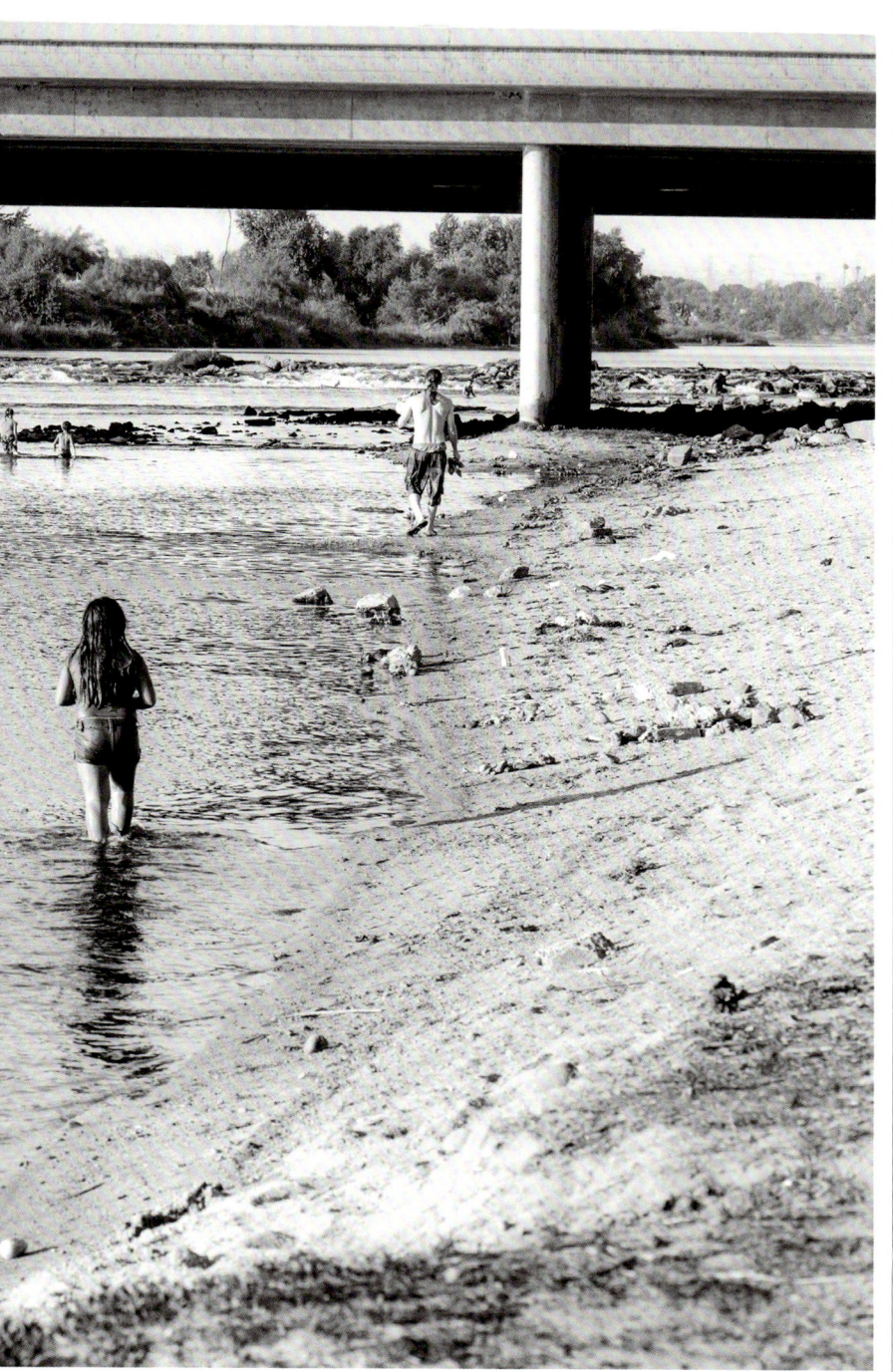

KG: Yes, you're absolutely right. The dynamic is complicated, for sure. It's not one thing or another, it's both collaborative and transactional. But over the course of five years, we've become a big, dysfunctional family. I talk to everyone regularly; I probably get half a dozen calls a day, and when I don't hear from Kiki, especially, I start worrying. It's kind of exhausting, but I really love them and I miss not seeing them every week. I visit as much as I can.

SM: It occurred to me that the apt comparison perhaps isn't Lange, but Walker Evans and James Agee's *Let Us Now Praise Famous Men* (1941). I kept thinking about Agee's sense of anguish and curiosity and guilt about what it means to embed yourself with your subjects, to both invade the lives of others and feel the weight of the responsibility of representing them, knowing that there is actually no good way. There's only the way you find, through your reactions.

KG: For sure, there is no perfect way, or at least no tidy way to do this. I'm always battling those demons, those unresolvable questions. I think it's a cop-out to avoid what's uncomfortable. Life is messy; that's the deal. But I'm clear about my intentions, and I believe in the work. What's the alternative? If I ruffle some feathers, so what? Maybe they needed a little ruffling. I think there's a lot of liberal white guilt, frankly. We're so worried about offending, about always doing and saying the correct thing. We convince ourselves that we don't have permission to go outside our own little bubbles. But we're more than the circumstances of our daily lives, and ignoring this fact just creates more distance.

I never pretended to be from the Nine or to have lived on the street. I earned their trust over time, and got to know people long before we started making the film. They didn't understand why anyone would care—some people were suspicious, and a few were convinced I must have been with the FBI.

SM: The work does something else that *Let Us Now Praise Famous Men* did. You sense Walker Evans's desire to concentrate hard enough with the camera to lift people out of a kind of generalized sociological explanation, the taint of pathology, and to provide just one second of transcendent connection. He would refuse the romanticism of that description, but that's the effect those portraits have always had. And they, too, have made people uncomfortable for the same reason.

KG: I think you're right about the source of the discomfort. For some reason, people want that distance, maybe because they don't want to look closely at themselves. I don't know, maybe it's a fear of being vulnerable, because once you acknowledge that fact, there you go, down the existential rabbit hole.

SM: We're all stuck between our feeling that it makes fun of somebody to photograph them, and the way we prioritize visibility in this culture; to be visible is to be recognized as a person. We're caught in our own conflicts about the value of looking.

KG: We're asking a lot from photography—we want it both ways. I do think that my most recent photographs, when seen in a gallery context with a price tag on them, raise some important questions that don't have easy answers. I've had a hard time reconciling this. So I decided a while ago that any profit would go directly back to the Nine. I don't want to make money from these pictures or the film. It's not something I've ever spoken about. I didn't feel like I needed to talk about it publicly, but it was an important decision.

This page:
*Ghost of the Kern River,
Bakersfield, California,*
2014

Opposite: *Man Holding
Milk Carton by Room 24,
Shiva's Motel Courtyard,
Modesto, California,* 2011
All photographs courtesy
the artist; Fraenkel Gallery,
San Francisco; and Salon 94,
New York

There's a kind of freedom in relying on our imagination to try and make something out of the chaos. But I don't think it's the job of art to entertain or offer reassurance.

When I started making the film, my attitude was that their time is worth something. On the Nine, every hour is about survival. They're doing incredibly demeaning work to make fifty dollars or eighty dollars to pay rent for a shitty motel room. So I established a day rate, which covered food, rent, and then of course a million other things crept in. They're pretty savvy—it's all about the hustle—and I wasn't very good at creating boundaries, unfortunately. But this freed them up to spend time with me, to just hang out and make a film together. When I was in town, that was their job. I wasn't interested in filming women turning tricks. It's implicit; it didn't need to be shown. It's what an audience might expect to see, but I was more interested in the way ordinariness and horror coexist.

SM: **The current political discourse is all about the white working-class man who is forgotten in the contemporary economy, and yet, as we've seen, still has a huge claim on political power and cultural representation. The community you worked with on *The Nine* is not that kind of "forgotten man." You were working with people of all races, transgender people, addicts, the homeless…**

KG: Yes. The Nine doesn't discriminate. There are people on the Nine with PhDs; there are guys with Superbowl rings; there are R&B singers. People from the mountains and from East Oakland. They're stranded on a street that's an hour from Silicon Valley—they're right in front of us, but it's as if they don't exist.

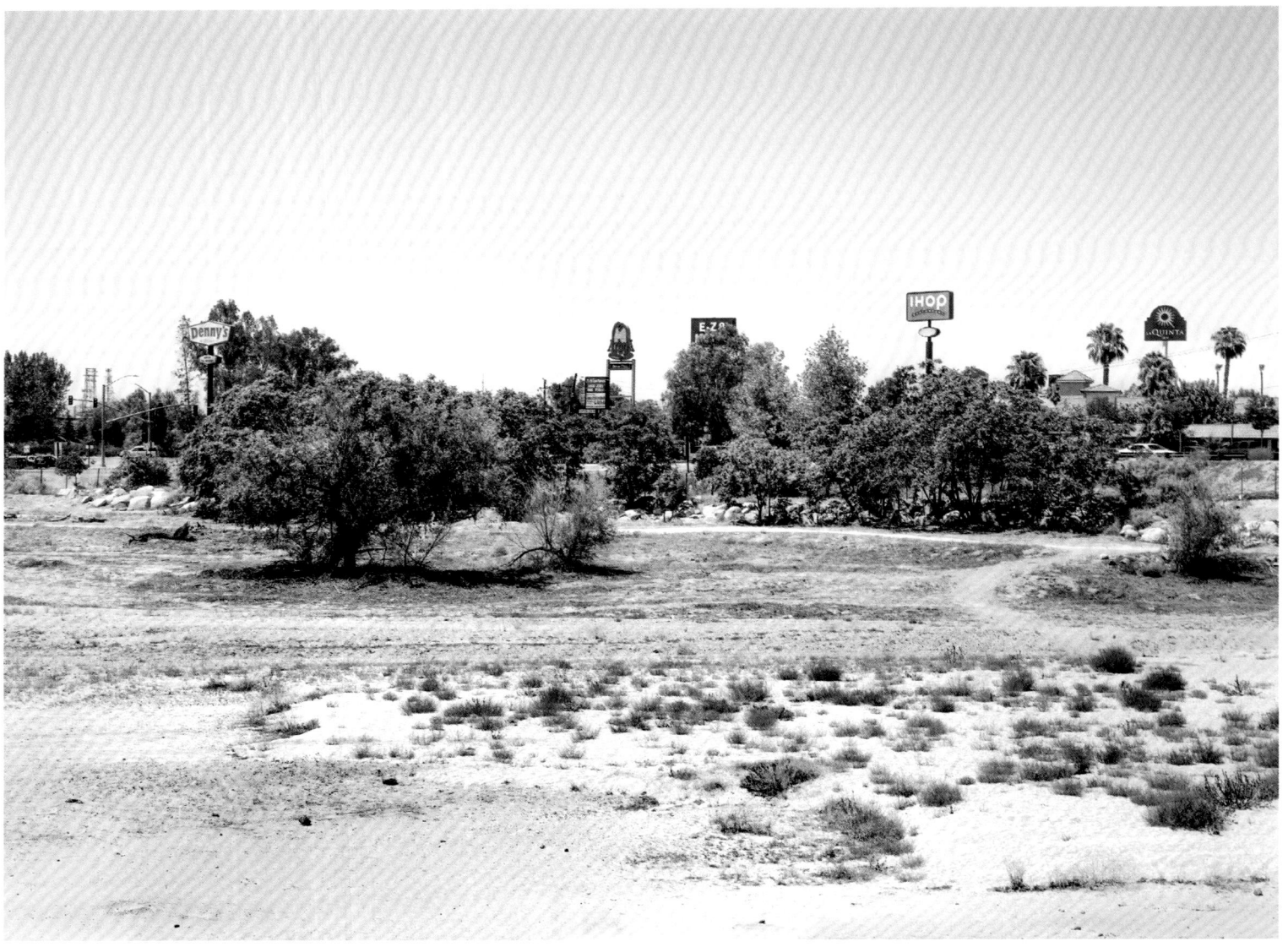

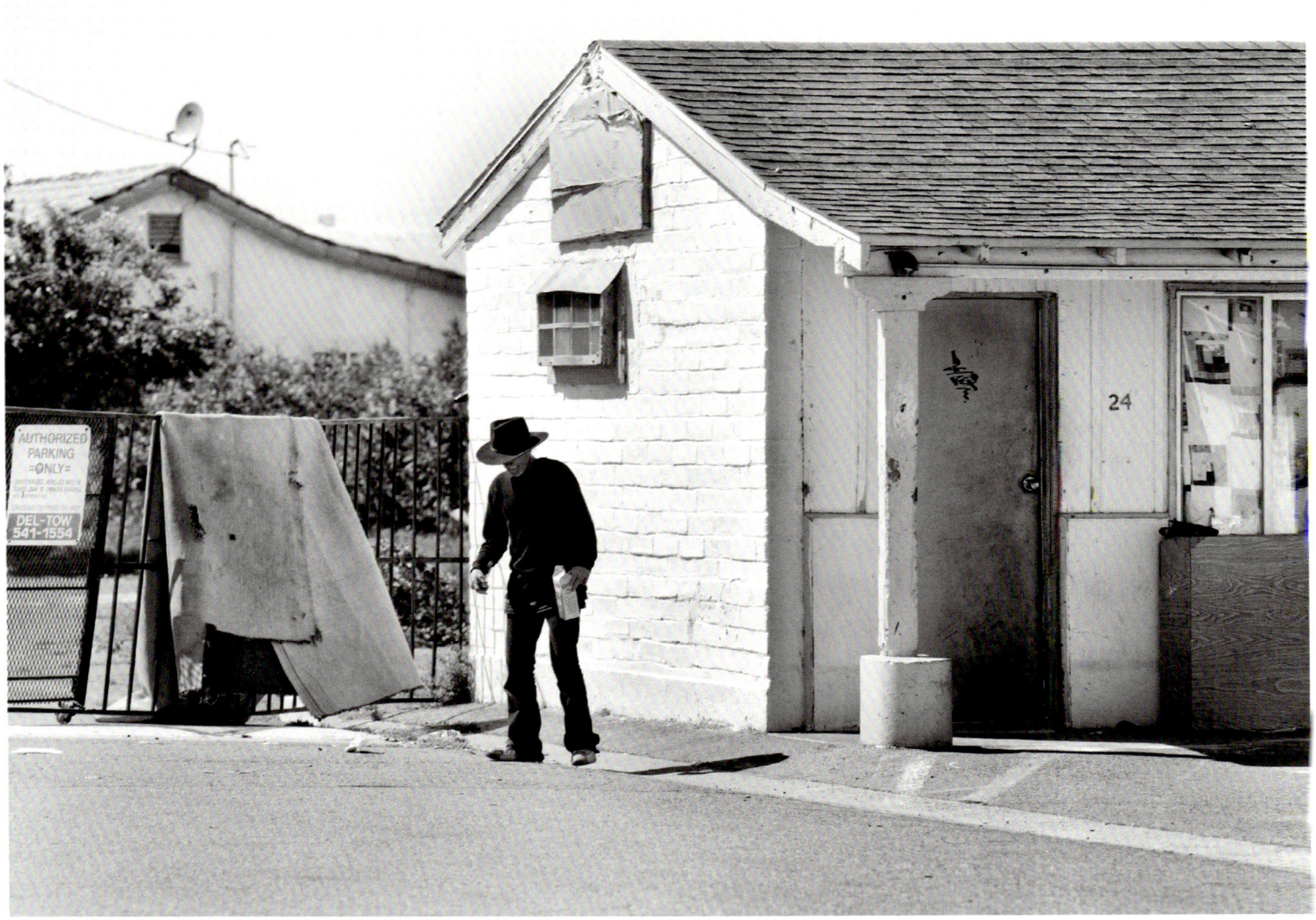

SM: **Last fall, you undertook a project on first-time voters for *The New Yorker*, people who were claiming a place in the political process and expressing their identity politics to you as you photographed and interviewed them. What was the experience like in terms of broadening the discussion about identity in America today, especially for people who feel that they are overlooked?**

KG: This was a dream assignment for me. I love going out into all the corners of the United States, seeing the breadth of experience and the micro-communities, and getting a better understanding of why people care about very specific issues and not others. Plus, the magazine asked me to make a short film for them, and gave me free rein to do whatever I wanted. That was an incredible opportunity—to be able say something about this crazy time in our history.

I noticed that there was a disparity between what we hear in the media and what people are actually talking about in their daily lives. In fact, I only heard one person, a white "nationalist," speak about his contempt for immigrants, and he was unabashedly racist. He was elated that he and his fellow white/right guys had permission to come out from the shadows. That was particularly disturbing. But no one else, in all of the states I visited, spoke like that. People are worried about jobs; they want to protect the Second Amendment; and they resent politicians, especially Congress. They weren't particularly thrilled with Trump, either, but they're exasperated. I can't remember who said that Trump was the "fuck it" vote, but I think that's spot-on.

SM: **Do you think of invisibility as a spectrum in American life? I was assuming that the kind of invisibility you've dealt with in Modesto is so extreme that it potentially trivializes everybody else's claim to feel overlooked.**

KG: Our culture is obsessed with money and celebrity. And politics, of course, is ruled by money and power. It's become obscene. Most Americans are left out of that equation; they don't feel like their issues are being addressed, and they're angry. They have a right to be angry and disillusioned. But then there are so many people who are *entirely* powerless. They have nothing.

On the Nine, people are desperate and they're just lingering in a kind of purgatory. Then the river and the animals are collateral damage. It's tragic—for a while I tried to bring home every stray dog and cat I found, but it was unending. I'd like to make a film that shifts the perspective, that illuminates the point of view of a river or the wilderness. Or a stray dog. Imagine what they're witnessing. Plus, I could use some quiet time alone in the woods.

For me, I think the heart of making art is about trying to make some sense of a world that is so utterly chaotic and inexplicable. I'm not necessarily coming up with answers, but I'm looking. There's a kind of freedom in relying on our imagination to try and make something out of the chaos. But I don't think it's the job of art to entertain or offer reassurance. There are hard truths without easy answers. Maybe discomfort, in some way, can actually lead to illumination.

Sarah M. Miller is an independent scholar, teacher, and critic based in Oakland, California.

Kathya Maria Landeros

West

Sandra Cisneros

Their names are Nicanor, Nato, Adrián, Lupita, Victor, Arturo, Antonia, Cristian. Even without the captions, I can tell the photographer knows who they are. They're not anonymous props in a wild landscape, not statistics, not "others" to be afraid of. The subjects Kathya Maria Landeros captures are above all presented as people, the land presented in context to these individuals. Her camera lets them tell their own stories.

Landeros documents with deep familiarity California's Central Valley and those bound to that land by labor. Millennia before European nations entered the New World, commercial routes were already connecting native communities from ocean to ocean, from the arctic north to the southern tip of Patagonia. The people in these photographs, the descendants of the survivors of conquest, land appropriation, and ethnic cleansing, continue to migrate across arbitrary borders, the product of the clash between the European and the native views of land. It is the same earth cultivated over thousands of years, the same routes followed north and south. This continuous thread is Landeros's visual narrative as well as her own story.

"There are histories we know intimately because we have lived them," Landeros tells me recently. "I come from a close-knit family from Mexico who came to the United States in search of work, in the canneries, in the fields, cleaning homes, whatever work they could find. Their power was in being unified. If history has shown me anything, it's that our survival depended on that."

Landeros lives in a time when the world is divided by borders. She is born on the U.S. side. This makes it possible for a scholarship, and her own intelligence, to launch her to another coast. What if she had been born in Mexico, where the working class create "folk art," not art? What if she had stayed in the California Valley—would she have worked in the fields? How does an unmarried daughter convince her parents to let her go off to a university, let alone one on the other side of the country?

"Until I went off east to college, art photography was something I didn't even know about," Landeros says. "It was storytelling, and poetry, and social activism, and everything I loved rolled into one magical package."

The irony is that her education does bring her home to work in the fields. One day she accompanies her father to the farm labor camps. She begins to take pictures. "Those were the first photographs I made that gave me a sense of purpose," she says. "My experience represents so many people in this country, yet in some ways I'm working in a vacuum. Latinos in this country aren't being represented photographically. Photos of the American West exclude so many people of color."

The series *Verdant Land* (2011–13) and *West* (2011–ongoing) obliged Landeros to follow ancestral paths south and north over a decade. In this contentious moment in history, the stories we tell are a social responsibility. Landeros tells them with humility. And in service. In my opinion, to be of service to those one loves is the highest of the high arts.

Sandra Cisneros is a novelist, poet, essayist, and the author of *The House on Mango Street* (1984), *Caramelo* (2002), and *A House of My Own: Stories from My Life* (2015).

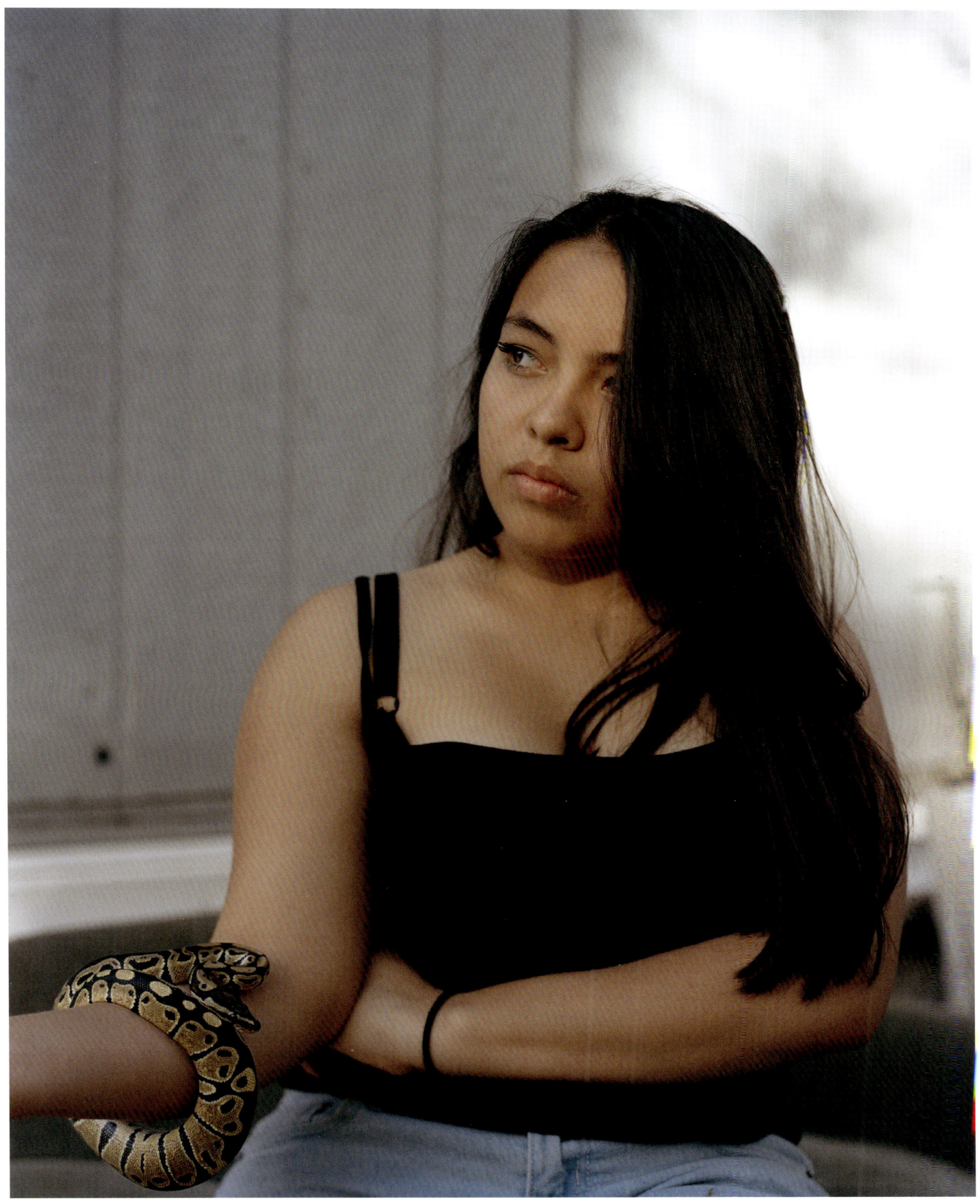

*Leslie, Elk Grove,
California, 2015*

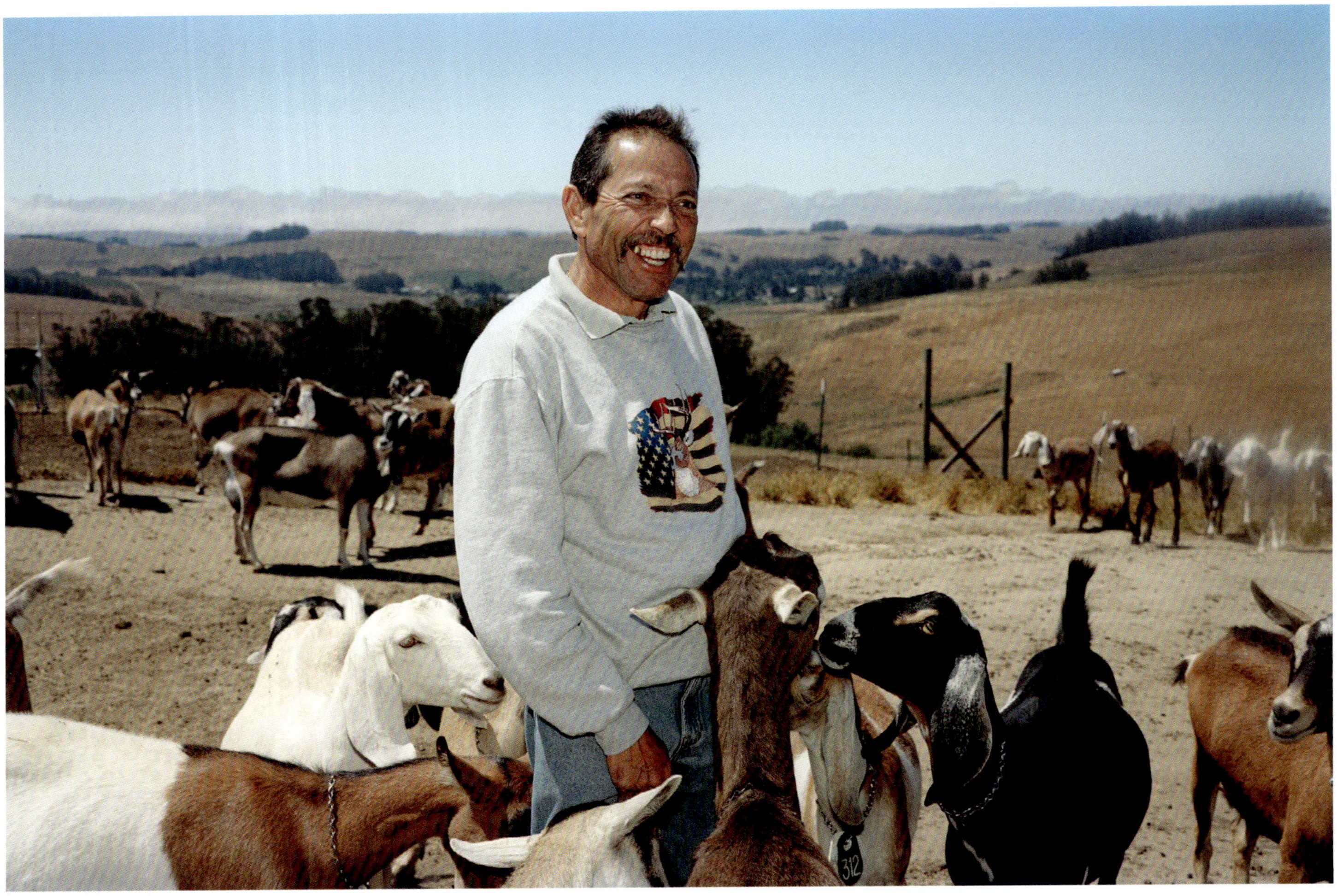
312

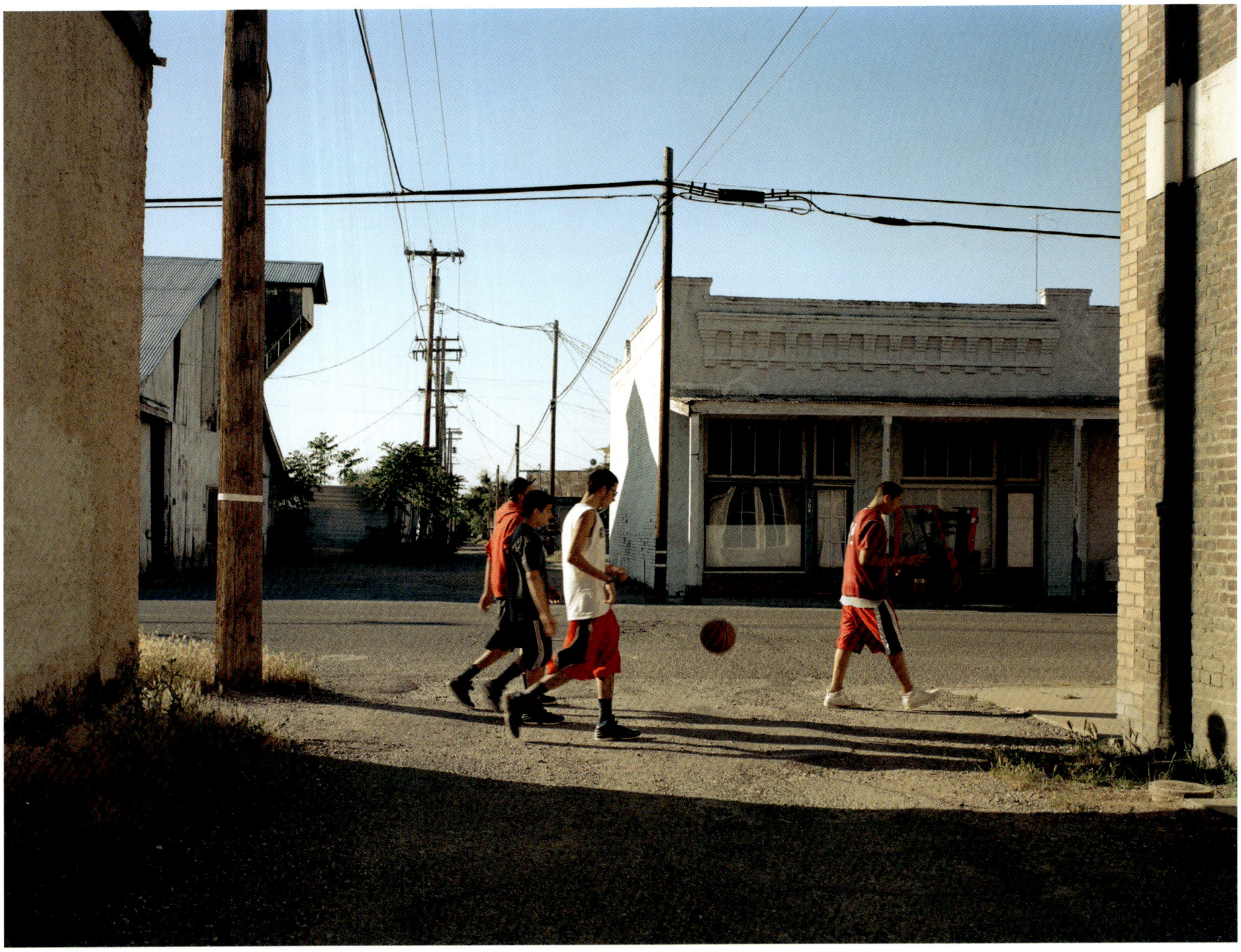

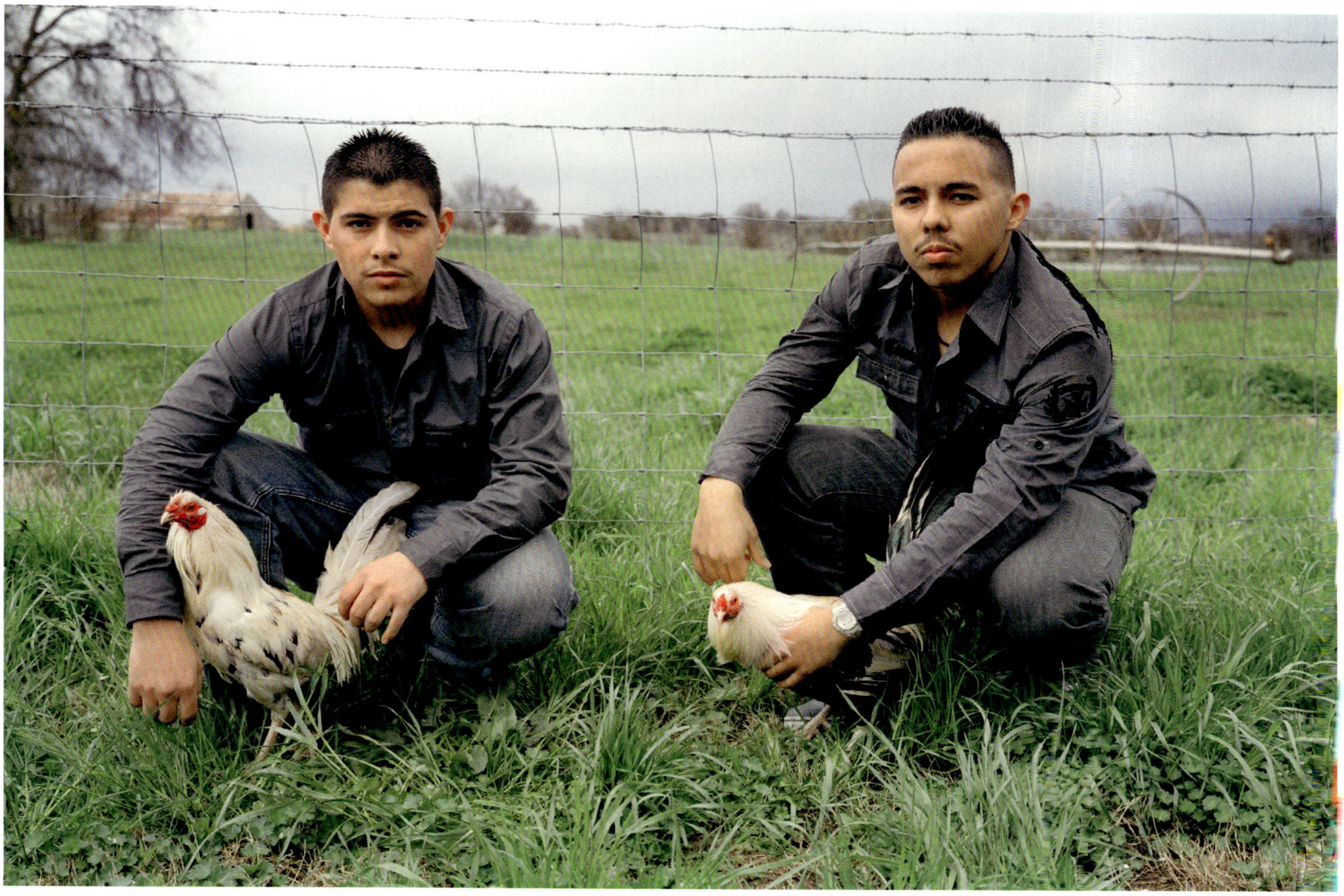

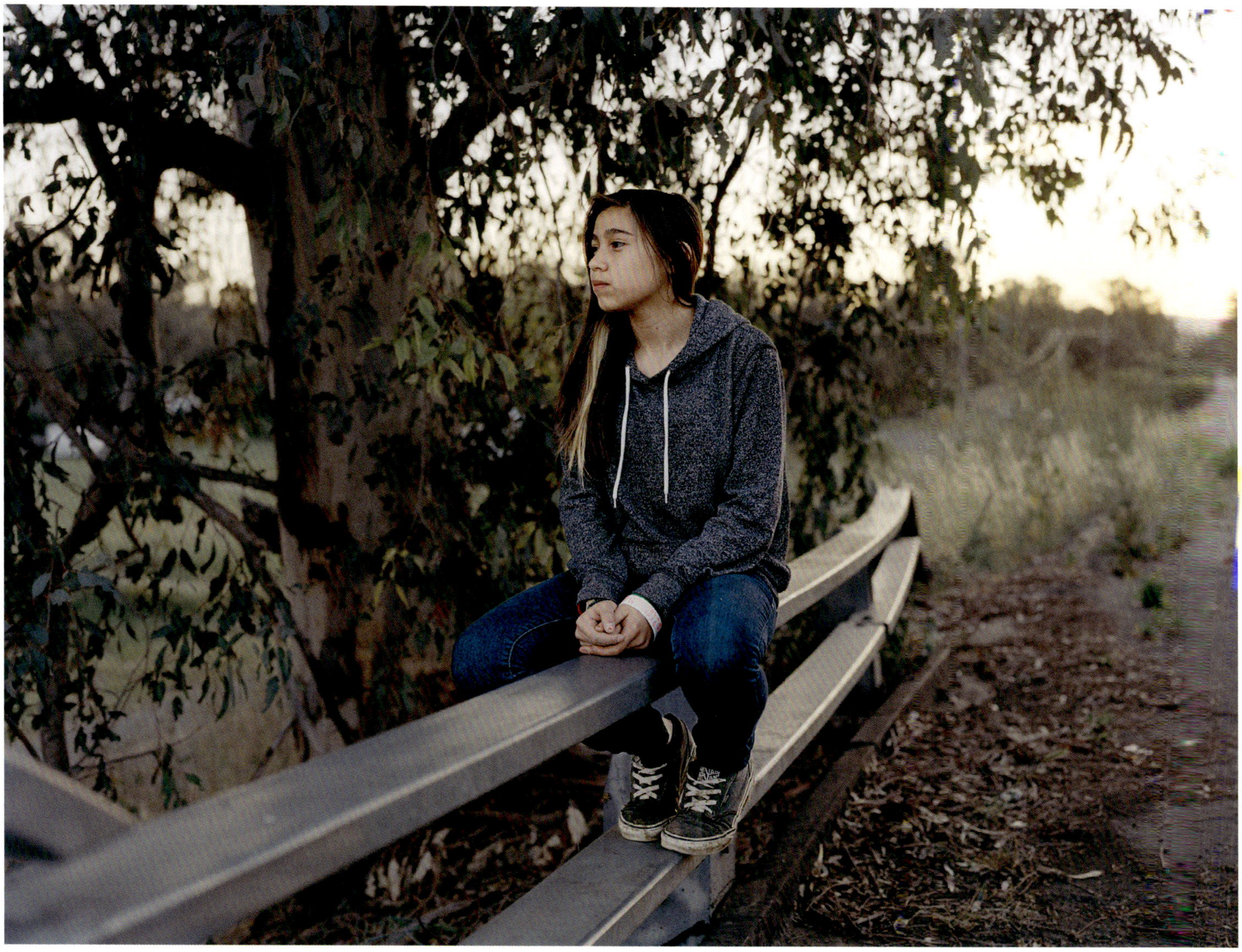

Previous spread,
clockwise from top left:
*Javier on goat farm,
near Petaluma, California,
2011; Cristian and Edgar,
Elk Grove, California,
2012; Mariah overlooking
Interstate 5, Dunnigan,
California, 2013;
Hall Street, Arbuckle,
California, 2013*

This spread:
*Main Street laundromat,
Methow Valley, Washington,
2012*
All photographs
from the series *West*
Courtesy the artist

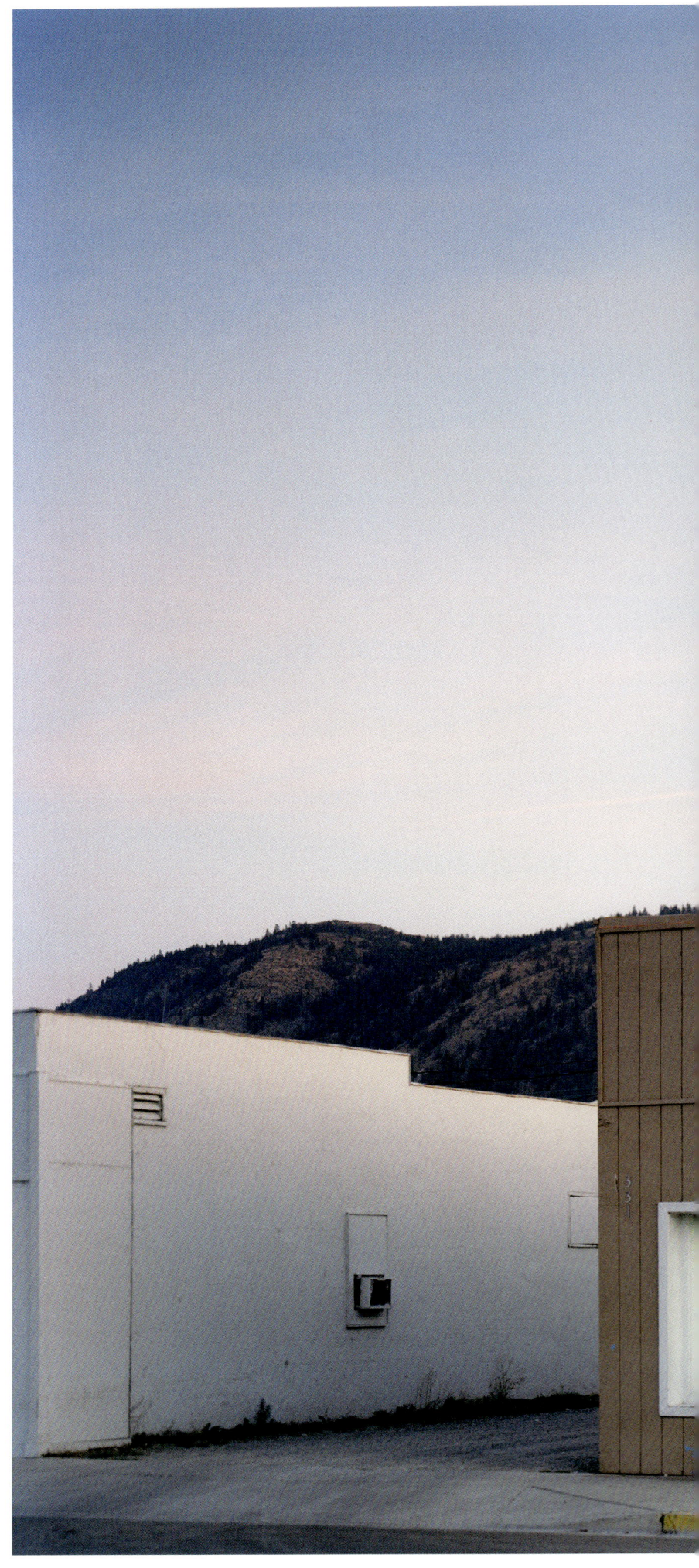

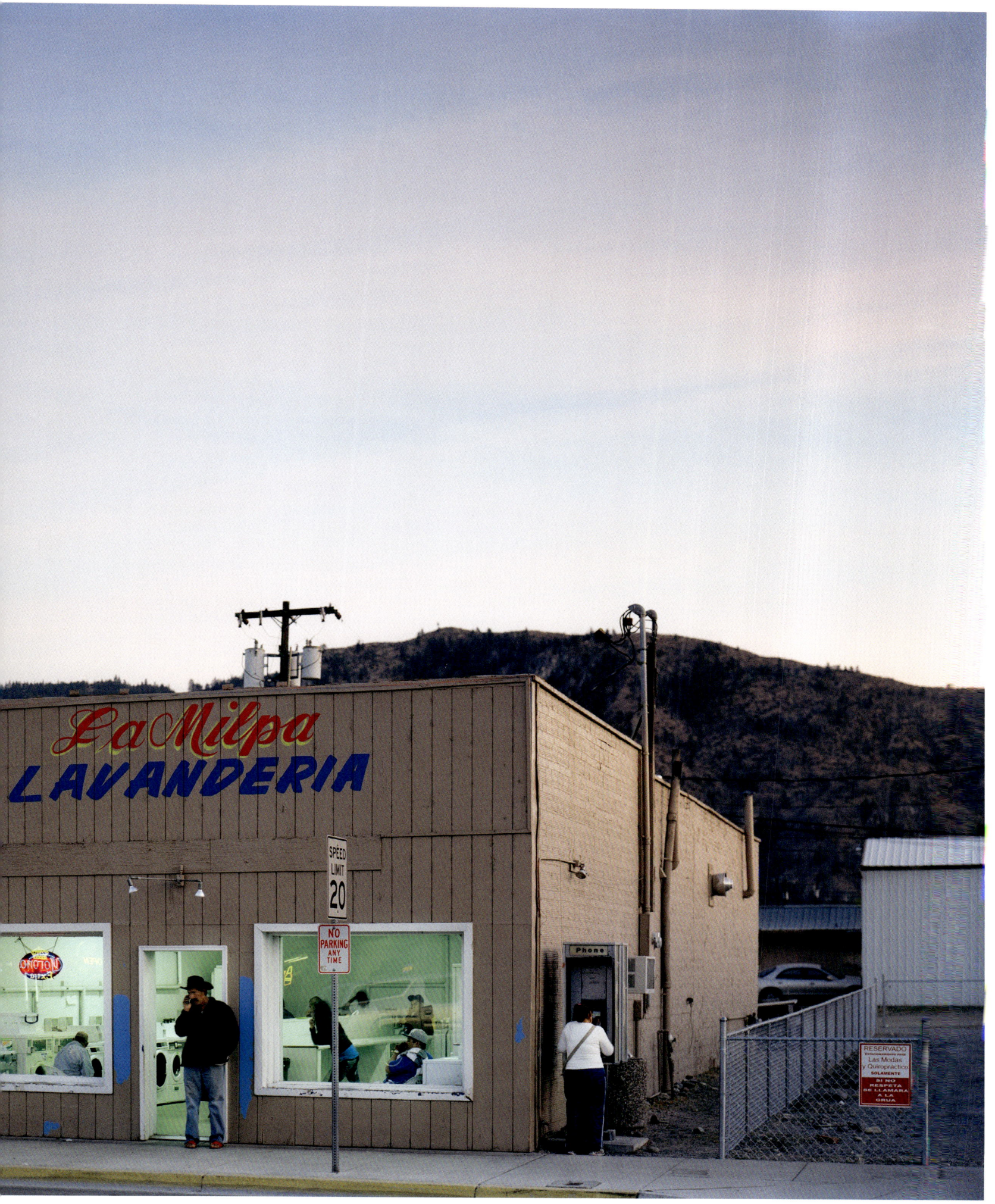

Anthony Lepore

Bikini Factory

Jonathan Griffin

For Christmas in 2012, Anthony Lepore's father gave him a section of a bikini factory in eastern Los Angeles—rows eleven to fifteen, to be exact. A few months earlier Lepore had inquired whether his dad might have any surplus space that he and his partner, the artist Michael Henry Hayden, could use for a studio. Real estate in Los Angeles is increasingly expensive but Lepore's father, whose bikini business has been declining since the 1980s, had more than he needed.

At its zenith, the company—founded by Lepore's grandfather in 1971—employed some three hundred people. Now there are four: seamstresses Lupe, Rosa, and Ligia, and Otilia, who does the finishing. Lepore has known these women for almost all of his life. While the majority of bikinis sold in the United States are currently made in China, the company has stayed afloat by specializing: today it solely manufactures plus-size swimwear.

Lepore and Hayden were grateful for the gift, although they asked if there was any space less central and intrusive to the workers. Lepore's father replied that this was what he had to offer, since he had begun subleasing sections of the factory to other businesses several years before. In 2007, he encouraged his head seamstress to start her own swimwear company under his roof. Her thriving business now outperforms his. The fabric cutting, which still takes place on a seventy-five-foot-long table built by Lepore's grandfather, is subcontracted. Nearby, a small team of master saddlers from northern Mexico now produces premium gay bondage wear.

So the artists put up their studio walls in the middle of the building. Lepore, conscious of blocking the seamstresses' view across the factory floor, asked them to choose colors they would like the walls to be painted. A pale blue with a darker blue upper section was selected, evoking the ocean horizon—the eventual backdrop for the swimwear once it leaves the factory.

Lepore has said that the factory is "like a river, through which a rainbow of color and pattern flows every single day." His studio is midstream. Within a short time of his moving there the factory began to infiltrate Lepore's photography, which often operates by confounding viewers' perceptions of depth and flatness. Initially, it was simply a case of using pieces of Lycra as backdrops. Then Lepore's mischievous torquing of foreground and background, of illusion and reality, began to seem reflected—sometimes literally—in the industry that envelops his studio space.

One evening, after factory cleaners had mopped the studio floor, Lepore dropped something and, stooping to pick it up, was astonished by the dazzling reflection of a striped fabric in the puddles. It is hard to believe that the resulting photographs were made without the aid of Photoshop, but Lepore rejects digital postproduction, and established an early rule that he would use only the factory's fluorescent lighting.

One exception to the latter rule is Lepore's series *Factory Chairs* (2015), in which he photographed seamstresses' chairs at the end of the working day in raking sunlight, isolating them against a white wall in the parking lot. These chairs, often custom upholstered by their owners with swimsuit Lycra to make them more comfortable, serve as surrogates for the women: not only for their bodies but also for their creativity, humor, and individualism. While the workers' daily labor can be hard and repetitive, Lepore also emphasizes the factory's enduring social role—a family business that, like many others, has itself become something like an extended family.

Factory Chair #1, 2015

Jonathan Griffin is a writer based in Los Angeles and a contributing editor of *frieze*.

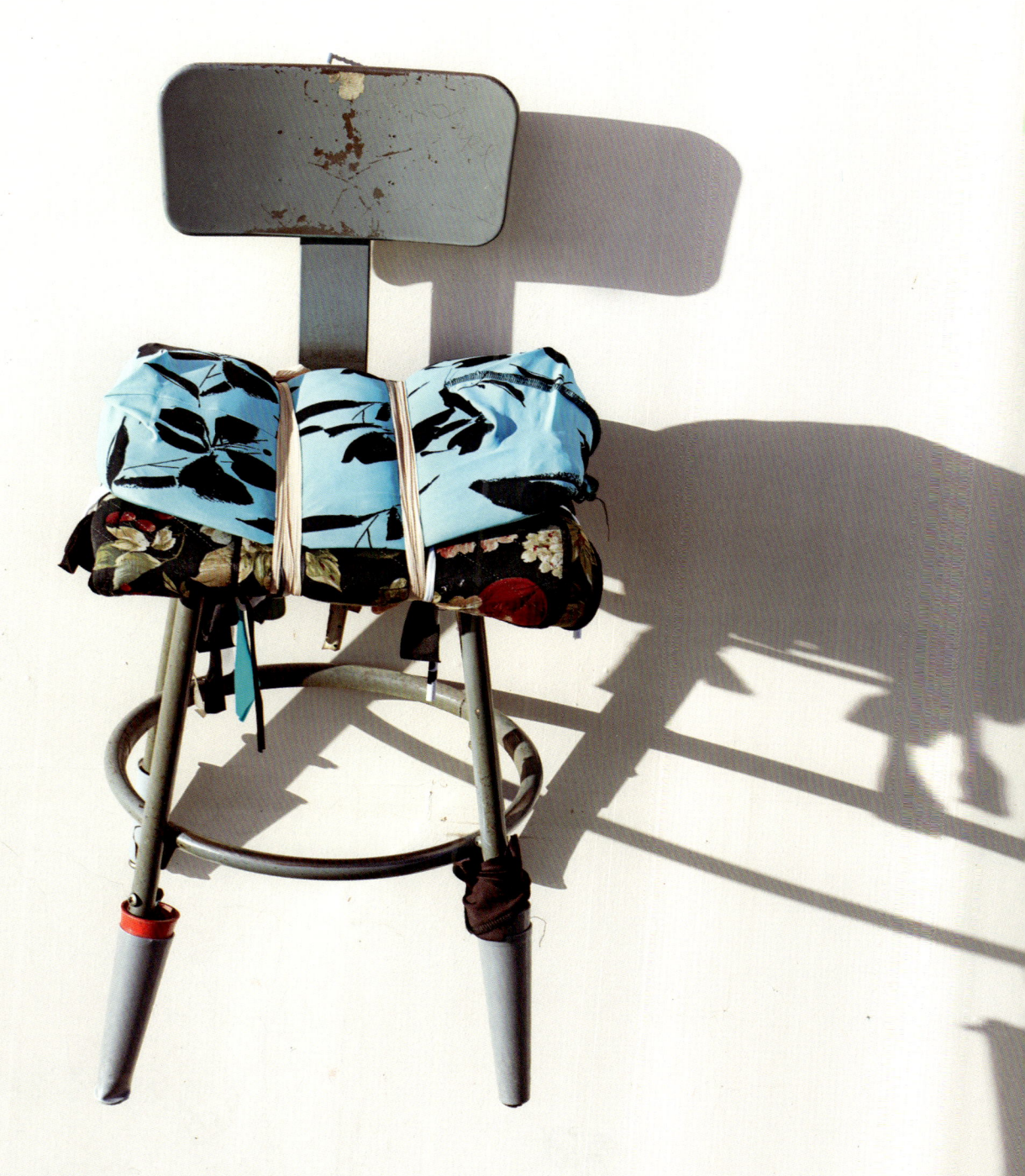

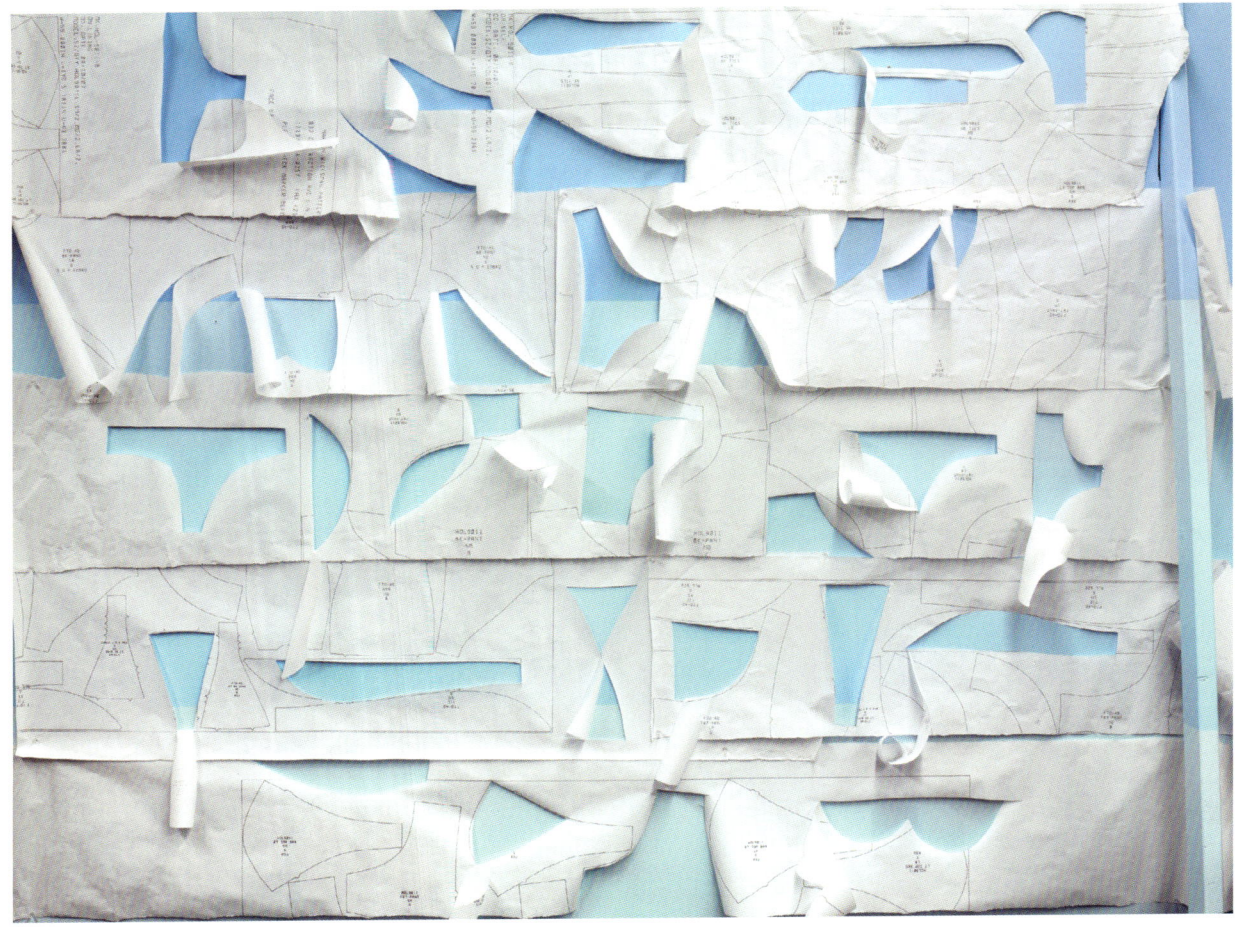

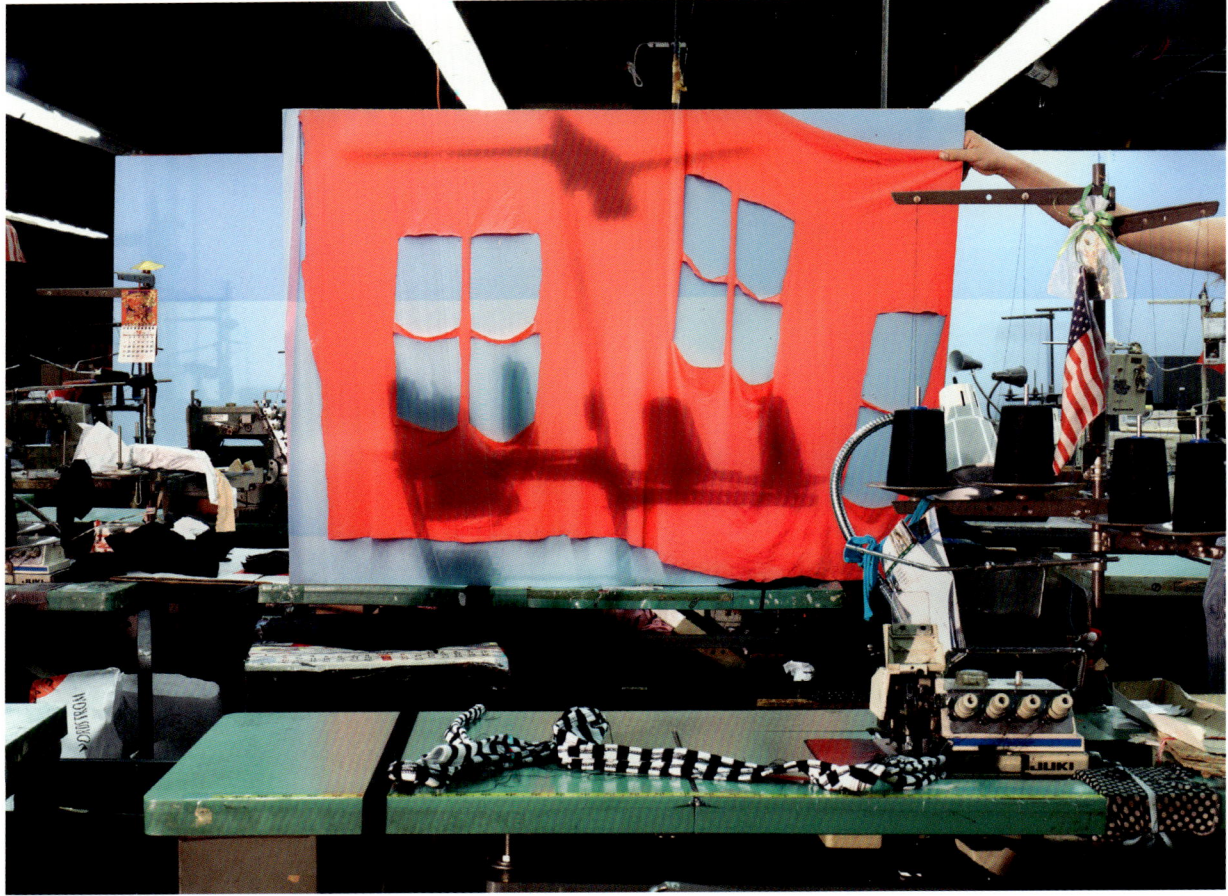

Top:
Blue Print, 2015

Bottom:
Window Dressing, 2015

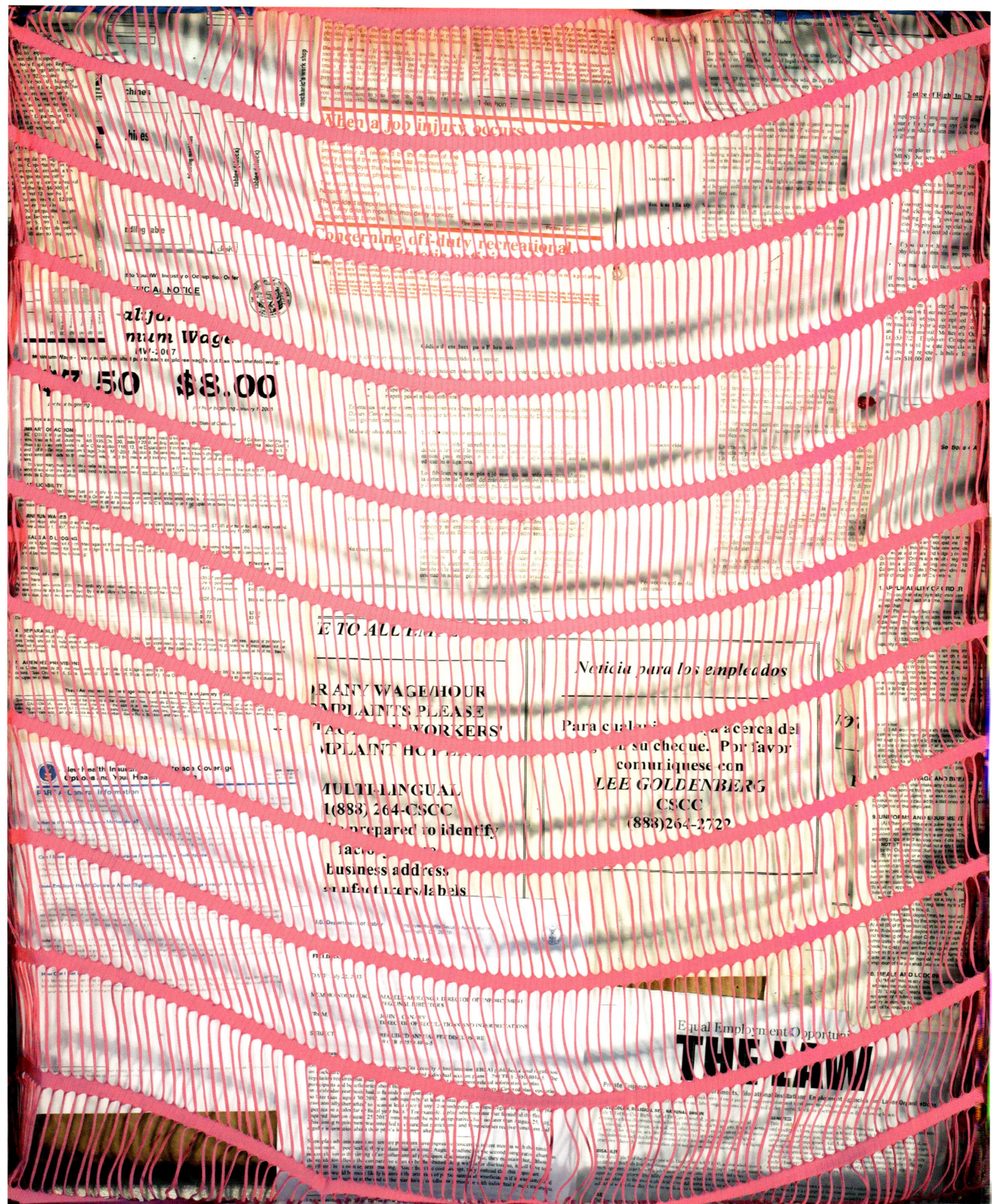

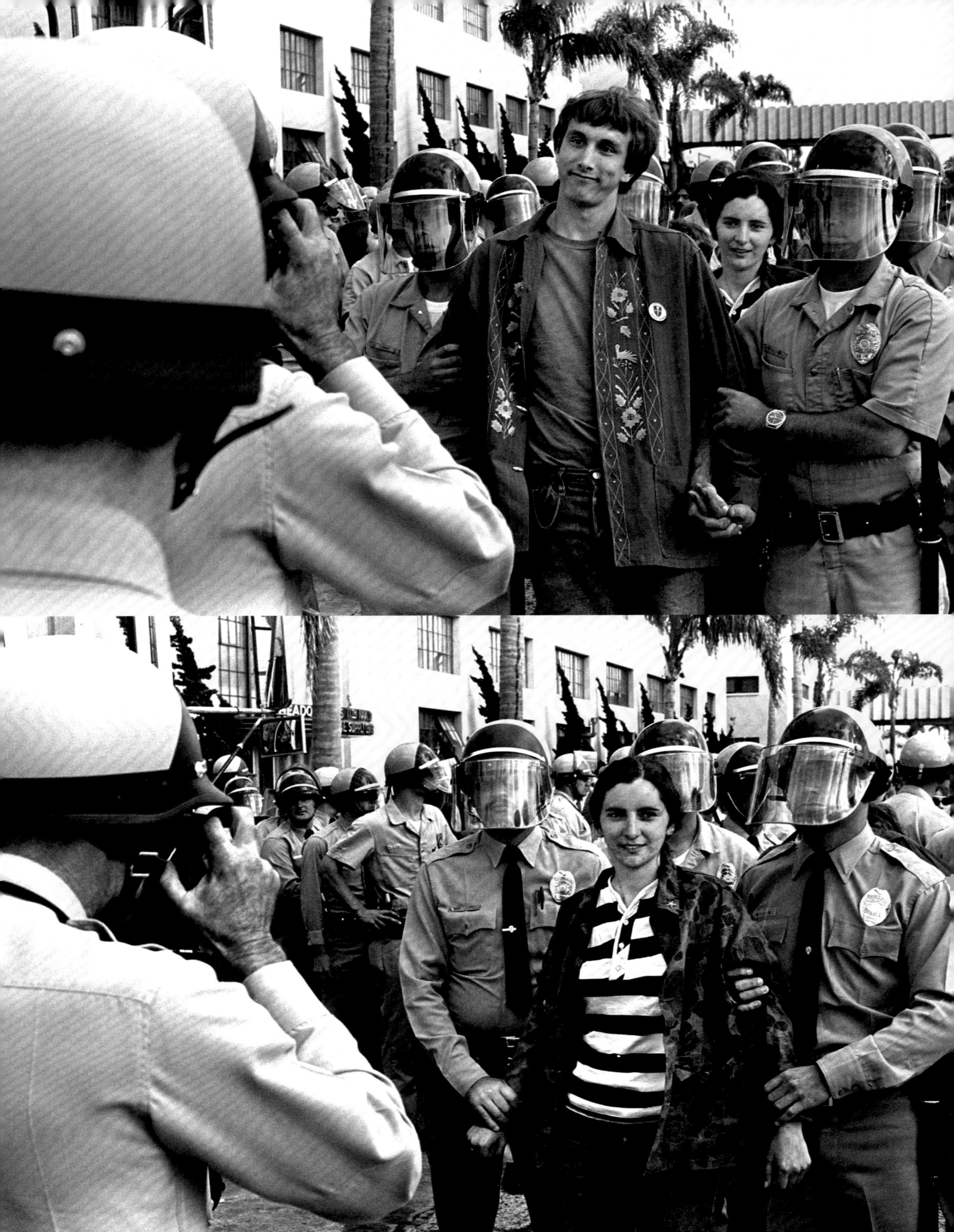

How did a former teachers' union president, Peace Corps volunteer, and Vietnam War resister disrupt the documentary tradition?

Fred Lonidier The Agitator

Brian Wallis

29 Arrests (detail), 1972

When photographer and social activist Fred Lonidier was selected for the 2014 Whitney Biennial, it came as a surprise to some. The last time the seventy-two-year-old professor had shown at the Whitney was his debut in 1977, nearly forty years earlier. But what always distinguished Lonidier's rigorous documentary work— his unwavering and unrepentant focus on labor and class struggle— was in 2014 suddenly at the forefront of American politics. And many of the most pressing issues of the 2016 presidential election and in recent social activism—including Occupy Wall Street, Black Lives Matter, and the insurgent Democratic primary campaign of Bernie Sanders—continue to be about labor issues. Numerous problems and discourses affect workers today: achieving income equality, fighting racial discrimination, compensating for outsourced production, accommodating guest workers and immigrant labor, raising the minimum wage, revising global trade policies, and adjusting to the information-economy workforce. Lonidier directs his photography toward these concerns and the workers struggling with them. He has served as president of the local teachers' union, and his artworks have been commissioned by unions and exhibited in spaces where workers gather. As Lonidier said to me recently, "My work is for, by, and about class struggle through organized labor."

This page:
Installation view of *I Like Everything Nothing But Union*, CLAP (Council of Freelance and Precarious Workers), Meeting Room, Officine Zero, Rome, Italy, 2015

Pages 103–4:
I Like Everything Nothing But Union (details), 1983

The forum through which Lonidier engages workers is an expanded documentary practice that combines straightforward photo-text panels with direct action. In the mid-1970s, Lonidier was a key member of a tight circle of photographers and artists at the New Left hotbed of the University of California, San Diego (UCSD), which included photographers Allan Sekula, Martha Rosler, and Phel Steinmetz. As part of what was then called the New Documentary movement, these ardently Marxist photographers used theoretical texts and innovative photographic projects to mount a trenchant critical and artistic challenge to postwar humanist photography. Their coherent program of oppositional cultural practices disputed the patronizing sentimentality of much liberal documentary, with its banal construction of victims without agency, arguing that such images were merely a politically disengaged form of artistic self-expression. They challenged traditional fine-art venues, such as museums and galleries, and argued for a more militant and engaged documentary photography, one that would democratize the medium by undercutting its purported objectivity, expose the systemic economic and political systems that shaped photographic "truths," allow voiceless workers and oppressed minorities to speak for themselves, and yoke their activist cultural criticism to pragmatic political change.

Of these artists, Lonidier was in many ways the most politically engaged and most committed to broad-based critiques of American capitalism. A former Peace Corps volunteer and convicted Vietnam War resister, Lonidier initially studied photography at UCSD as a way to make a living, possibly as a commercial photographer. But his MFA thesis project, a piece titled *29 Arrests* (1972), already demonstrated his sly understanding of Conceptualism and how to disrupt the conventions of photographic tradition while foregrounding political activism. The work consists of a series

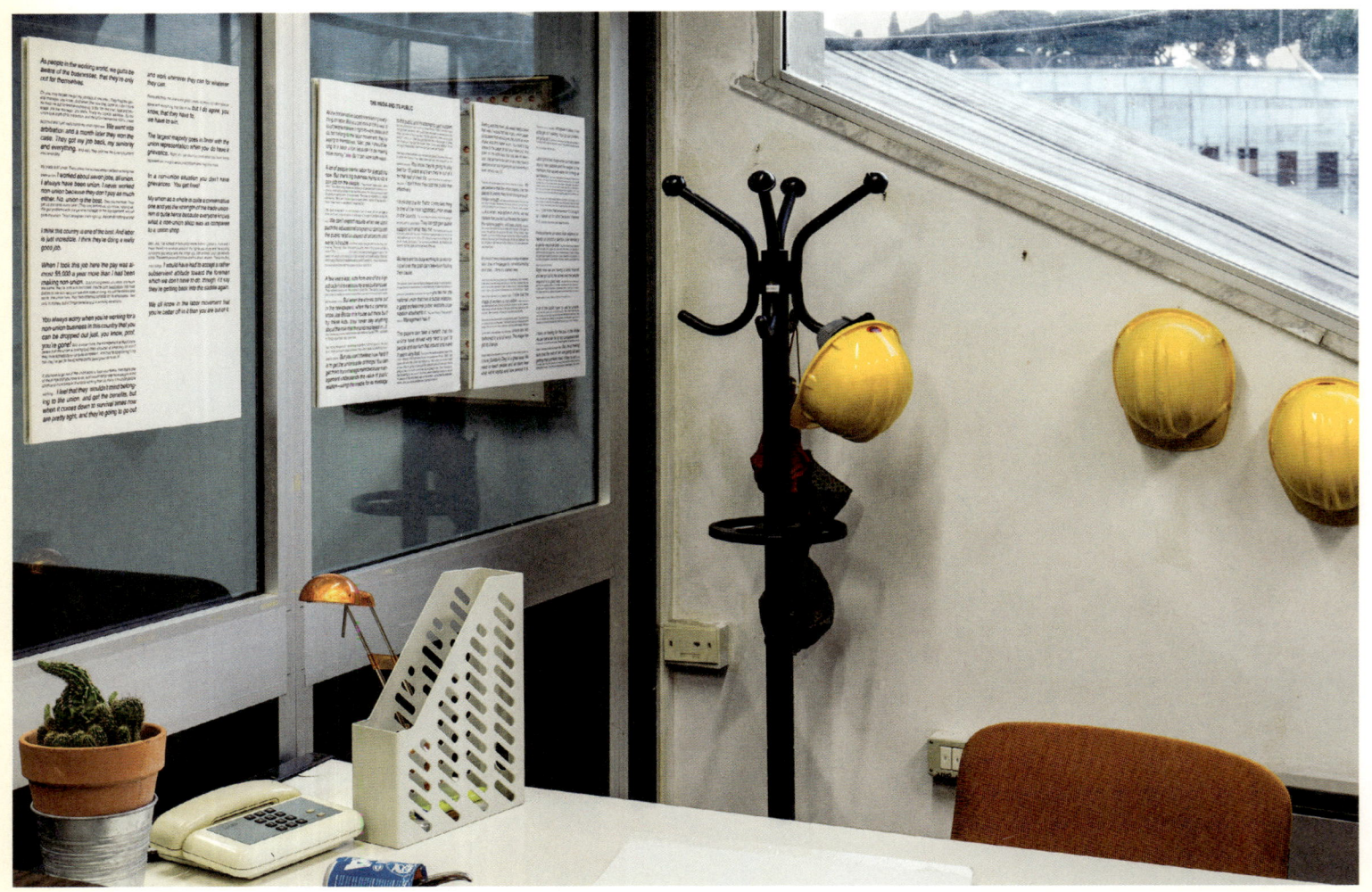

OFFICE AND PROFESSIONAL EMPLOYEES INTERNATIONAL UNION
LOCAL 139

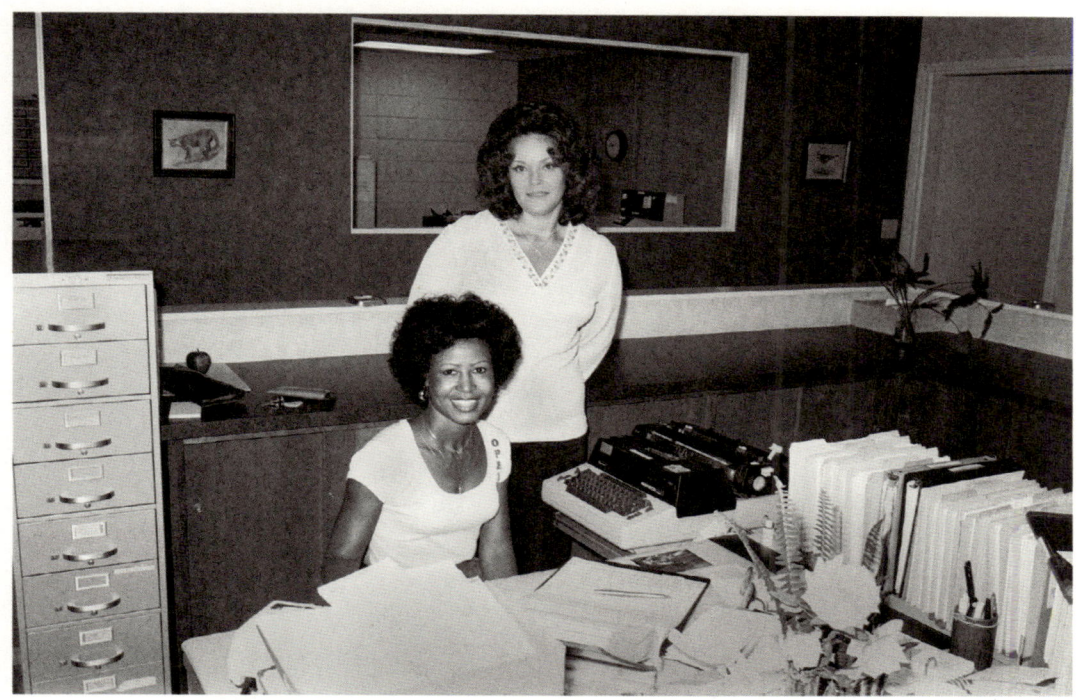

—— **Juanita Whetstone**, OPEIU and **Pat Harte-Johnson**, IAM ——

Sometimes unions are employers and workers work for unions. Many of our locals have office staff that belong to OPEIU.

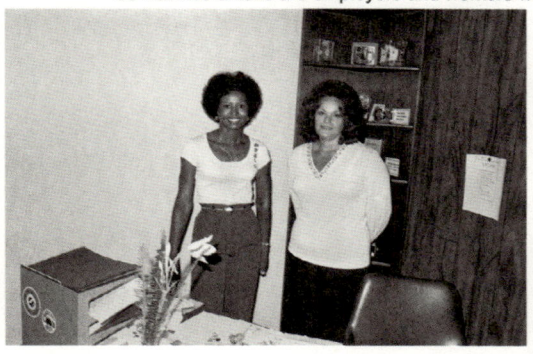

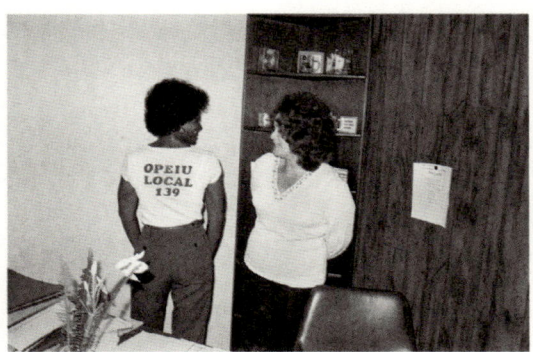

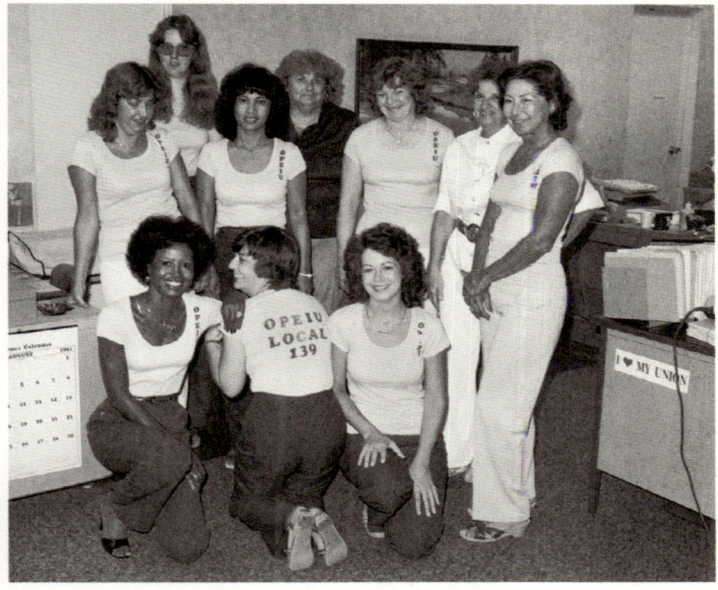

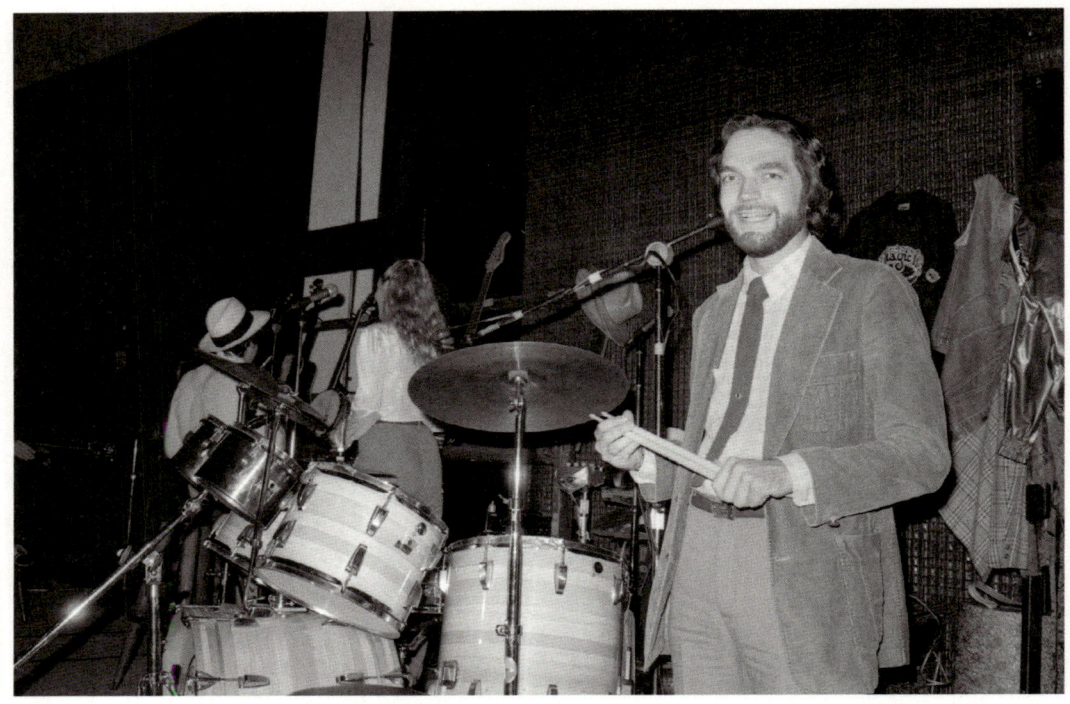

— Don Carney —

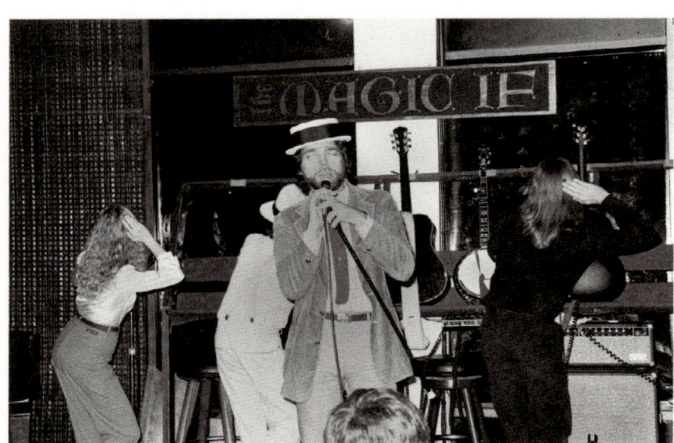

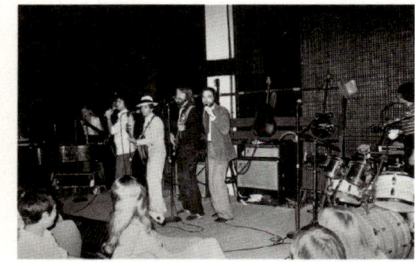
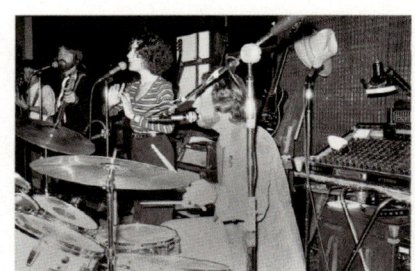

Photo License (detail),
1978

Lonidier presents a diverse, articulate, and highly opinionated community of workers with clear ideas about how best to achieve constructive political change.

of near identical shots of twenty-nine student antiwar protesters, each being held by cops while a police cameraman takes the person's portrait. Lonidier adopted a position just behind the official photographer, offering a framing perspective that the mug shots would block out: the legions of seemingly unnecessary police surrounding the nonresistant protesters. Lonidier's point of view and deadpan style mock the protocols of professional photojournalism. His images almost comically avoid the protest's dramatic confrontations, showing instead the bureaucratic processing of the accused and the state apparatus in which they are enmeshed.

Lonidier's best-known work, *The Health and Safety Game: Fictions Based on Fact* (1976–78), is an extended rumination on the brutality of the workplace and the casualties that result. He examines in explicit detail the routine violence of on-the-job injuries, which he portrays as a deliberate calculation sanctioned by the economic "game" of American industry. Across twenty-six panels that look like part of a science fair, Lonidier exposes the impact of corporate decision making, which coldly weighs the negative aspects of workers' injuries against the steep costs of preventing them. Many of the photo-text panels feature case studies of specific incidents ("Oil Worker's Burns," "Office Worker's Nerves," "Graduate Film-maker's Nail"), offering garish photographs of the injuries, as well as step-by-step timelines of the wounds, statements from workers, responses of employers, and testaments to the drawn-out struggles for treatment and compensation. Other text panels explain the various moves available to workers and management within the game. When confronted with health and safety concerns, management can, for example, bust the union, lobby politicians, move to another state, hire undocumented workers, underreport, counter with public relations, or simply violate the standards. Against such tactics, employees have few remedies. Lonidier's project reveals to workers the corporate logic and patterns that lie behind specific incidents and complaints, and encourages solidarity and activist responses. "I always look for the submerged, missed, or forgotten

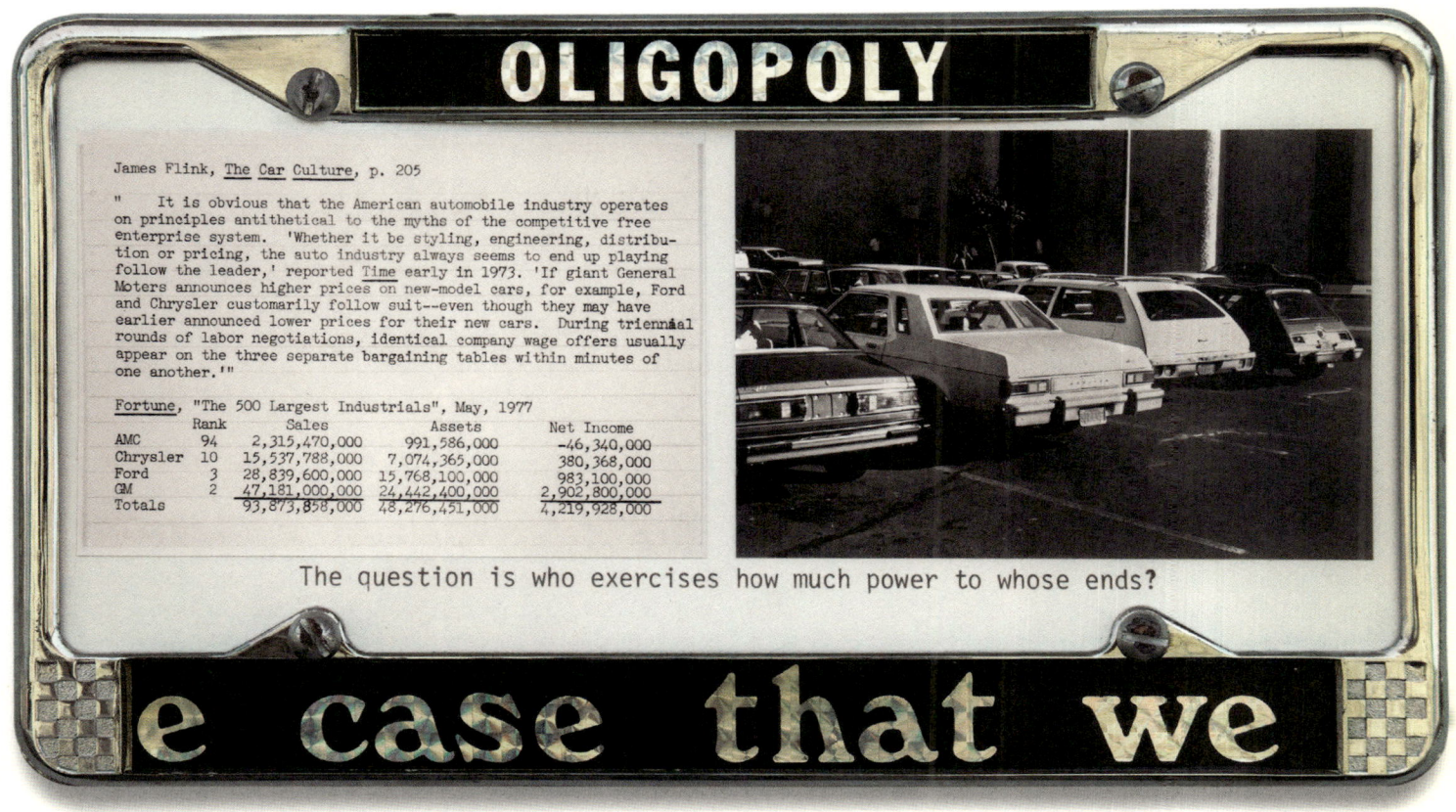

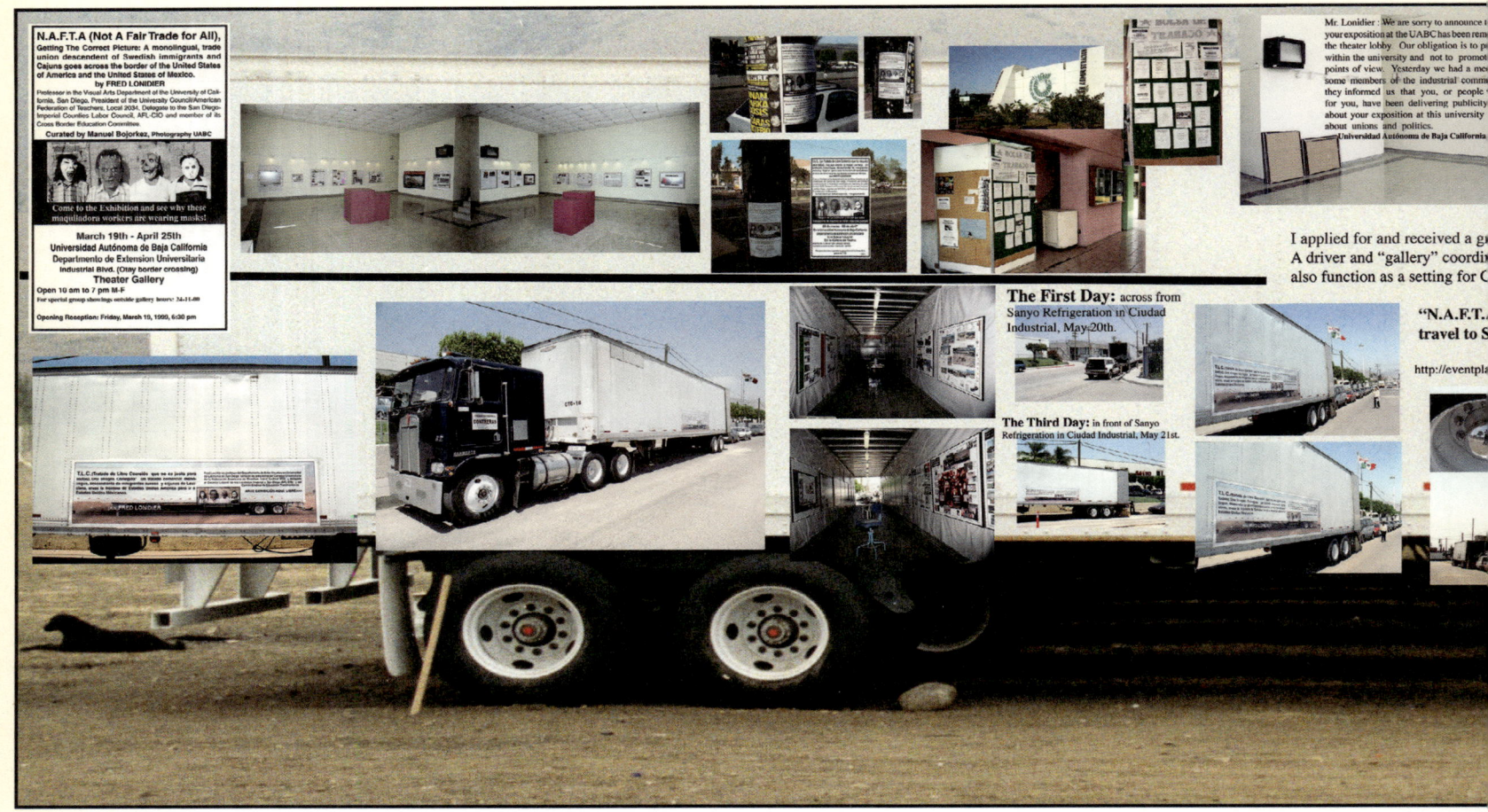

N.A.F.T.A. #16 A/B:
N.A.F.T.A... Returns to
Tijuana / T.L.C... Regresa
a Tijuana (detail), 2005
All images courtesy
the artist; Essex Street,
New York; Michael
Benevento, Los Angeles;
and Silberkuppe, Berlin

When one version of the project was shown in Tijuana, administrators closed the exhibition, claiming that Lonidier was an agitator.

labor issue," Lonidier once wrote. "Much of what I have to say is already known and discussed or suspected by workers themselves. It may only be a question of legitimizing or distilling and organizing certain ideas rather than teaching in the one-way sense."

But if *The Health and Safety Game* is critical of labor relations, other works, like the fifty-six panel *I Like Everything Nothing But Union* (1983), constitute a wholesale glorification of union workers marching in solidarity. Commissioned by the San Diego-Imperial Counties Labor Council, AFL-CIO and permanently installed in San Diego's Labor Council Hall, this work was designed specifically to honor the diversity of the union, a view that goes against the univocal stereotype of blue-collar labor. Lonidier's photographs depict a range of union members at their jobs, from clerical workers to musicians; accompanying text panels quote pithy statements from the laborers that freely offer views on the role of the union, pride in their work, and the ways labor conditions affect their lives, both on and off the job. The dedicated voices captured in this massive and optimistic study counter the conventional view of a silent workforce, grumbling about their lot and unable to represent their own interests. Instead, Lonidier presents a diverse, articulate, and highly opinionated community of workers with clear ideas about how best to achieve constructive political change.

As much as Lonidier's work reflects a mutating transformation of documentary photographic practice, it also engages with a reawakened social art movement. His long-standing documentary project *N.A.F.T.A. (Not a Fair Trade for All)*, begun in the mid-1990s, suddenly seems timely as it dovetails with widespread political condemnation in the United States of the North American Free Trade Agreement (NAFTA), which eliminated tariffs for trade between Mexico, Canada, and the United States. Even former president Bill Clinton, who signed the treaty in 1993, had insisted on amendments for granting worker and environmental protections and, more recently, has acknowledged some of NAFTA's negative consequences. As Lonidier shows in the various iterations of

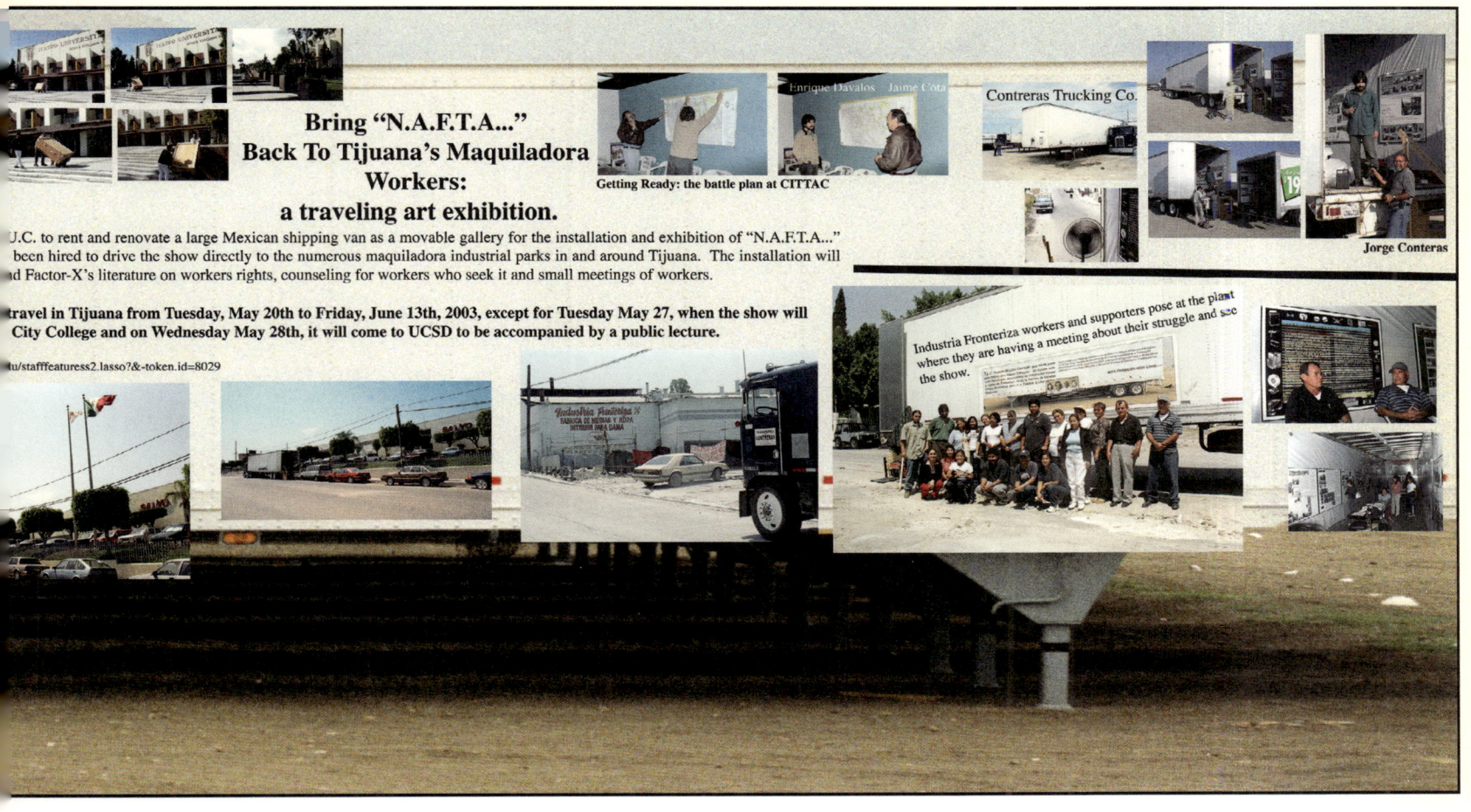

**Bring "N.A.F.T.A..."
Back To Tijuana's Maquiladora
Workers:
a traveling art exhibition.**

Getting Ready: the battle plan at CITTAC

Enrique Davalos   Jaime Cota

Contreras Trucking Co.

Jorge Conteras

J.C. to rent and renovate a large Mexican shipping van as a movable gallery for the installation and exhibition of "N.A.F.T.A..."
been hired to drive the show directly to the numerous maquiladora industrial parks in and around Tijuana. The installation will
d Factor-X's literature on workers rights, counseling for workers who seek it and small meetings of workers.

travel in Tijuana from Tuesday, May 20th to Friday, June 13th, 2003, except for Tuesday May 27, when the show will
City College and on Wednesday May 28th, it will come to UCSD to be accompanied by a public lecture.

tu/stafffeaturess2.lasso?&-token.id=8029

Industria Fronteriza workers and supporters pose at the plant
where they are having a meeting about their struggle and see
the show.

his NAFTA documentary project, American companies have
redirected production to low-cost light assembly plants, or
maquiladoras, just across the Mexican border, thereby paying
drastically lower wages and avoiding strict U.S. safety and
environmental regulations. Lonidier uses photo-text panels
to analyze in plain language and stark images the dire working
conditions in the *maquiladoras* and the recent attempts by some
Mexican workers to unionize. When one version of the project was
shown at the Universidad Autónoma de Baja California in Tijuana
in 1999, administrators closed the exhibition, claiming that Lonidier
was an agitator who had distributed leaflets to workers at a nearby
factory. Lonidier responded with *N.A.F.T.A. #16 A/B: N.A.F.T.A…
Returns to Tijuana / T.L.C… Regresa a Tijuana* (2005), in which he
mounted his photomontages on the outside and interior of a large
cargo truck, the kind used to carry immigrant laborers across the
border, and toured it to *maquiladora* zones near Tijuana and colleges
in San Diego.

Photographs of the truck highlighted Lonidier's contribution
to the 2014 Whitney Biennial, but the culmination of his
participation was undoubtedly the evening teach-in that featured
Lonidier lecturing on the connections between art and the working
class, and also included a rousing performance by the red-shirted,
fist-clenching New York City Labor Chorus singing "Solidarity
Forever." Foregrounding the voices of workers and emphasizing the
role of pedagogy, Lonidier symbolically delineated strategies for a
new alignment of social-movement art, bringing resonant cultural
iconography to the workplace, and inserting labor concerns into
the white-cube space of the art museum. "My commitment has long
been that the concerns and exhibition of social art be connected
in some way to organized efforts towards the same ends," Lonidier
says. "Art that intends to challenge the social world has its best
chance in tandem with social/political organizations and their
allies." This ideal remains the incomplete project of an expanded
documentary photography.

Brian Wallis is a writer and curator based
in New York.

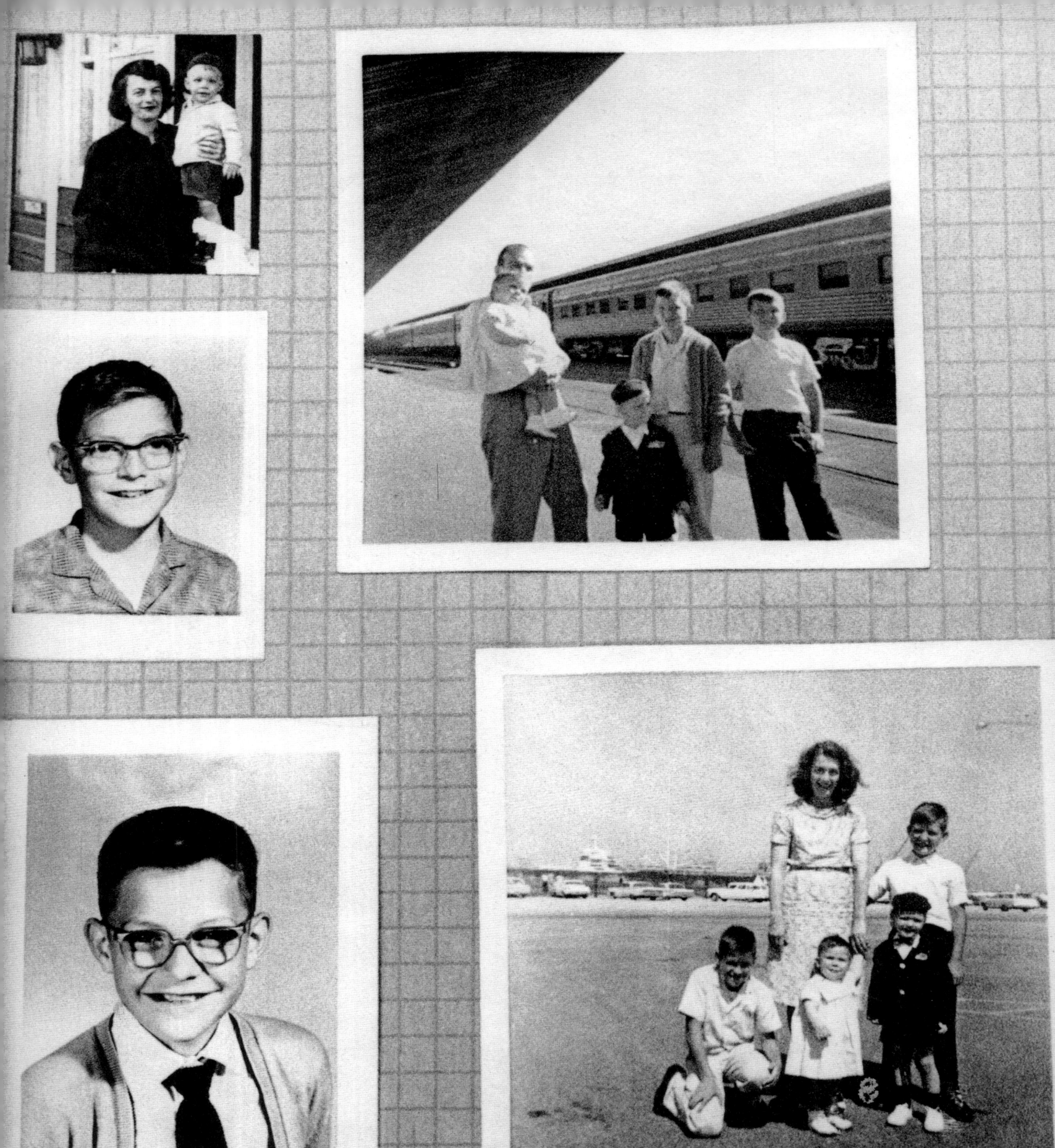

Allan Sekula

Aerospace Folktales

Drew Sawyer

In 1973, a year that marked the beginnings of a national recession and the signing of a peace treaty to end the Vietnam War, Allan Sekula's first major work took as its subject an aerospace engineer who had been laid off from Lockheed, then the single largest defense contractor in the United States. By combining intimate scenes of family life in a small Los Angeles apartment with various personal documents—family photo albums, a rental agreement, bookshelves filled with classic literature, the engineer's CV, and job rejection letters—*Aerospace Folktales* explores the daily life of this unemployed white-collar worker and his family as their class identity is being thrown into question. Sekula then goes on to disrupt the usual objective distance of social observation and documentary politics by revealing that the unemployed worker is in fact his own father.

Page 108, this spread, and overleaf:
Images from *Aerospace Folktales*, 1973
142 gelatin silver prints and eight title cards mounted to poster board; seven text panels mounted to poster board; four audiotape recordings, 75:24 minutes (loop)

Sekula forces both his subjects and viewers to consider the dissolution of the postwar American dream.

The result is a group portrait of an artist and his family in relation to each other and to their surrounding social and economic structures.

At its peak, in 1967, Southern California's vast aerospace industry accounted for nearly half a million jobs. But the waning of the Vietnam War and of the Apollo space program, along with a recession, brought a sharp falloff in military and NASA procurements that resulted in a succession of layoffs during the early 1970s. Many of those employees were, like Sekula's father, professionals and experts who had risen to the middle class after World War II by obtaining undergraduate and graduate degrees. Sekula forces both his subjects and viewers to consider the dissolution of the postwar American dream, and the artist himself wonders in an accompanying text what will become of his career as an "art engineer" once he completes his graduate degree.

In its original installation at the University of California, San Diego (UCSD), in 1973, *Aerospace Folktales* consisted of 142 black-and-white photographic images and text cards, along with four sound recordings of interviews between the artist and his father, his mother, and his mother's friend (whose husband was also unemployed). Sekula hung the 142 photographs in a single row with text cards breaking the sequence into smaller groups that suggested the narrative flow and format of a silent movie. In this first exhibition, the audio played in an adjacent room, but in a 1974 installation at the Brand Library & Art Center in Glendale, near the Lockheed plant, the speakers were hidden behind potted plants in the gallery. At UCSD, Sekula performed a reading of an explanatory text, typed on seven pages of letter-size paper and titled "a commentary," serving as a general narration but also "filling in for earlier omissions ... because of the limited representational range of the camera." In 1984, the year he published his seminal book *Photography Against the Grain*, Sekula

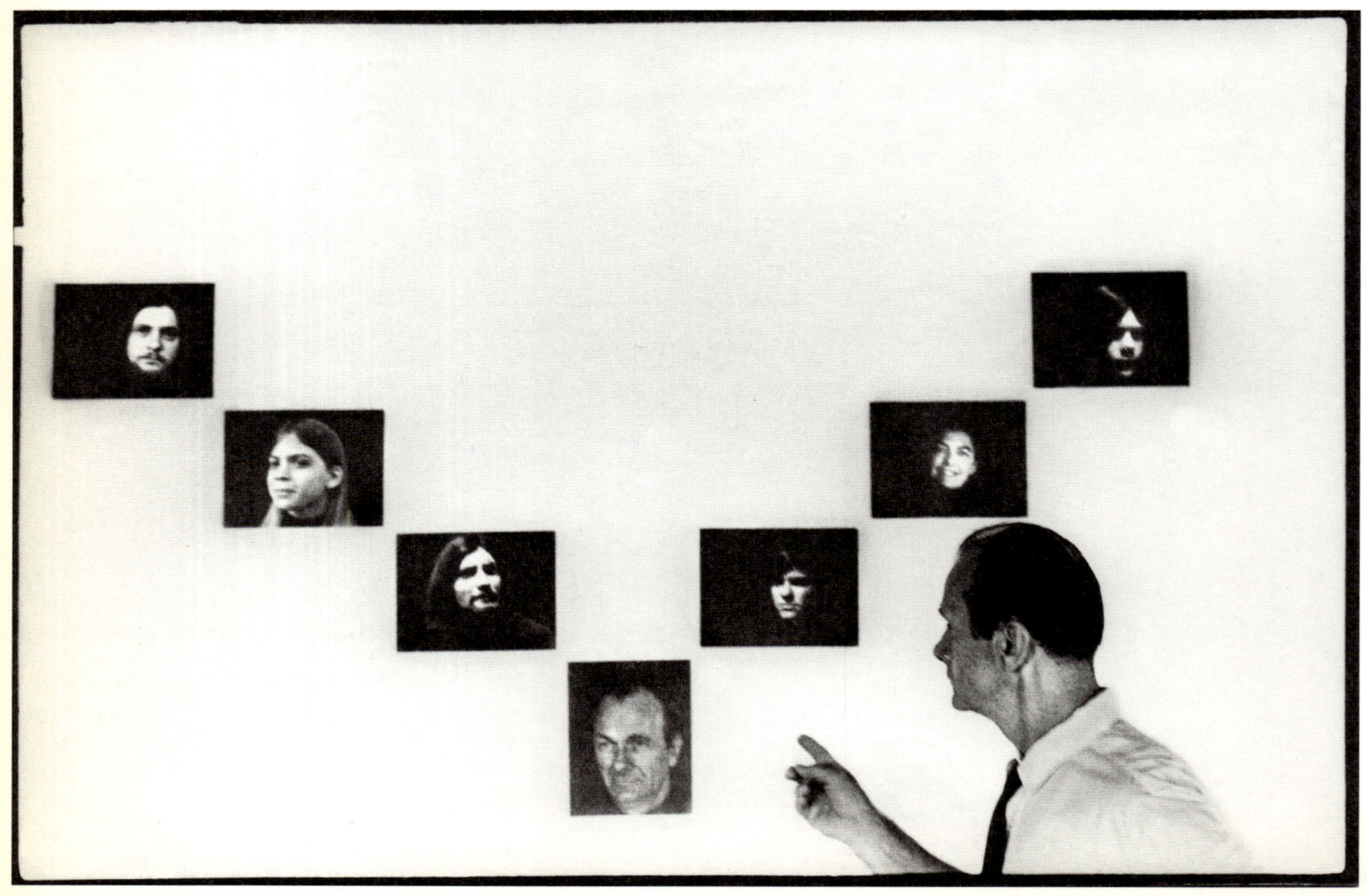

the engineer and his old friend stood in the empty
lockheed parking lot while i photographed them

unable to fathom my motives, they were uneasy

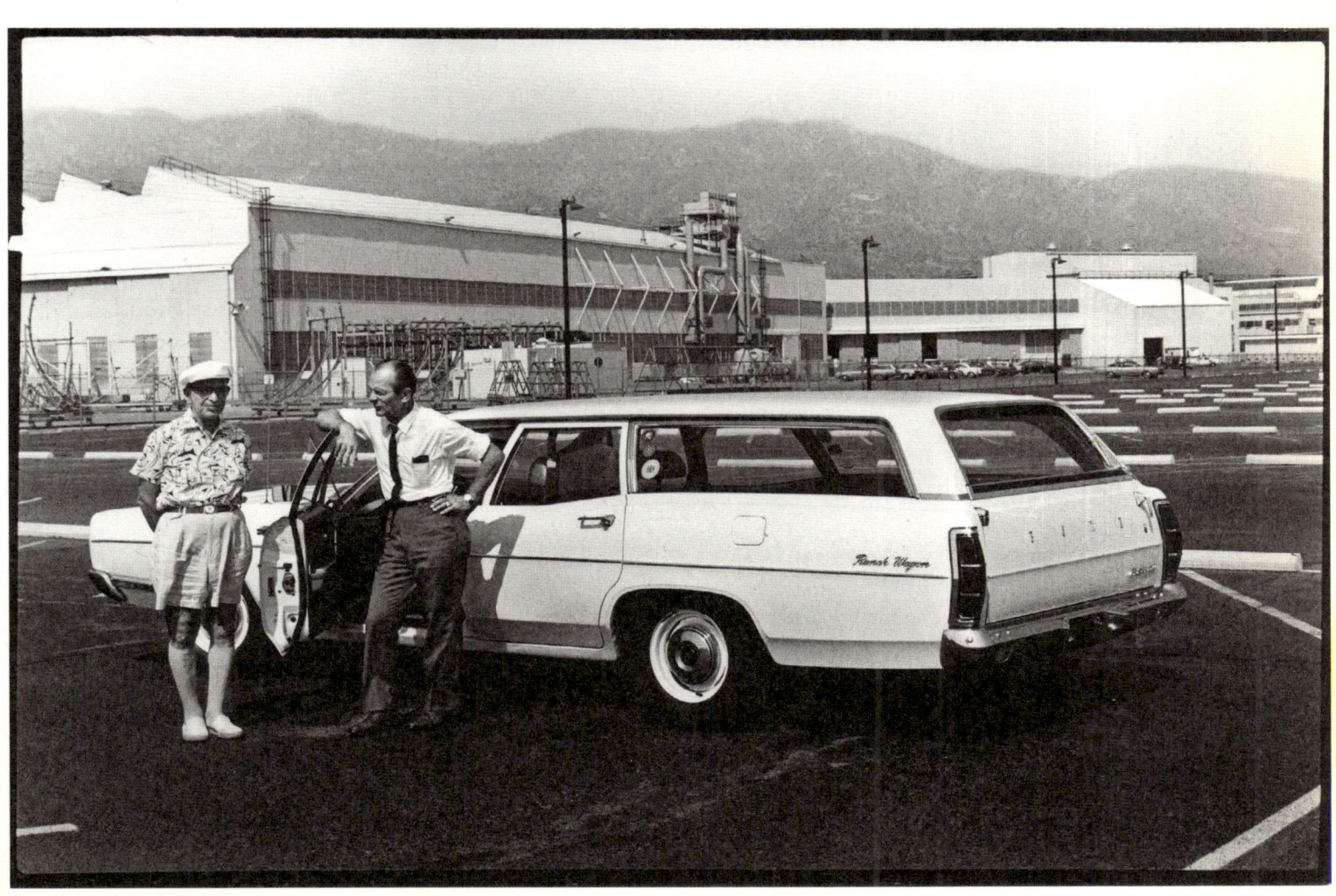

edited the work down to fifty-one photographs, often grouped as diptychs or in grids of four, and three sound recordings.

Sekula referred to the work, with its deconstruction of the essential elements of a film, as a "disassembled movie." He had already begun to experiment with this format in his 35mm slide show *Untitled Slide Sequence* from 1972. Here too he turned his camera on aerospace factory workers, but without the typical veneration associated with pictures of such laborers taken by photographers for the Office of War Information or popular magazines like *Fortune* during the 1940s. Instead, he chose to capture the workers just as they were leaving their shifts at a General Dynamics Convair Division factory in San Diego, where several of them likely helped produce the F-111 military planes that flew in Vietnam. The twenty-five images in this sequence depict a range of employees as they climb the staircase to a pedestrian overpass and are directly confronted by the artist's camera. Sekula had originally envisioned *Aerospace Folktales* as a slide show as well, but ultimately decided to keep separate image, text, and audio "tracks," allowing their formal discontinuities to underscore the contradictions inherent in the documentary genre as well as in contemporary life—both are their own kinds of folktales or mythologies.

Like a film, *Aerospace Folktales* begins not with an image, but with text. Included is a short excerpt from Lockheed's promotional materials, with typical corporate platitudes, and a quote from the company's chairman that declares: "Our competence has kept us in the forefront of the industry … I know that at Lockheed our eyes are on the future, and our efforts are in a large part directed toward realizing it fully." Several reproductions of archival newspaper photographs follow of what seem to be cheerful Lockheed employees and U.S. military personnel standing in a parking lot. Next appears a suite of straight photographs of Lockheed's Burbank plant and parking lot, where Sekula's father and a friend stand next to a Ford station wagon. The change from the archival halftone images to the documentary photographs conveys a movement forward in time, but the nearly empty parking lot and the uneasy engineer suggest the future is not quite what Lockheed had promised.

More often, though, Sekula takes viewers into the family's apartment in San Pedro, a working-class neighborhood in which the Port of Los Angeles is partially located. There, we witness the father's attempts to fill his days and evenings by reading the newspaper, writing letters, and fixing a lamp while Sekula's younger siblings do schoolwork and play. Sekula referred to these banal everyday activities as his parents' "white-collar art"—the patterns of thought and behavior that formed their worldviews and identities. Both his mother's and father's own words, heard in the interviews, reflect the frustrations of finding employment at middle age and their conflicting ideas about technology, the economy, and the future of the country. Why did his father, Sekula wondered in his commentary, mimic the rhetoric of Lockheed's upper management, when those beliefs went against his own economic and political interests? As the sequences and sound track progress, the focus shifts from father to mother, as she prepares dinner and arranges flowers in a vase. "Her unpaid labor," Sekula explains, "provides management with well-fed, well-cared-for labor, forty hours a week," an attentiveness to the gendered dimension of labor that places his work in dialogue with the feminist movement and related art practices of the decade.

While an MFA student at the University of California, San Diego, a school founded in 1960 with the support of the military and aerospace industries already located nearby, Sekula became close with the artist Martha Rosler, known for photomontages and videos that impugn traditional gender roles. Studying art with David Antin and John Baldessari, and Marxist philosophy

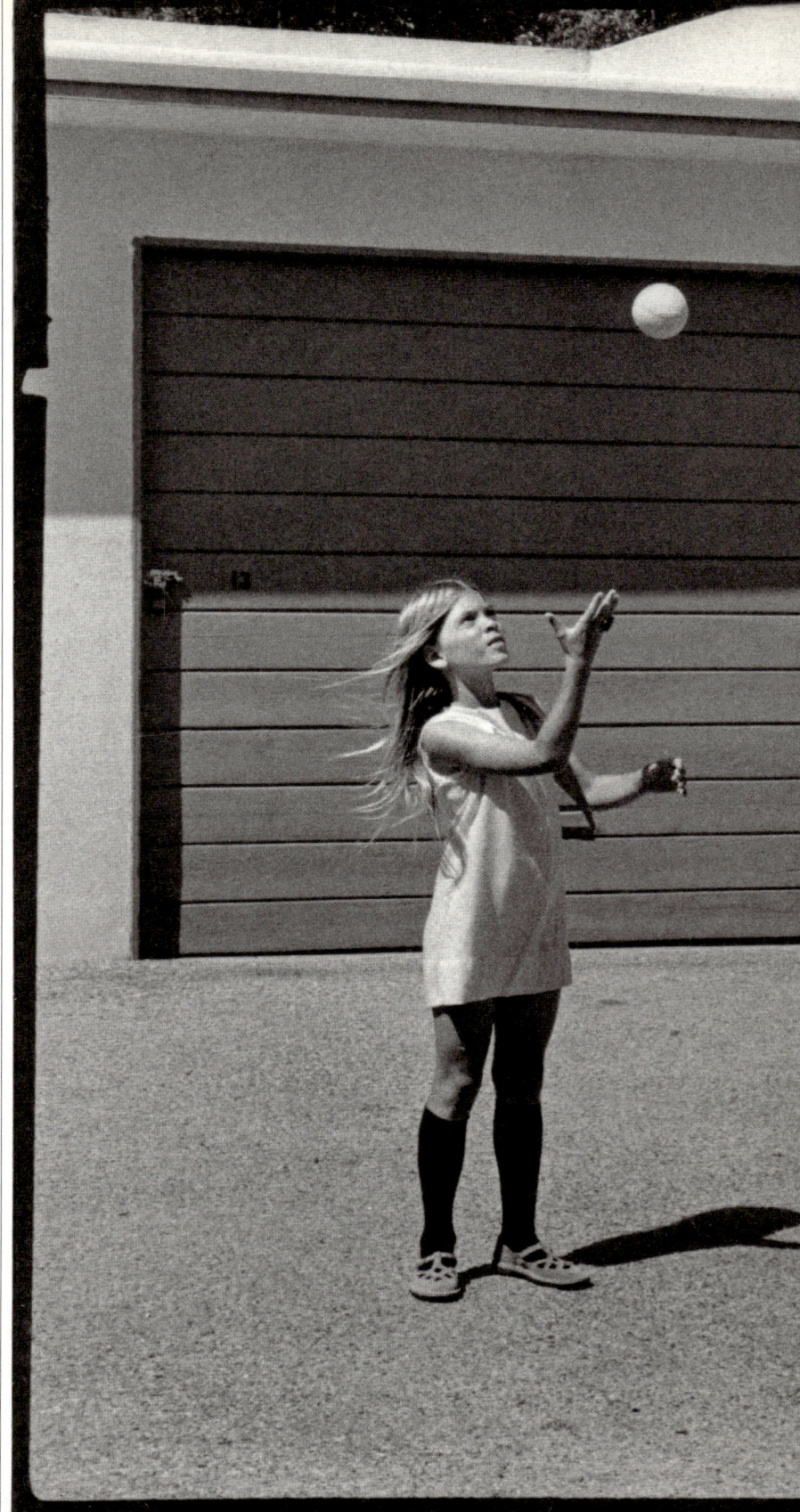

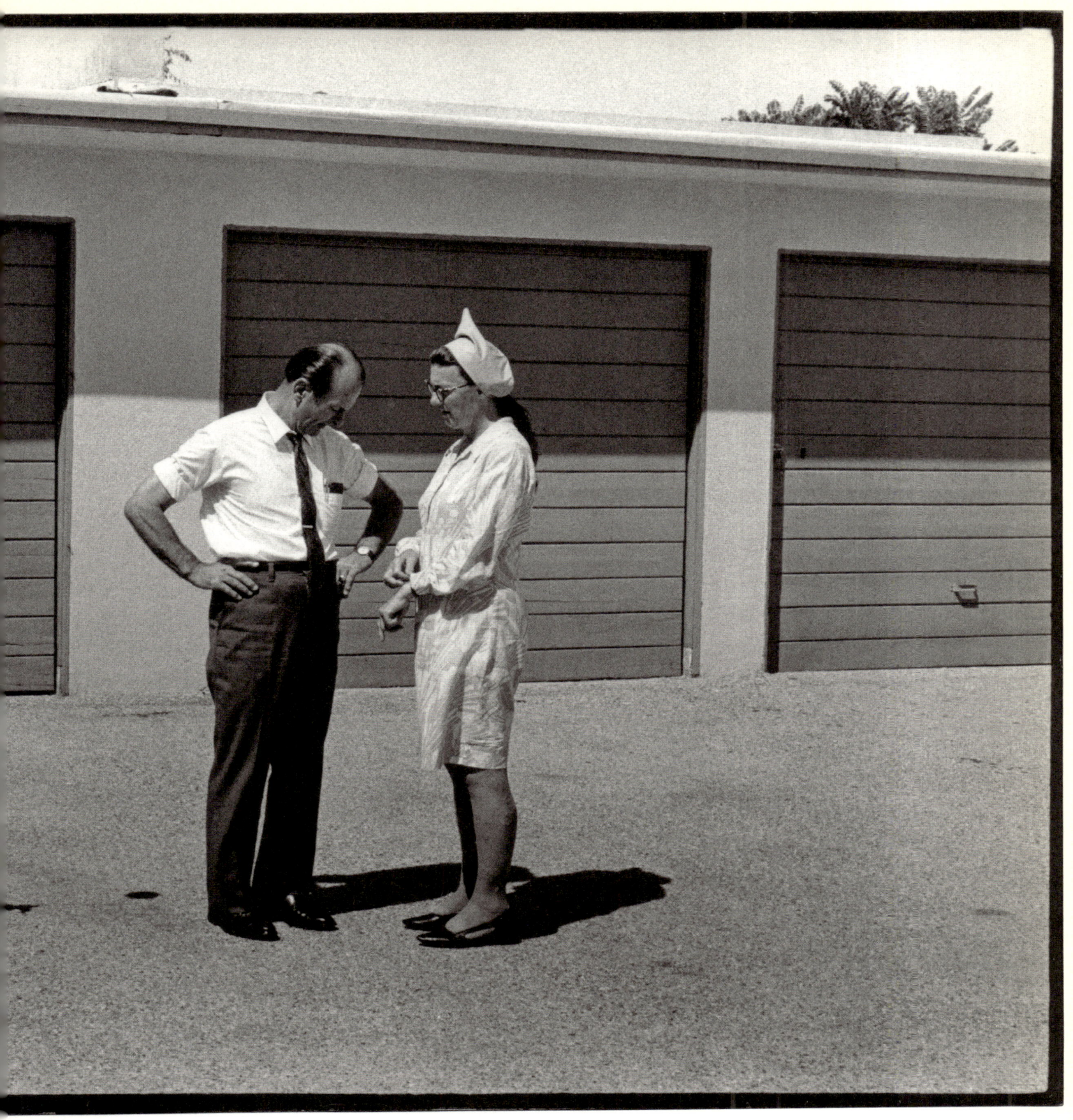

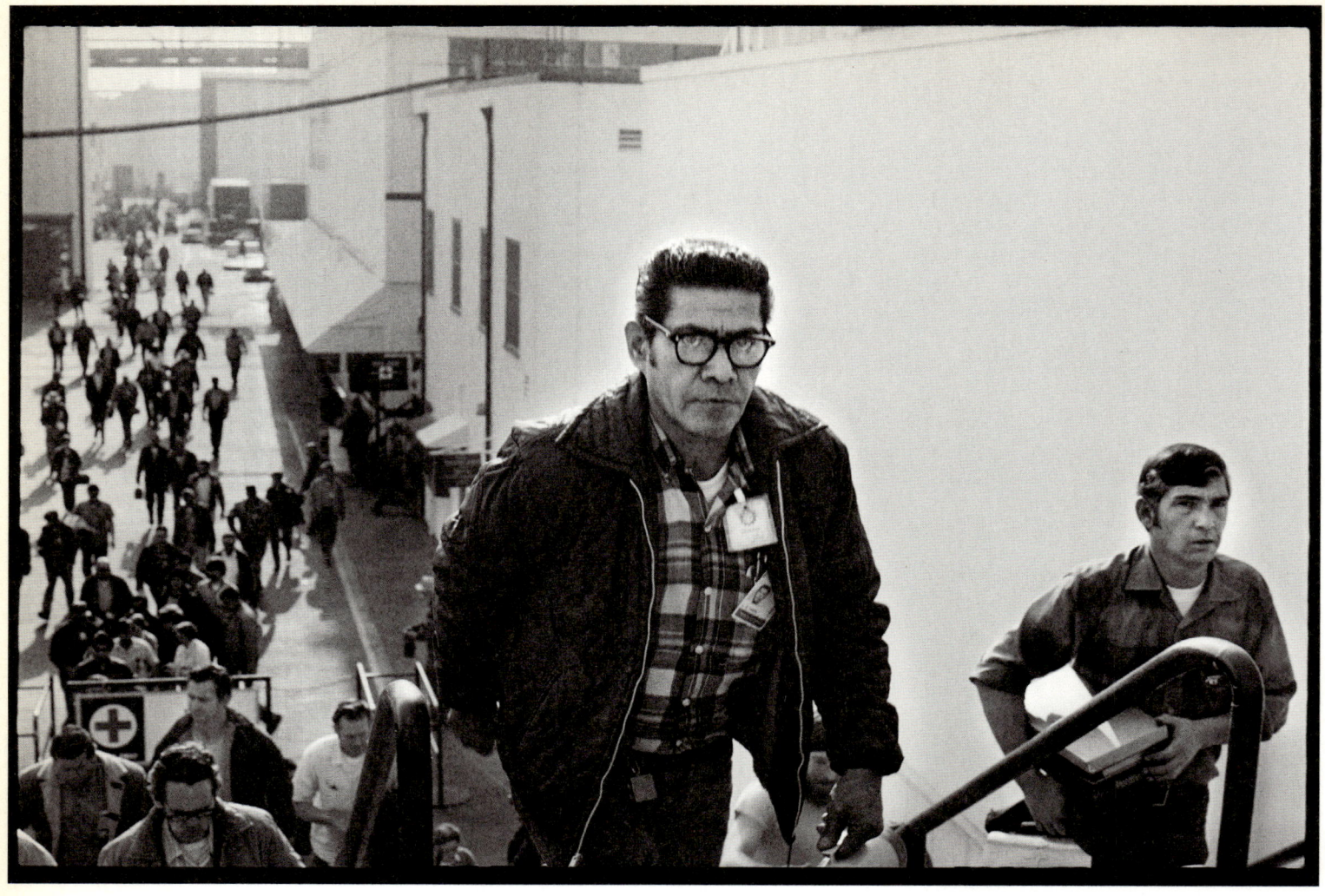

with Herbert Marcuse and Fredric Jameson, Sekula and Rosler, along with fellow classmates Fred Lonidier and Phel Steinmetz, utilized the strategies of Conceptual art and institutional critique to both challenge the orthodoxies of modernism and reestablish a political documentary artistic practice. In the 1970s, Sekula would publish a series of seminal essays, including "Dismantling Modernism, Reinventing Documentary (Notes on the Politics of Representation)" (1976–78), which questions the separation of art from everyday life and politics, the aestheticization of suffering and poverty, and the myth of photographic truth and neutrality. It became a manifesto for both his generation of artists and those to follow.

Over the course of Sekula's practice, his writings grew inextricably tied to his art, as he refused to concede the usual divisions between artist, critic, and historian. A deep appreciation and understanding of the histories of photography are reflected throughout his work. While *Untitled Slide Sequence* is in part a tribute to the Lumière brothers' first film, *Workers Leaving the Lumière Factory* (1895), *Aerospace Folktales* pays homage to Walker Evans and James Agee's 1941 experimental documentary book, *Let Us Now Praise Famous Men*. That book, which began as a picture story for *Fortune* magazine in 1936, documents the families of tenant cotton farmers in Alabama during the Great Depression and similarly separates the constitutive elements of documentary—image and text. Sekula's sequence of photographs of his parents standing against a slatted garage door outside their apartment building is perhaps the most obvious reference to Evans's iconic portraits of farmers against their clapboard shacks, and stakes a claim to a lineage of challenging, if not radical, forms of documentary from the first half of the twentieth century.

Sekula's art was about making visible those unseen, or at least undocumented, aspects of our economy.

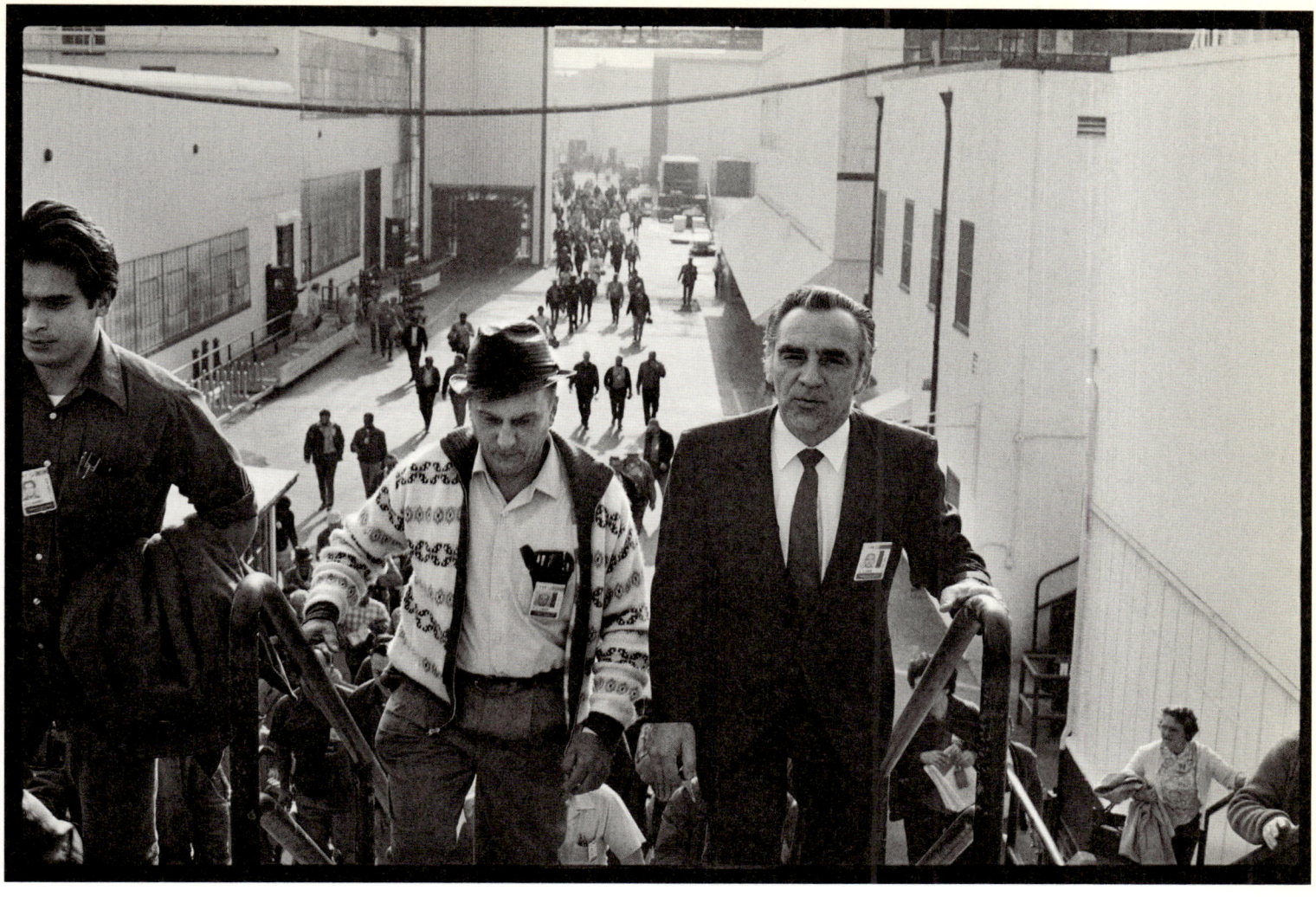

Opposite and this page:
From *Untitled Slide Sequence*, 1972
All photographs courtesy Allan Sekula Studio and the Columbus Museum of Art

While Sekula remained based in Los Angeles for much of his working life (he died in 2013), teaching photography and critical theory at the California Institute of the Arts, his art would eventually take him to far-flung places, as his attention shifted to the accumulating effects of global capitalism. His photobook and multipart exhibition *Fish Story* (1989–95), along with his and Noël Burch's film *The Forgotten Space* (2010), track maritime space and the impact of the invention of the cargo container, or what Sekula called "the very coffin of remote labor power." For the artist, large seaports, like the one just down the street from his family's home in San Pedro, had remained relatively invisible, located on the outskirts of large metropolitan centers. Yet, they had radically changed manufacturing and the distribution of both goods and labor. "Factories are now like ships: they mutate strangely, masquerade, and sometimes sail away stealthily in the night in search of cheaper labor, leaving their former employees bewildered and jobless," he lamented. Sekula's art was about making visible those unseen, or at least undocumented, aspects of our economy. This was never an easy task, neither for the artist nor the viewer—photography was not merely a product, but always a process of labor.

Drew Sawyer is the William J. and Sarah Ross Soter Associate Curator of Photography at the Columbus Museum of Art, where he is organizing an exhibition on the original version of *Aerospace Folktales*, along with other slide and video works by Allan Sekula.

Jim Goldberg & Donovan Wylie

Laura Wexler and Chris Klatell

In New Haven

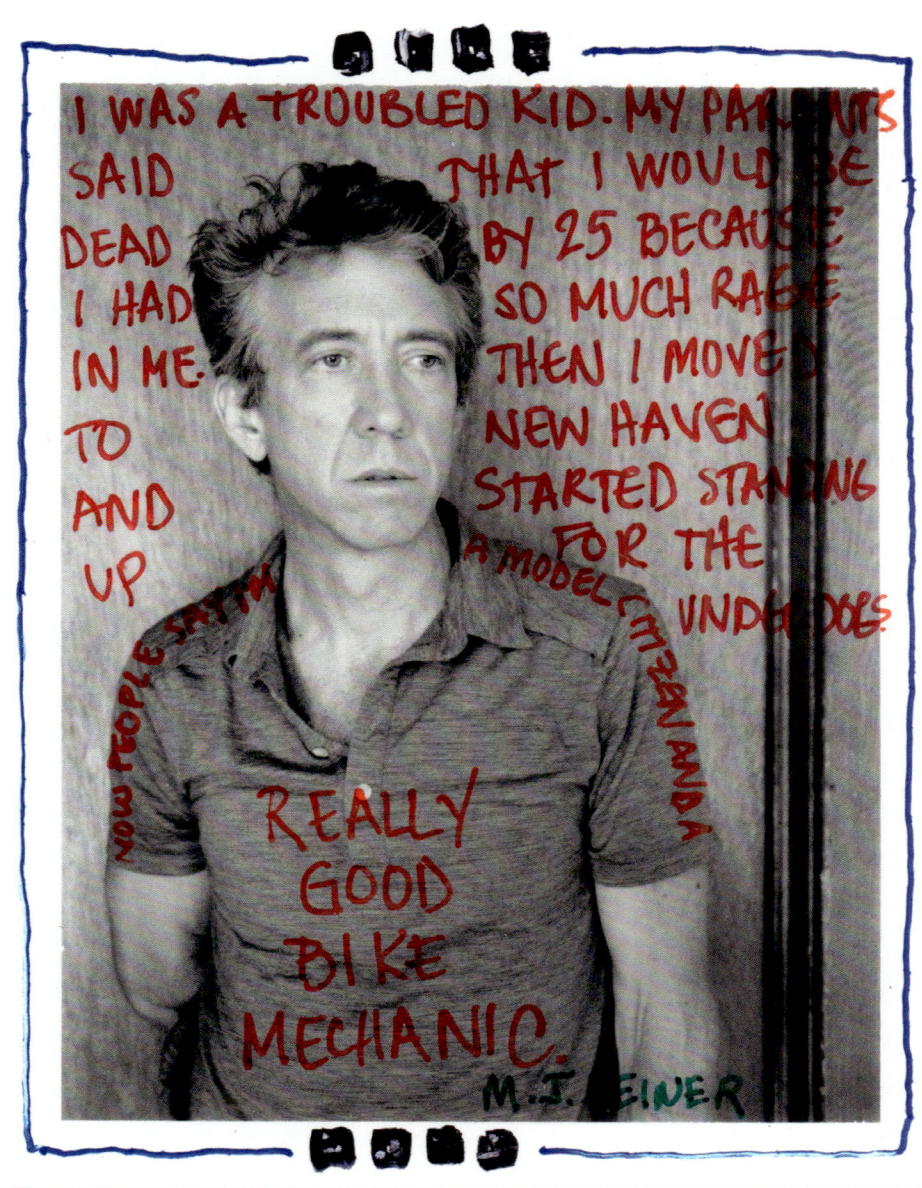

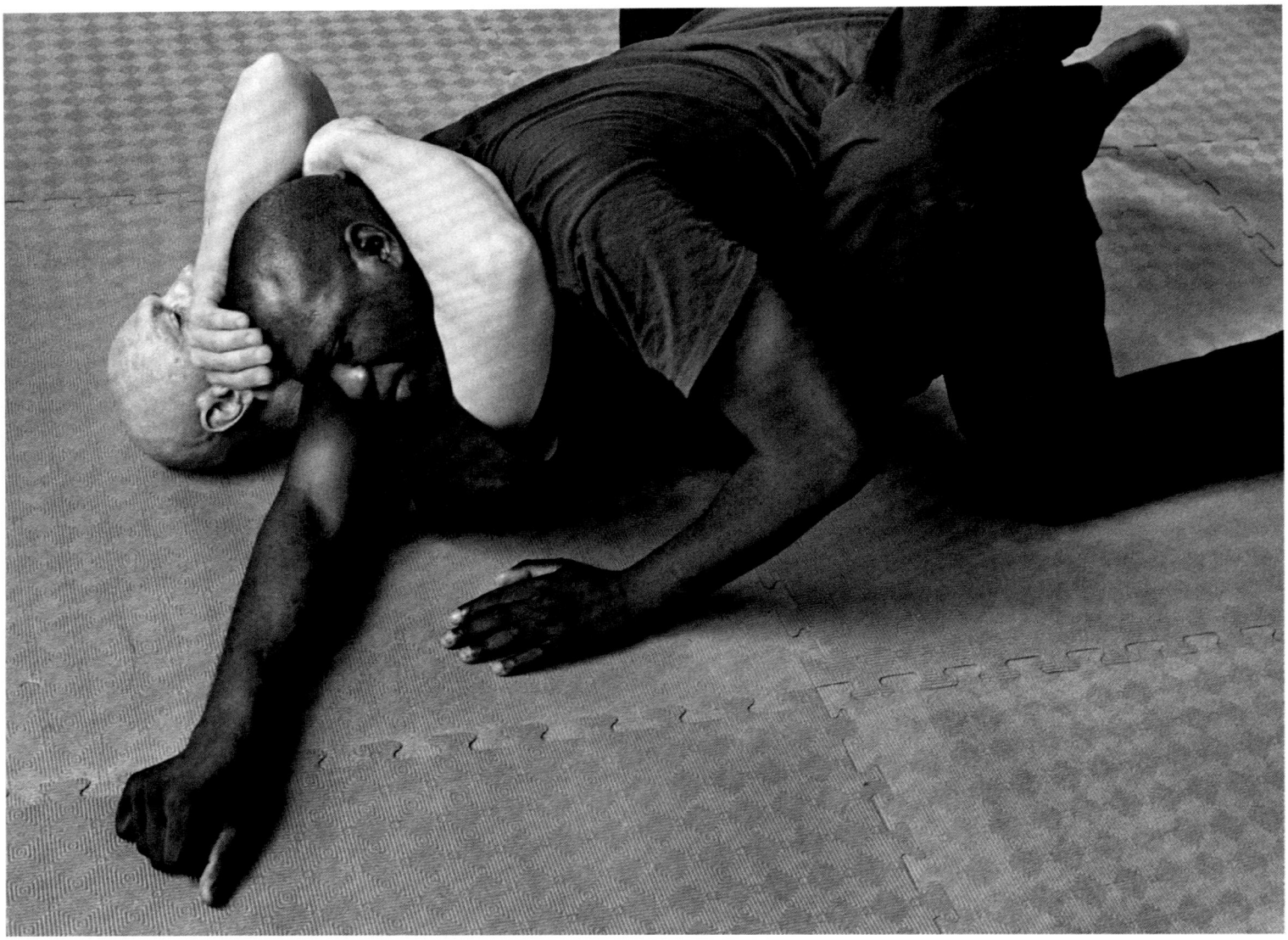

Connecticut was long the center of the North American armaments industry, home to Remington Arms in Bridgeport, Colt's Patent Firearms in Hartford, and Winchester Repeating Arms (manufacturer of the "gun that won the West") in New Haven. Colt .45s, Winchester model 1873s, Ruger pistols, Marlin rifles, and Thompson, Browning, and Gatling machine guns all rolled off Connecticut production lines, earning the state the moniker "the arsenal of democracy."

The gun industry is mostly gone, but the factories remain, crumbling just off multiple exits from I-91 and I-95, the two major highways that cut through the state and merge, with a particular force, in the middle of New Haven. Along the state's rivers other ghosted industries have also left their trace: brass, tobacco, fish, oysters, timber, ships, and clocks. The great industrial past looms over Connecticut's coastal and river roads like successive manifestations of a single impulse: the desire to dominate a continent that stretches inland to the west, whether by force, or by commerce, or both. The promise is implicit: a good and spacious land, covenanted to a chosen people, may all those who stand in the way be damned.

Perhaps it took an Irishman like Donovan Wylie to see this phenomenon engineered into the highways that were both strange and familiar; back home, the Ulster plantations were being settled at the same time as the Connecticut colony, and with similar violence. But Wylie is less interested in showing us the narrative than in revealing the material construction of the roads it generated.

A topography of empire, Wylie's series *A Good and Spacious Land* (2017) reveals the weight that everything beneath the highways, human and concrete, is asked to bear in the process of keeping the roads and their myth aloft.

Jim Goldberg, New Haven born, knows that weight first-hand. As a boy in the late 1950s and early 1960s he watched his father's candy store disappear to make way for I-91, and he remembers a kind of howl that arose when I-95 tore the city apart. Those were the days when New Haven was known as the Model City, and promises of "redevelopment" were plentiful and cheap. The people of New Haven learned that experts and planners, looking down at them from above, would engineer their home into a "slumless city," the nation's first, idealized and pure, a city on a hill. There was sweetness in those long ago New Haven days.

But slowly, the myth of the "model city" crumbled and then came crashing down. On May Day, 1970, at protests on the New Haven Green against the upcoming Black Panther trials, the supporting structure snapped. It was a moment of polyvalent disillusionment from which it seems that few have ever really recovered. Goldberg fled west, vowing to undermine the "model city" point of view and to expose its hypocrisy; he searched for it first among the extremes of San Francisco society in *Rich and Poor* (1985, reissued 2014), and then, a runaway himself, took to the streets in search of it again in *Raised by Wolves* (1995). Now he's back in New Haven for a reckoning, and to complete the trilogy. In *Candy* (2017), he's produced something like a

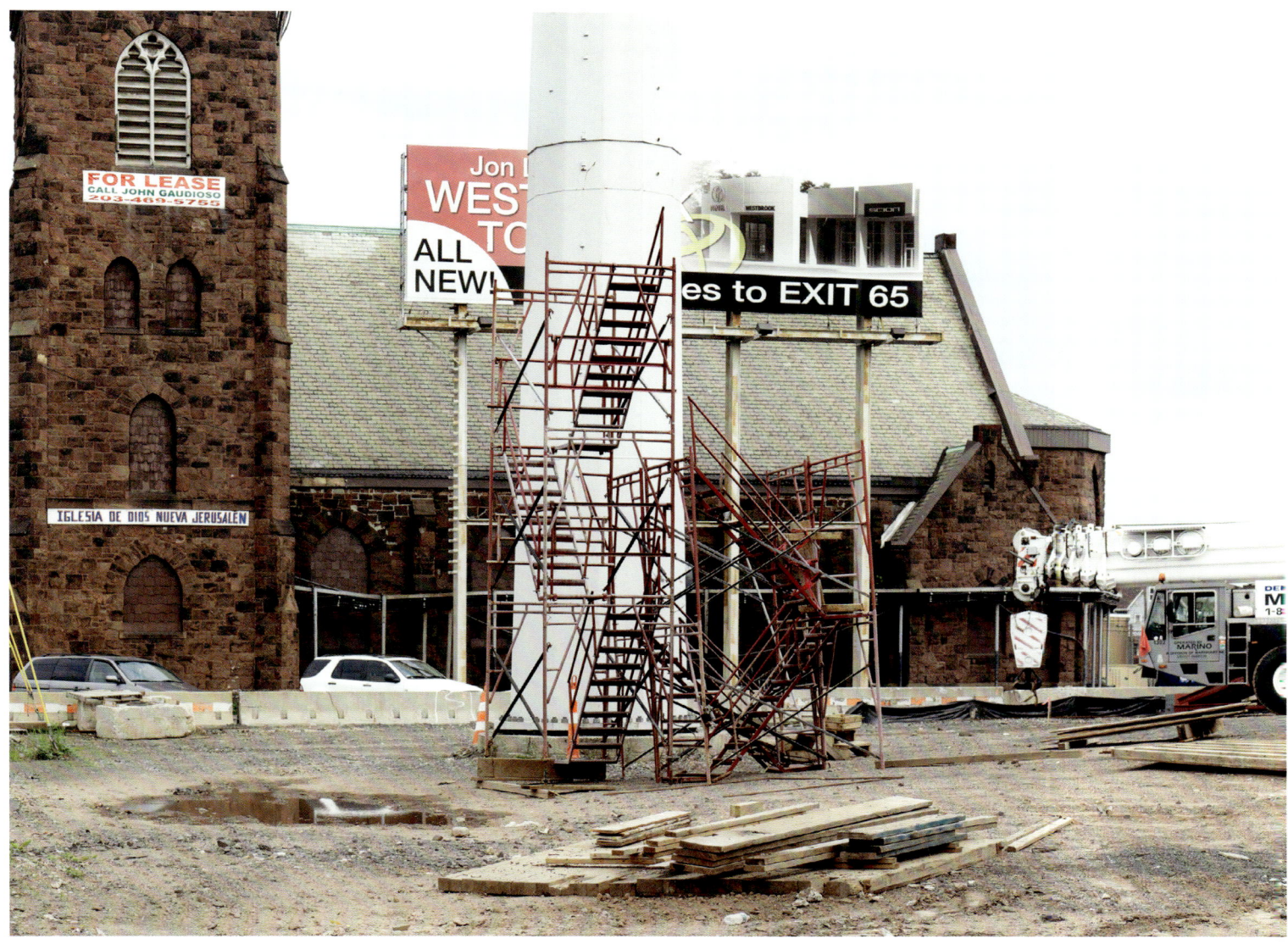

novel, a sprawling story based on the lives of three boys in the Model City: one who stayed, one who left, and one who was sent away, but none of whom could ever let it go.

Violence is a landscape, a set of connections between events, locations, memories, and monuments. New Haven's roads map the edges of a world-historical trauma, from the carefully planned grid of the Puritans' nine squares to the endlessly reconstructed merge of I-95 and I-91. The Model City was built upon the genocidal decimation of the Pequot tribe, the savagery of slavery, the inexorable demands of capital, and a demolished candy store. Beneath it all, beneath everything, lies betrayal. New Haven's hometown hero, believe it or not, is Benedict Arnold.

Taken together, the studies of New Haven that Goldberg and Wylie have produced also propose nothing less than a way out of the maze: that we look at and listen to every place and person in New Haven until we can make peace with both the real and imagined photographs through which they map the space. Ultimately, as Wallace Stevens wrote, the real and the imaginary in their photographs are simply two in one: New Haven, before and after one arrives.

Opposite:
Jim Goldberg,
Police Training, 2014

This page:
Donovan Wylie,
*Church of New Jerusalem,
Forbes Ave, New Haven*,
2014

Overleaf:
Jim Goldberg, *Joe Taylor's
Family Story* (detail), 2016

*Candy/A Good and
Spacious Land* will be
published as two volumes
by the Yale University Art
Gallery in June 2017.

Laura Wexler is Professor
of Women's, Gender,
and Sexuality Studies
and American Studies
at Yale University.

Chris Klatell is a lawyer and
writer based in New York
and New Haven.

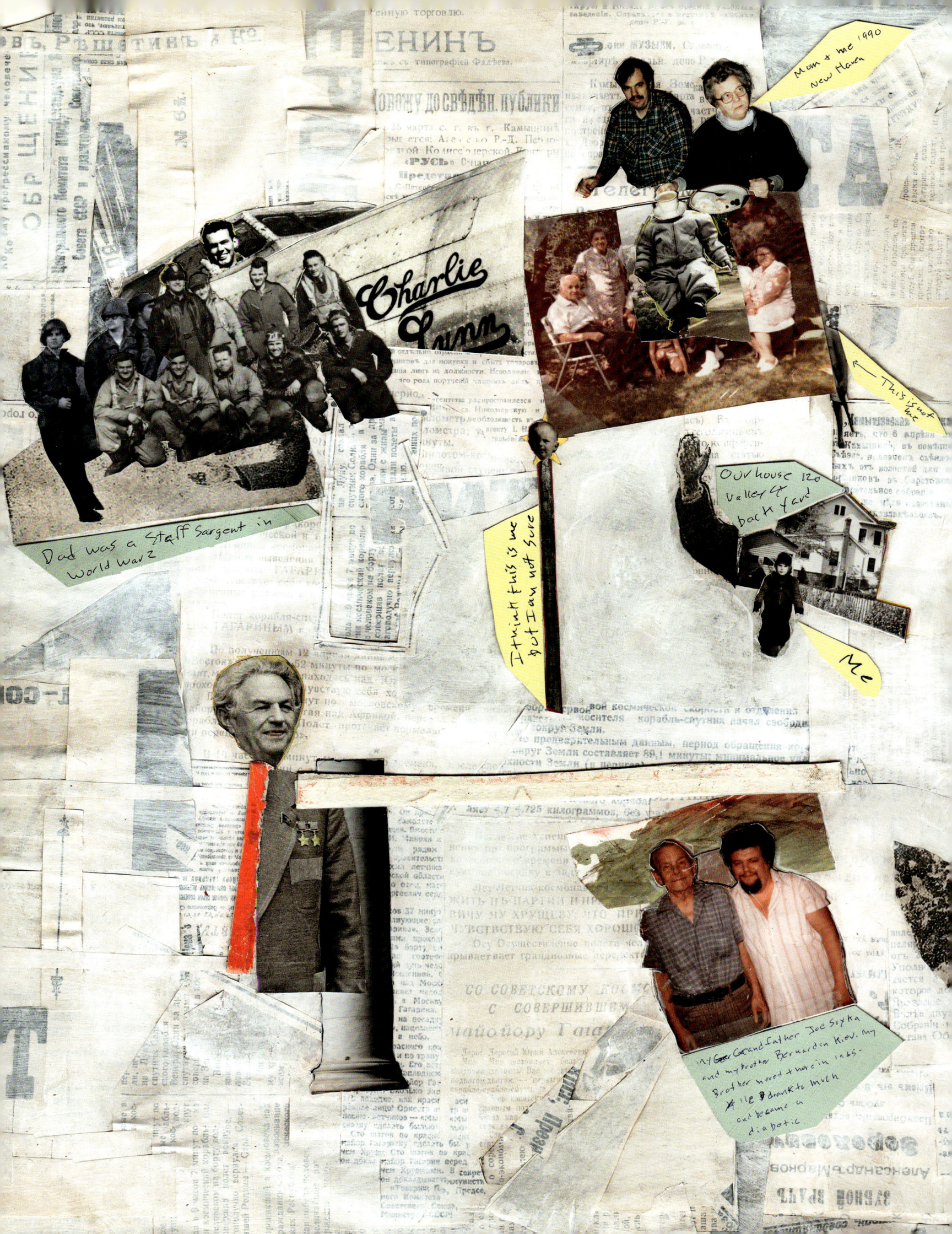

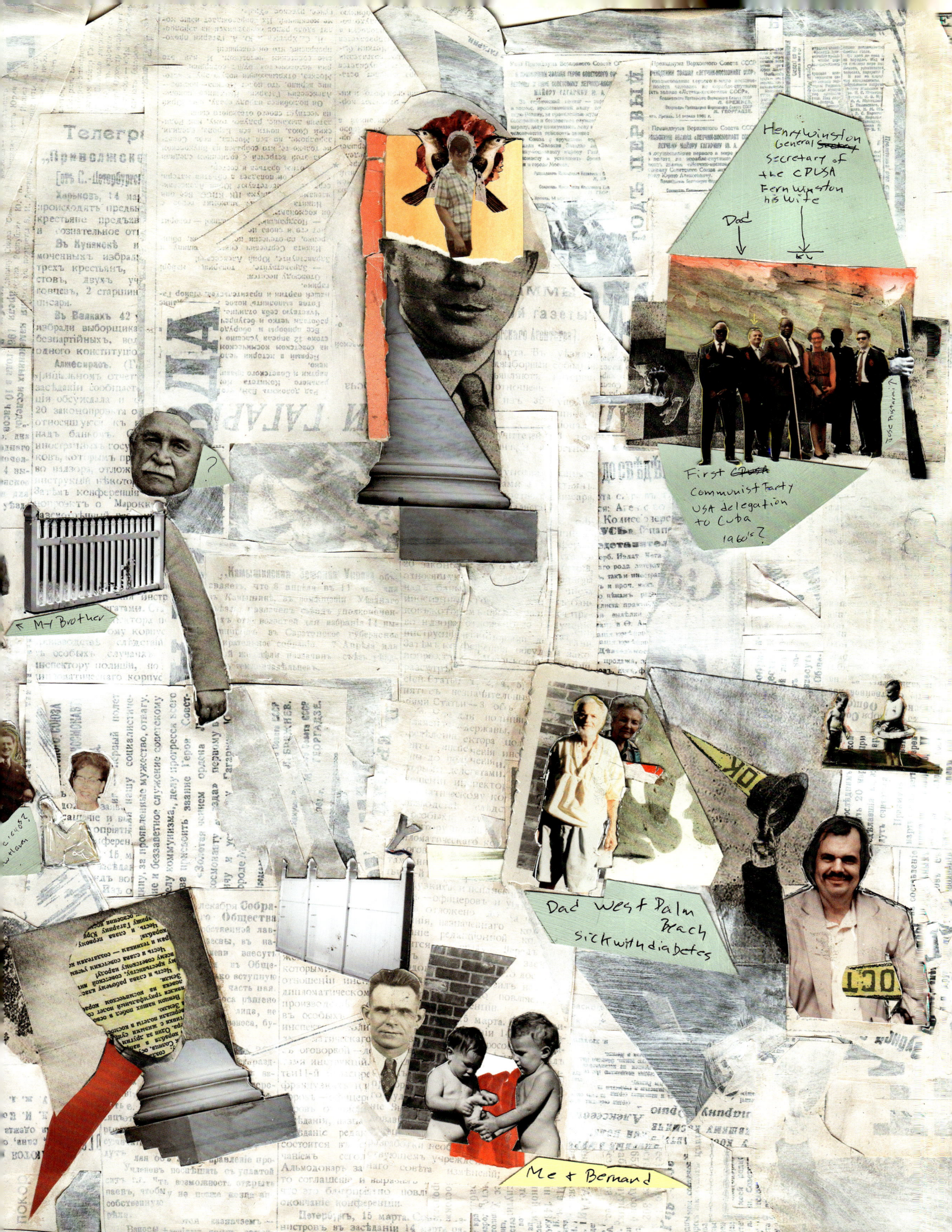

Henry Winston
General ~~Sec~~ Secretary of
the CPUSA
Fern Winston
his wife

Dad

First ~~CPUSA~~ Communist Party USA delegation to Cuba 1960's?

← My Brother

Dad West Palm Beach
Sick with diabetes

Me + Bernard

Donovan Wylie,
*Scavenging, Chapel Street,
New Haven*, 2015

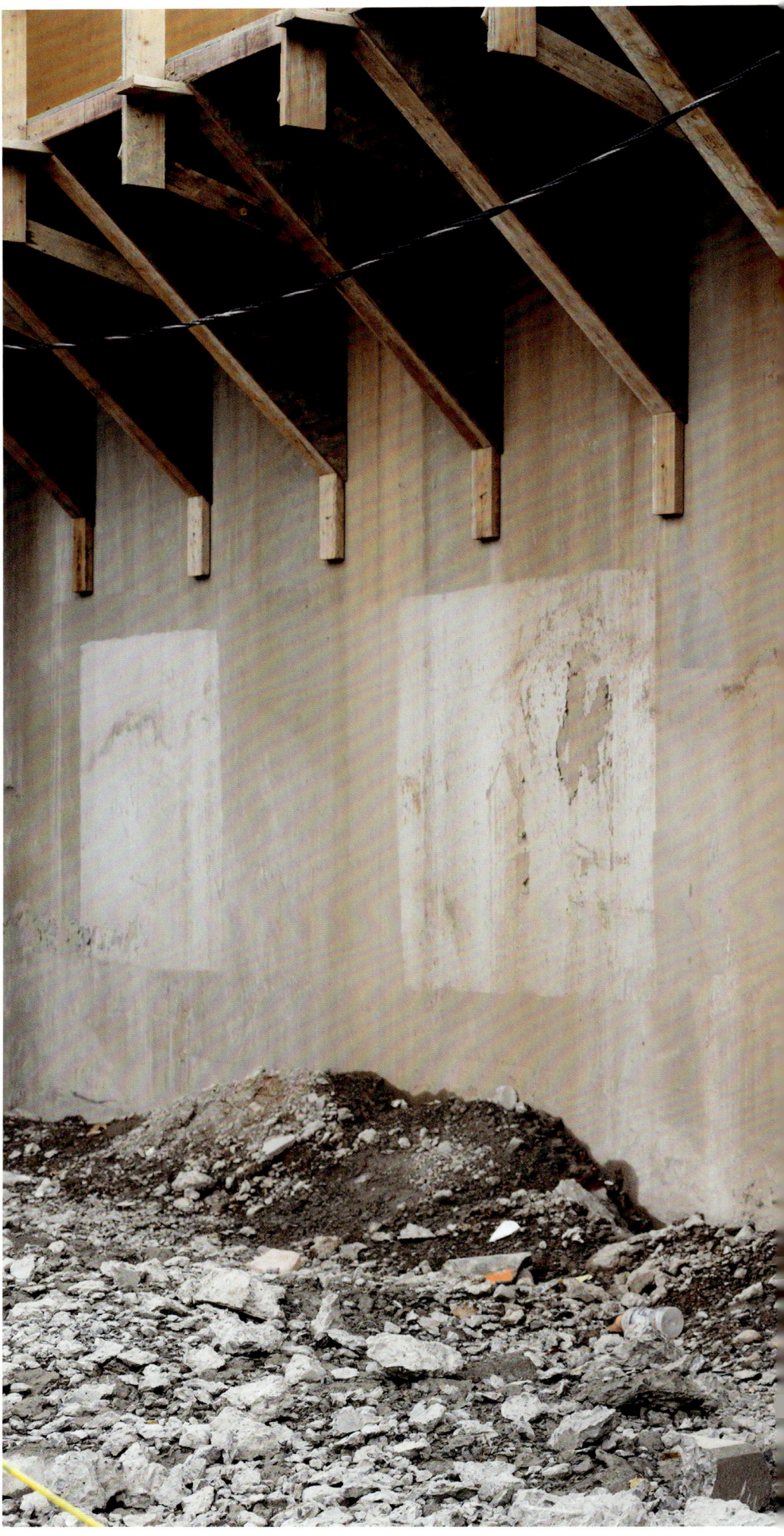

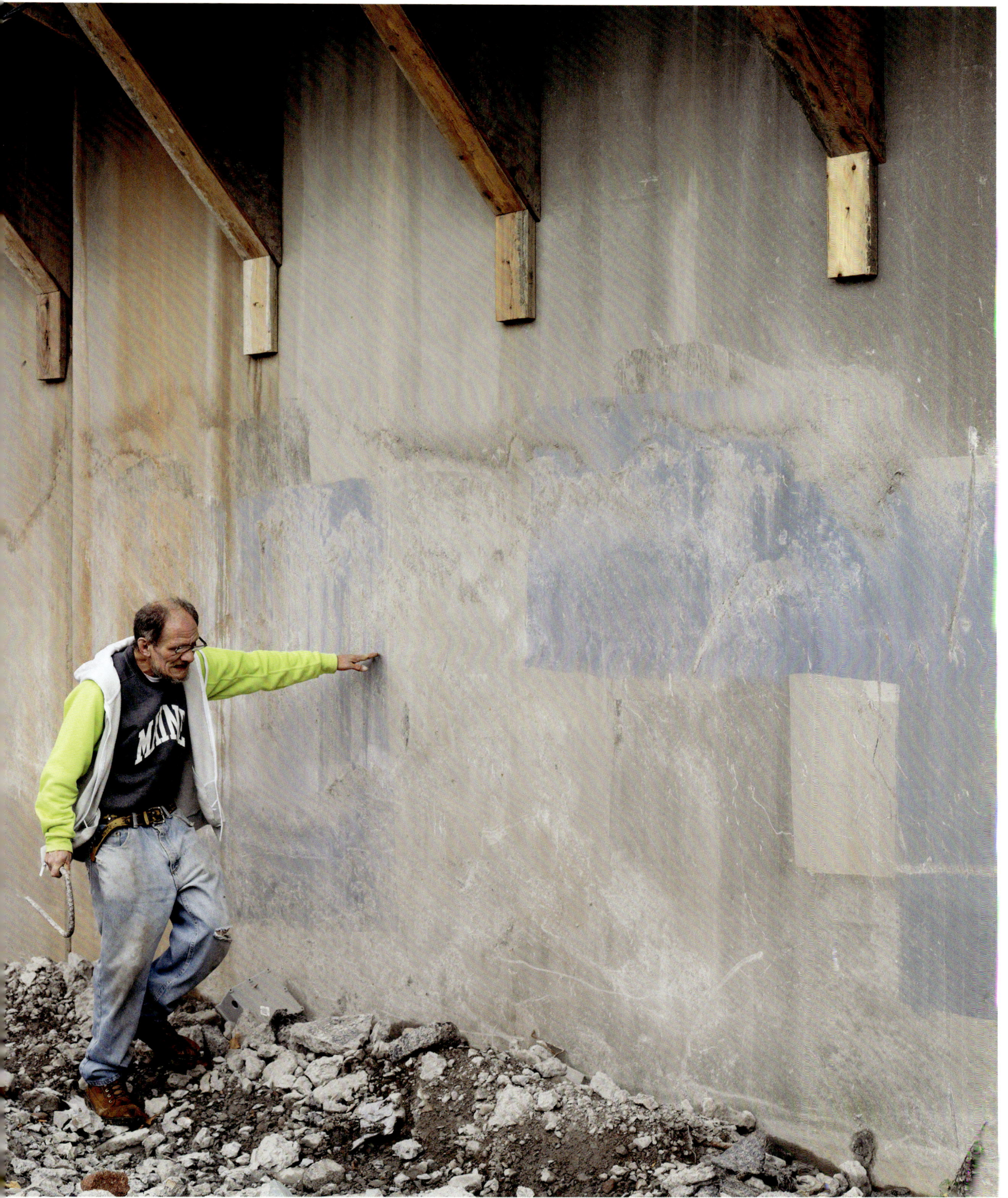

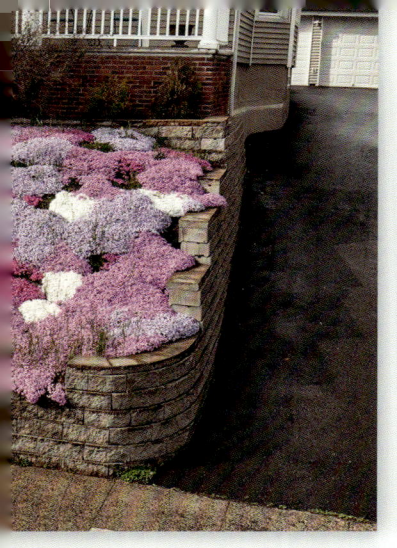
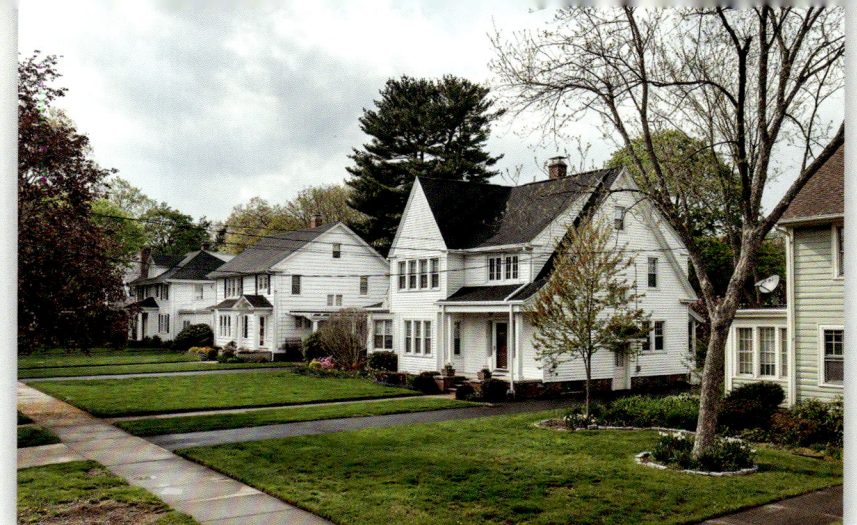
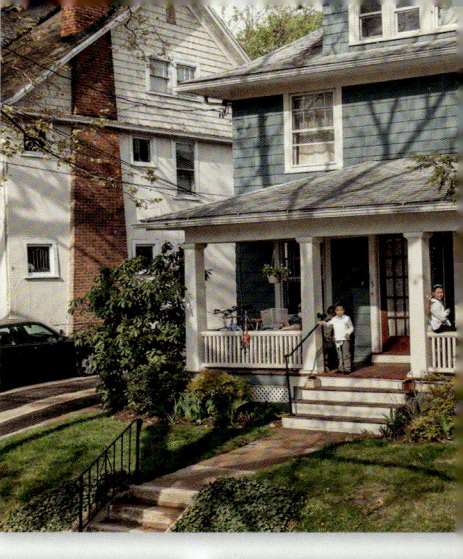
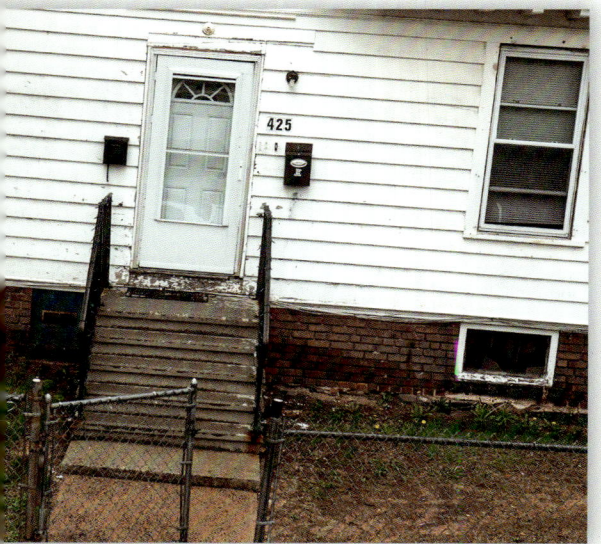
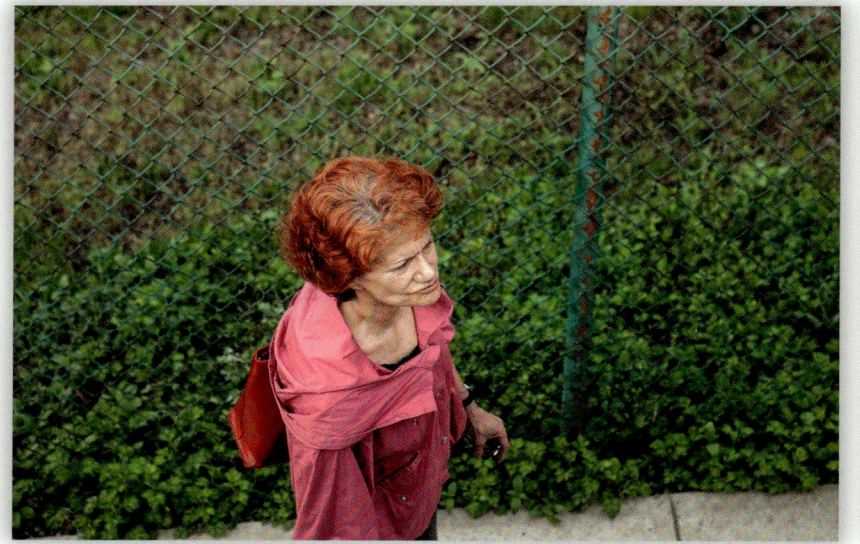
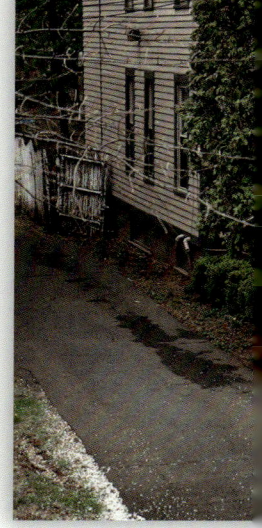
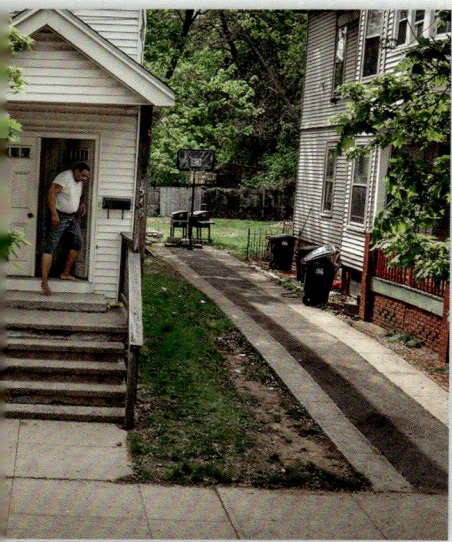
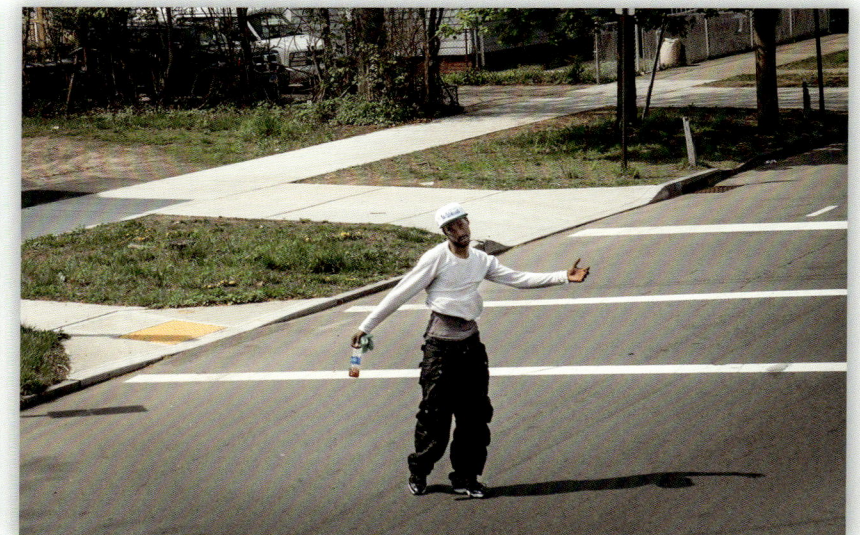
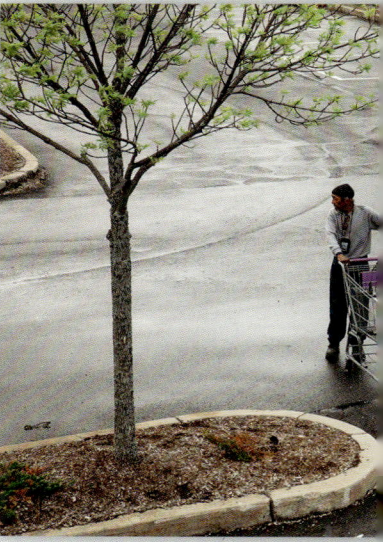
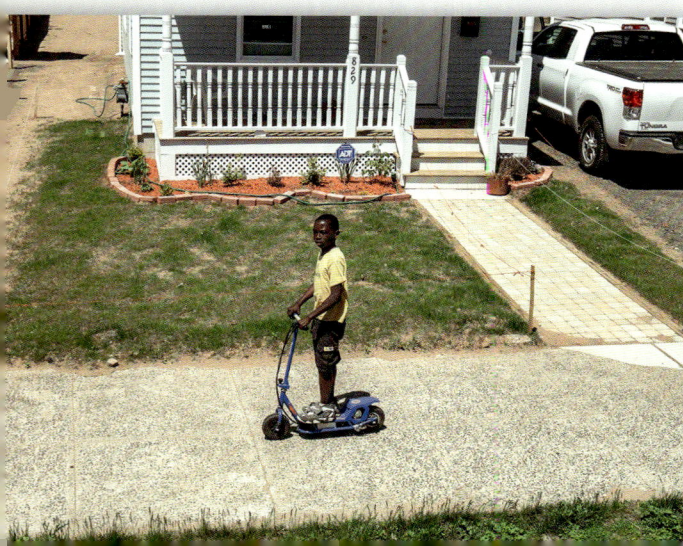
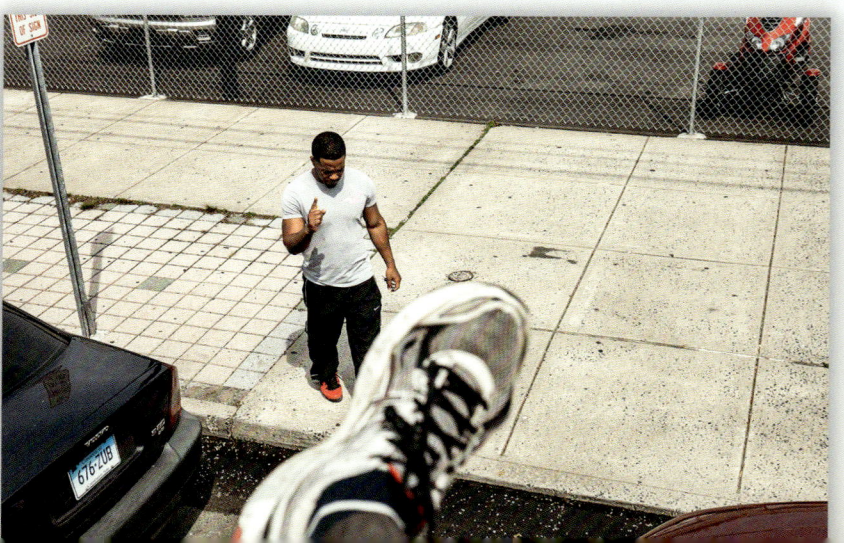
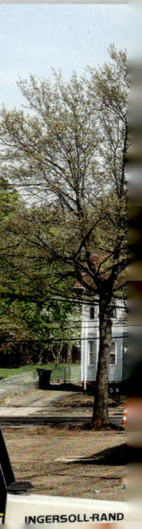

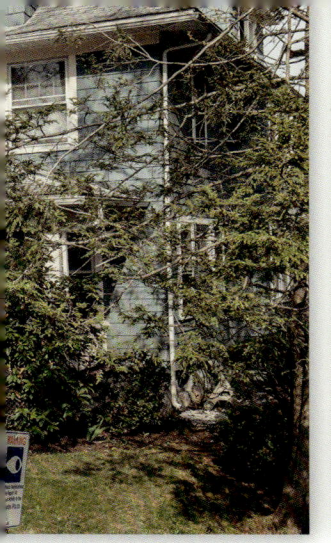
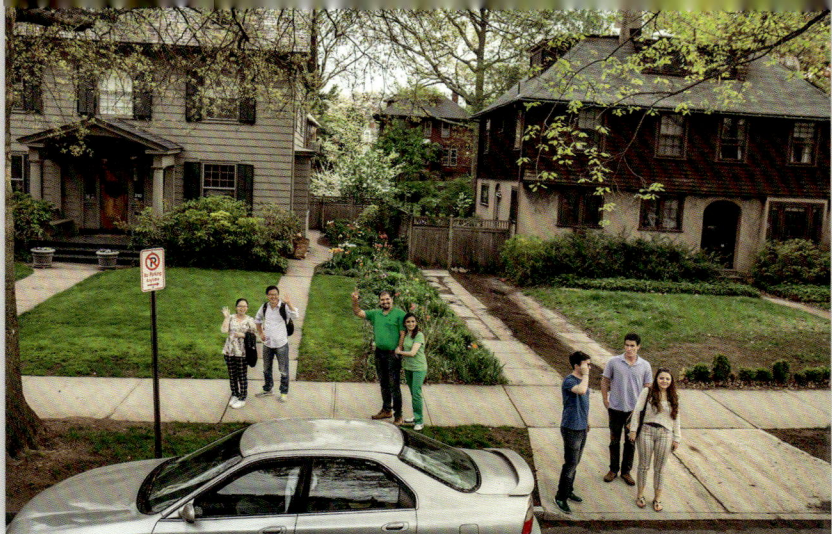
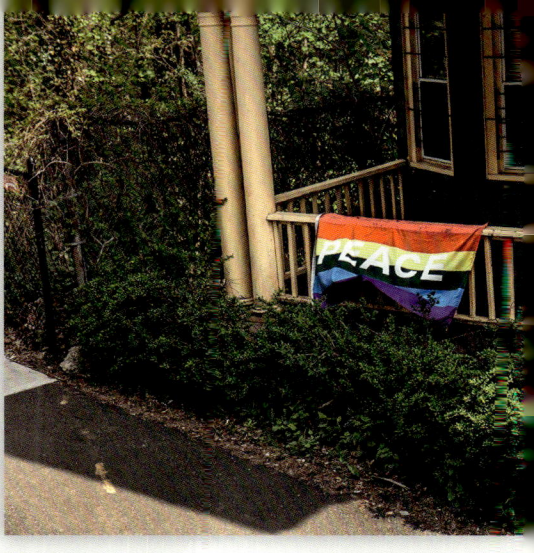
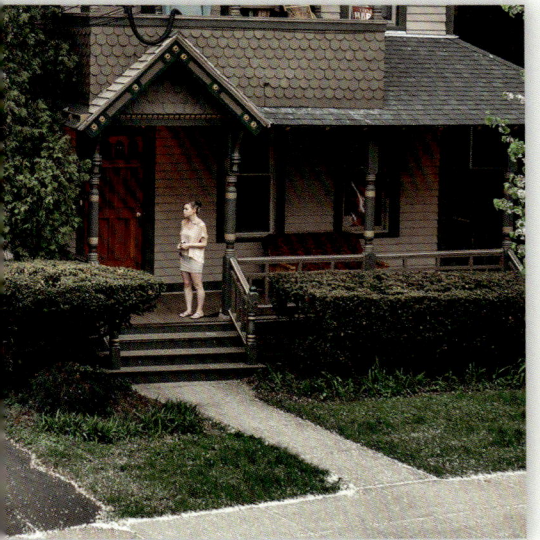
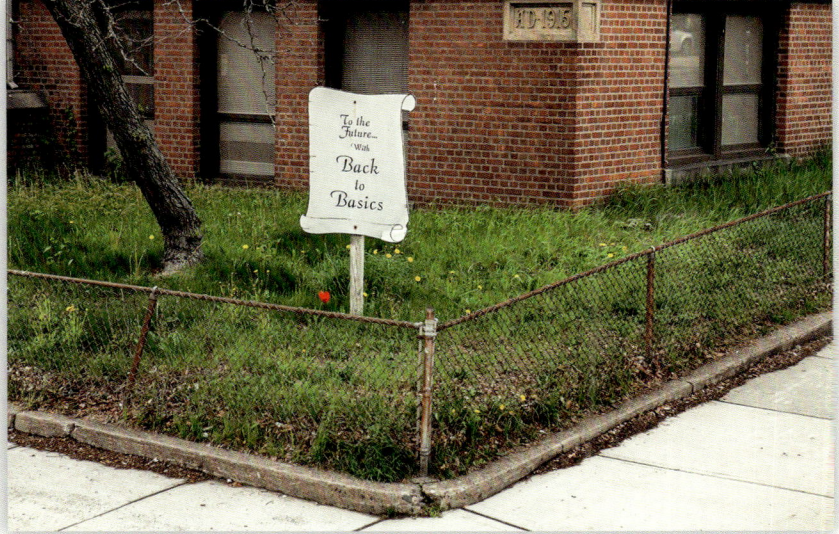
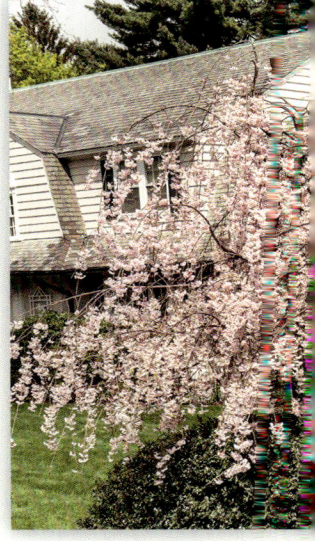
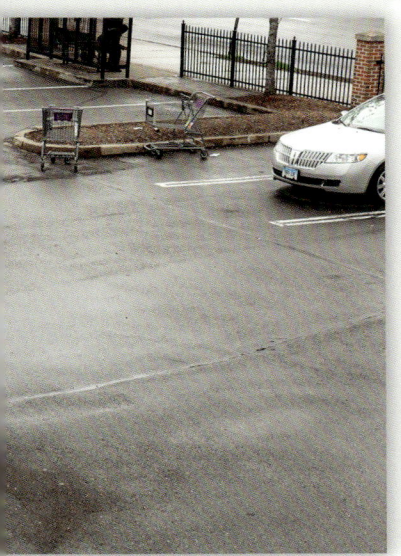
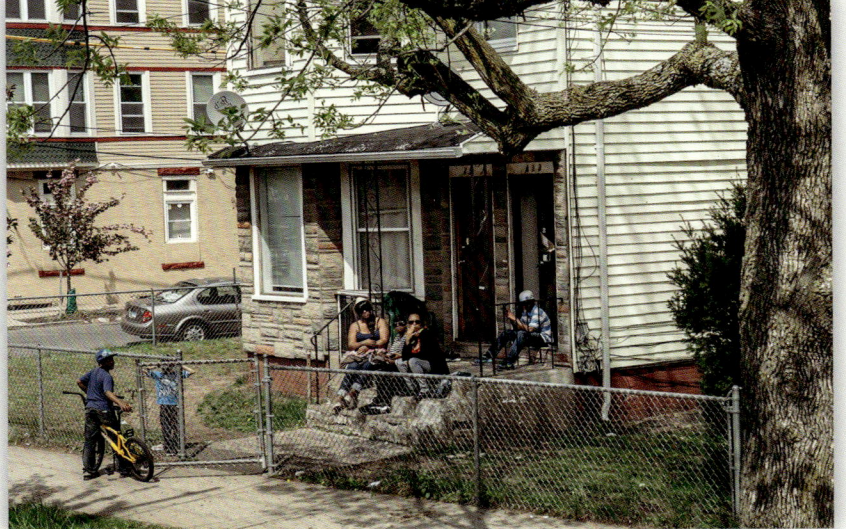
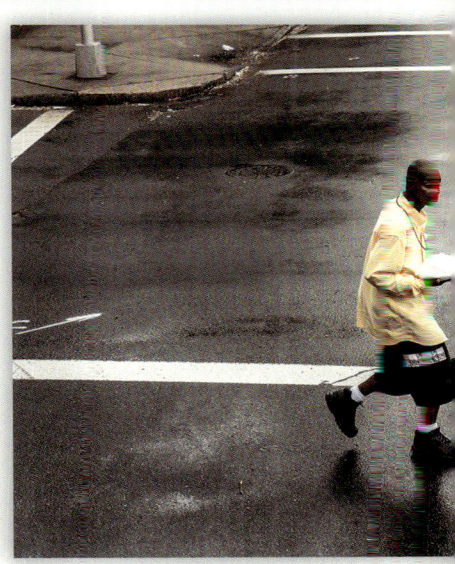
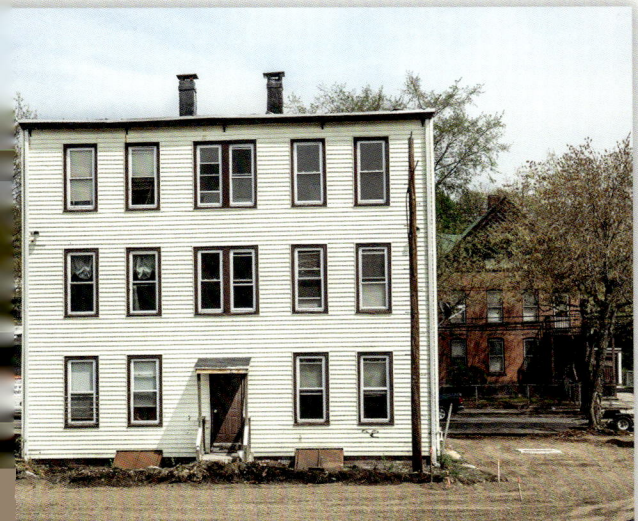
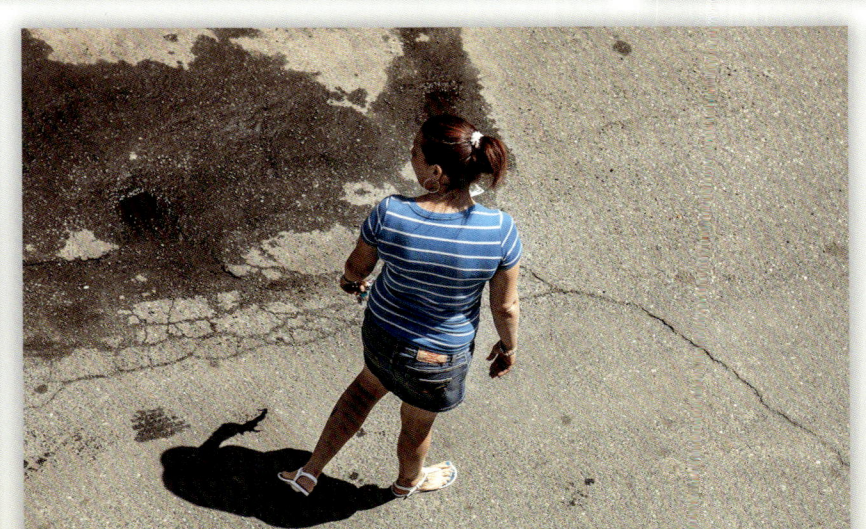
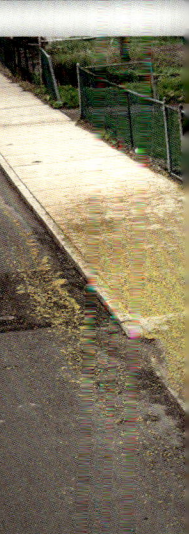

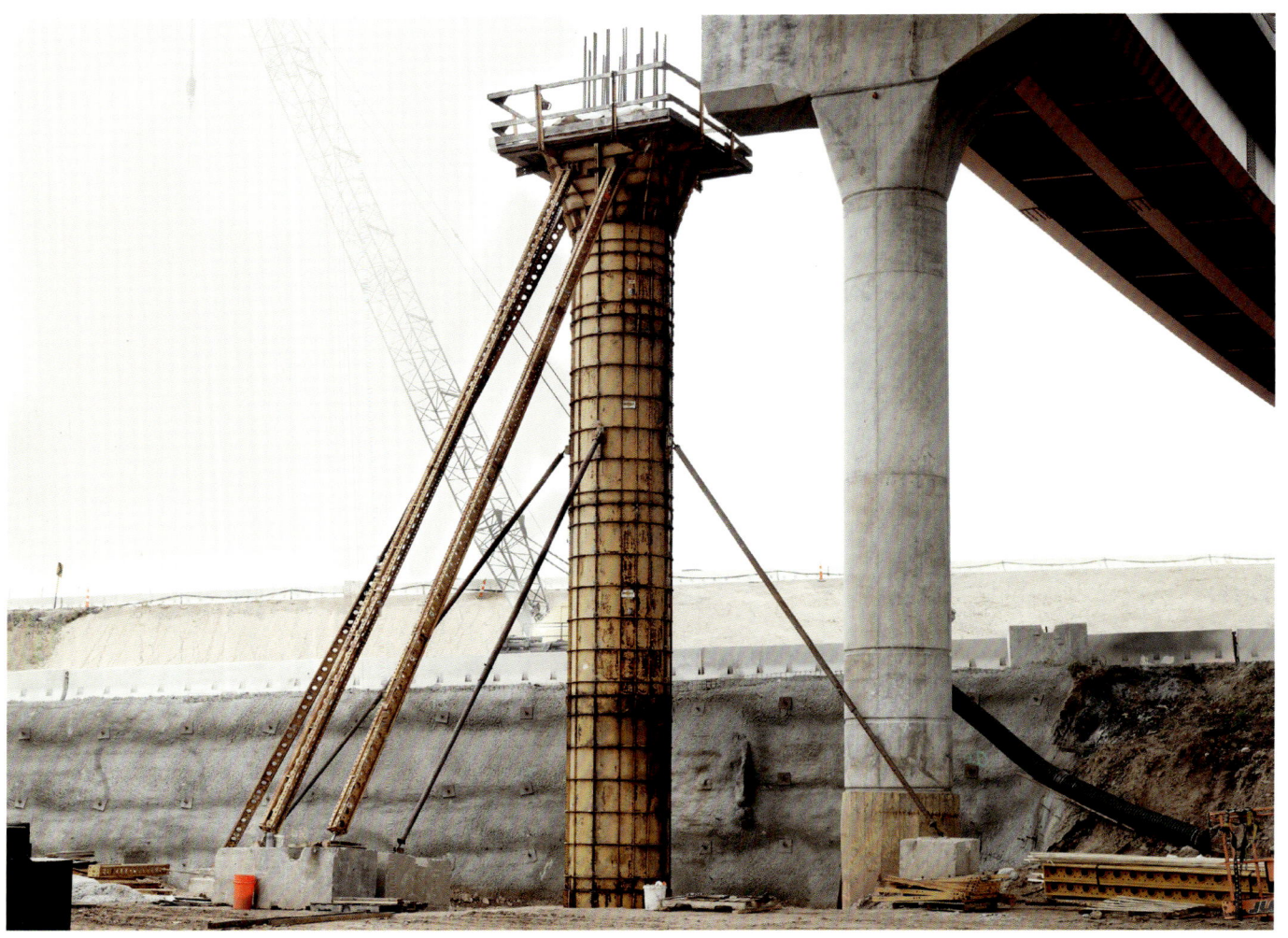

This page:
Jim Goldberg, *On US-1*,
2014

Overleaf:
Jim Goldberg, *Bus Stop, New Haven Green*, 2015–16
Jim Goldberg photographs
© the artist and courtesy
Pace/MacGill Gallery,
New York, and Casemore
Kirkeby, San Francisco

Donovan Wylie photographs
courtesy the artist

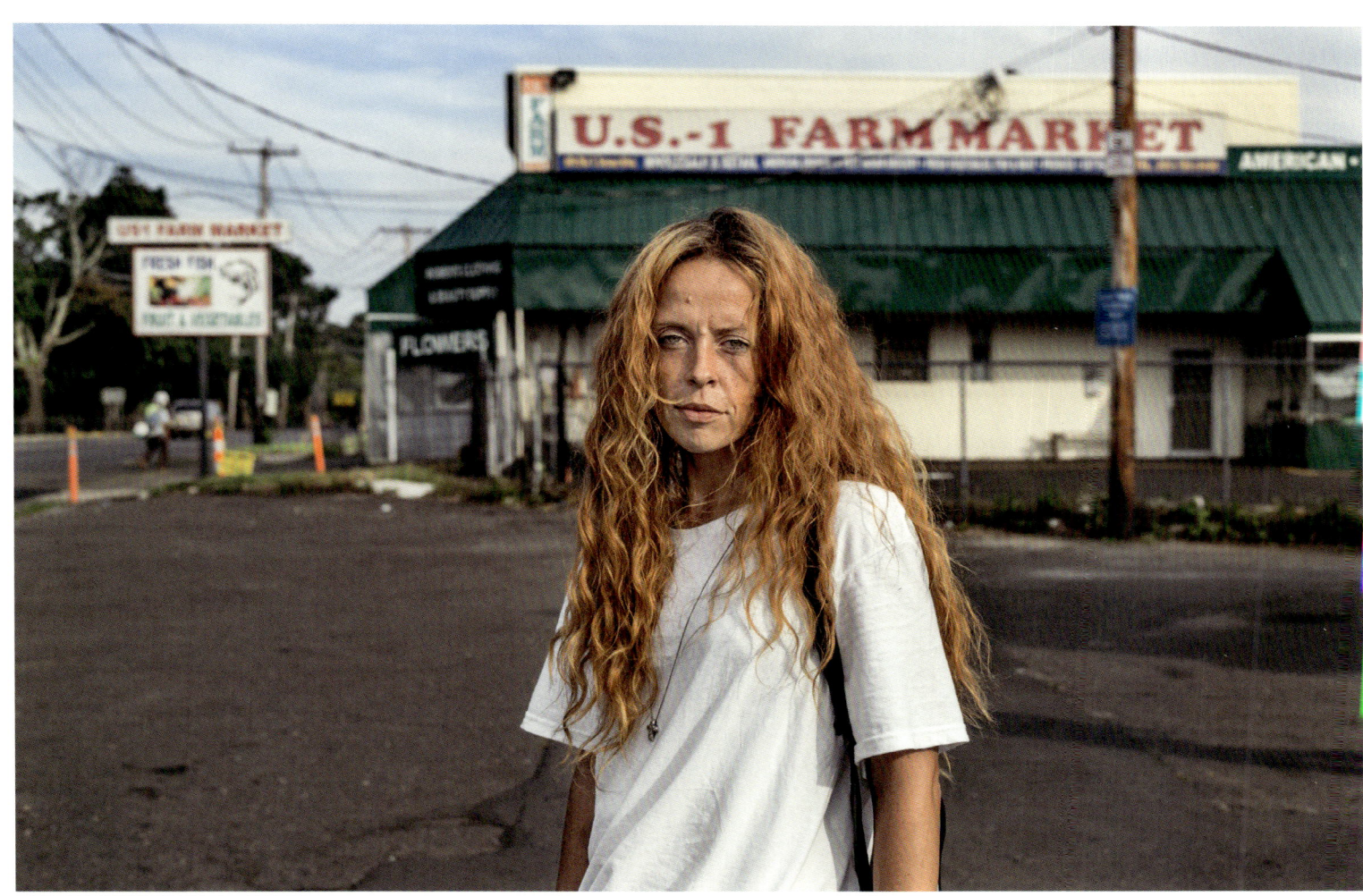

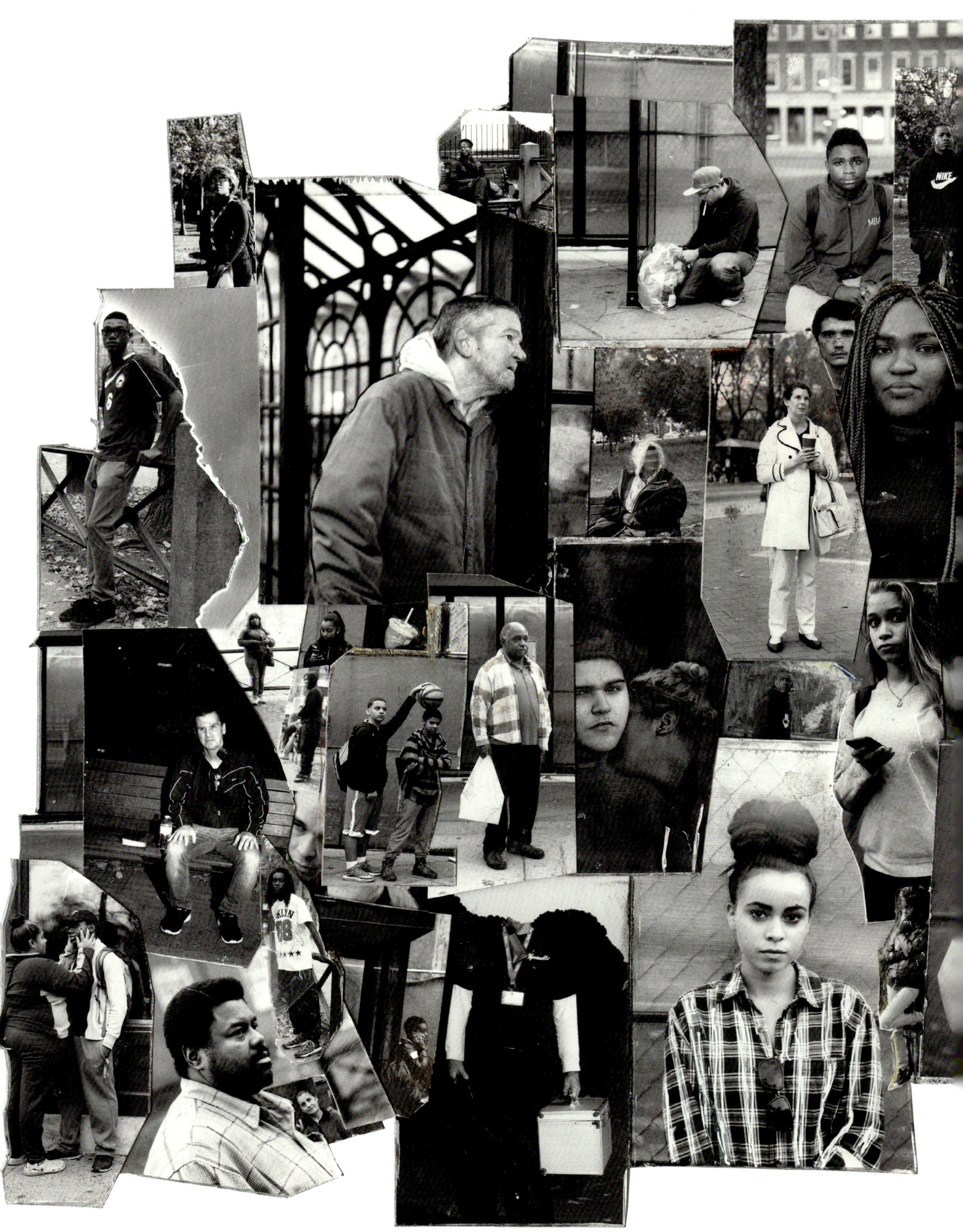

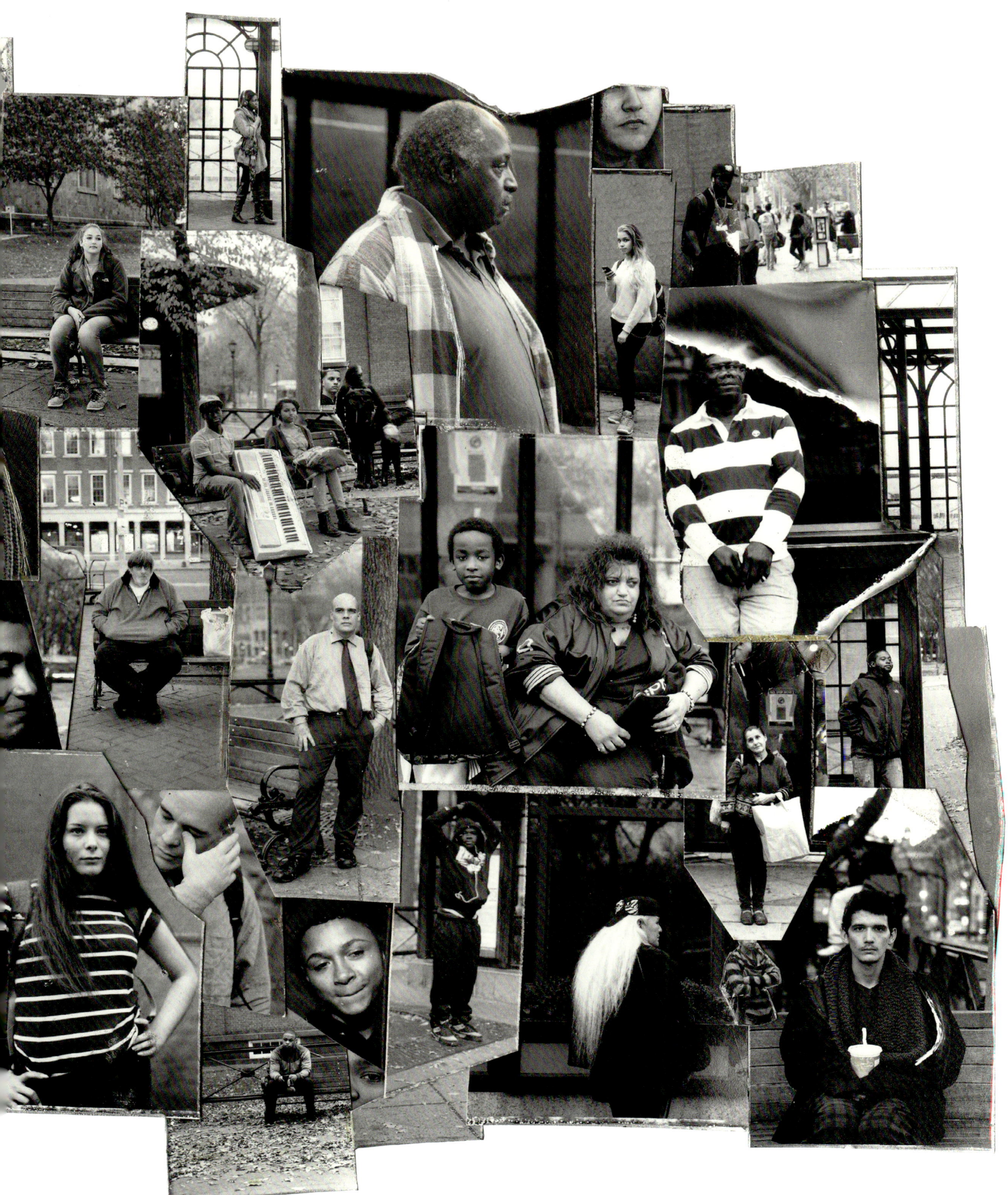

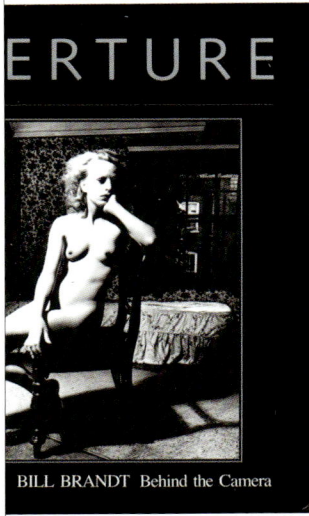
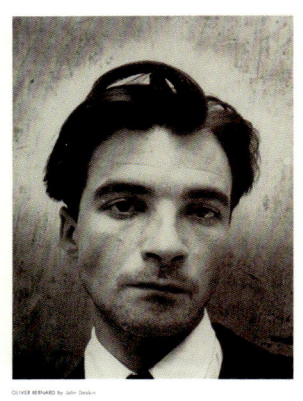
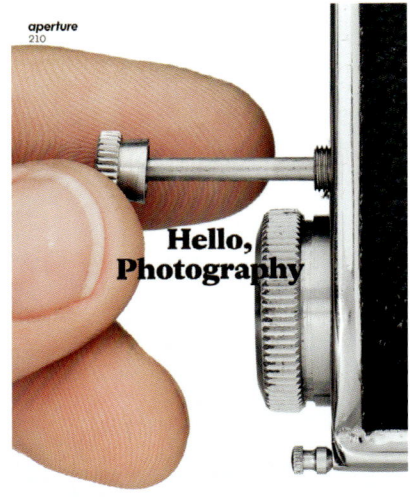
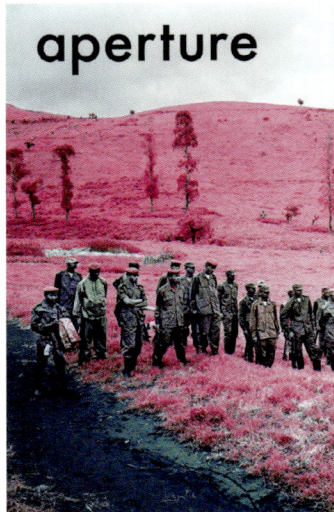
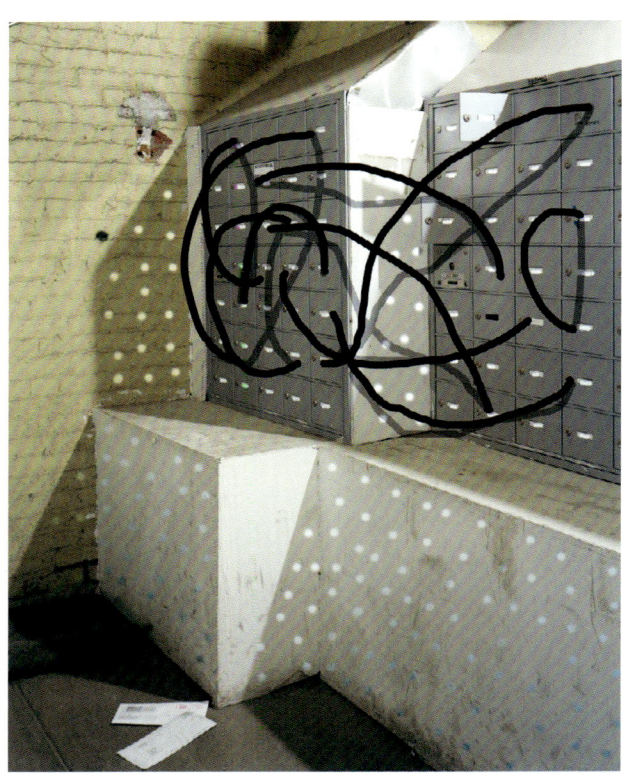

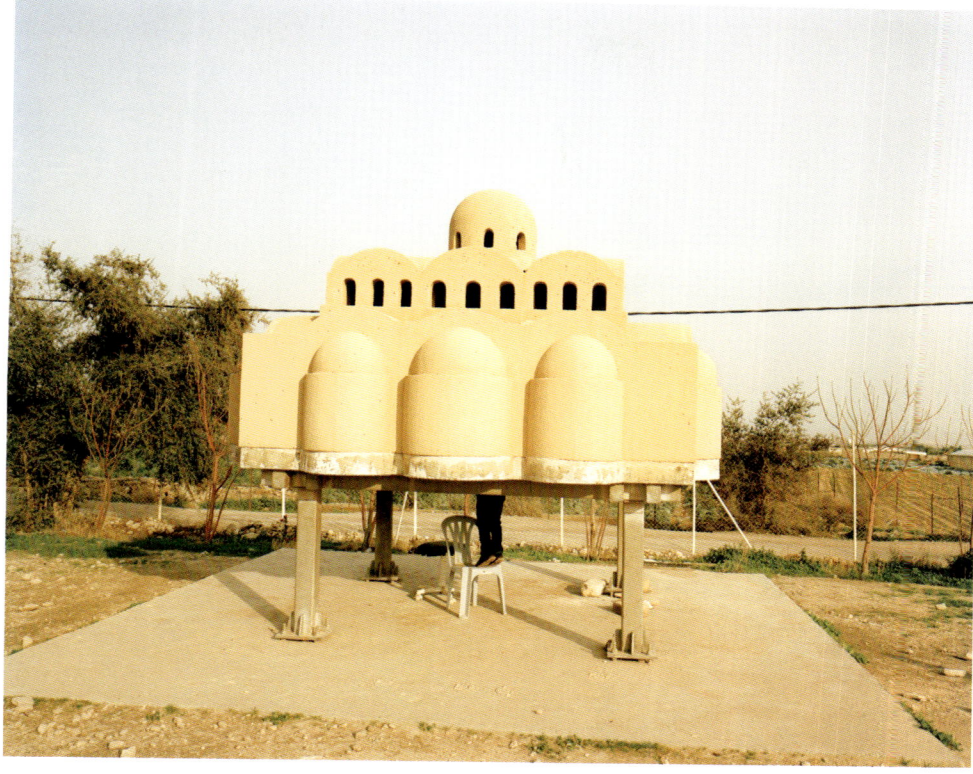
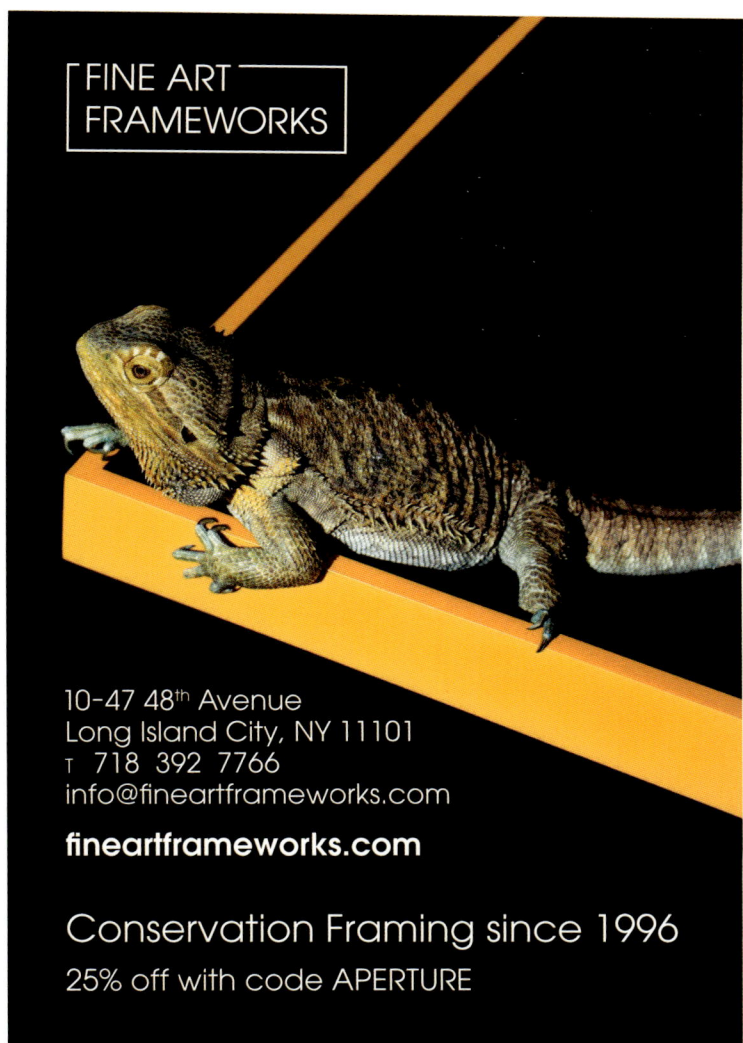
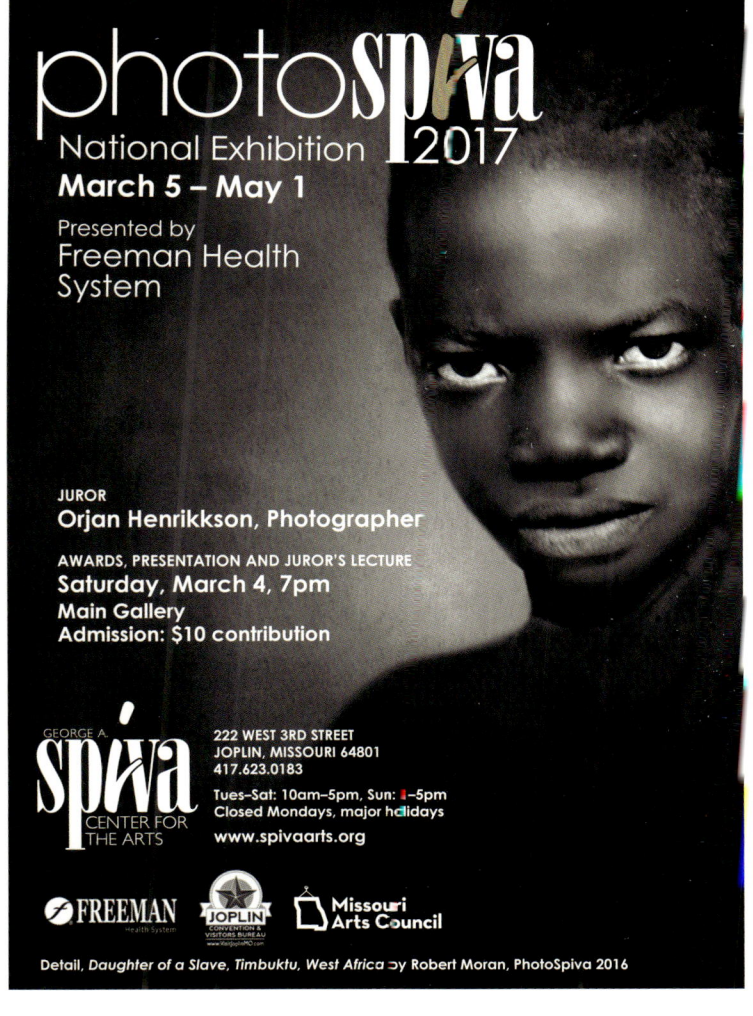

Object Lessons
Worker Badges from G. & G. Precision Works,
ca. 1940

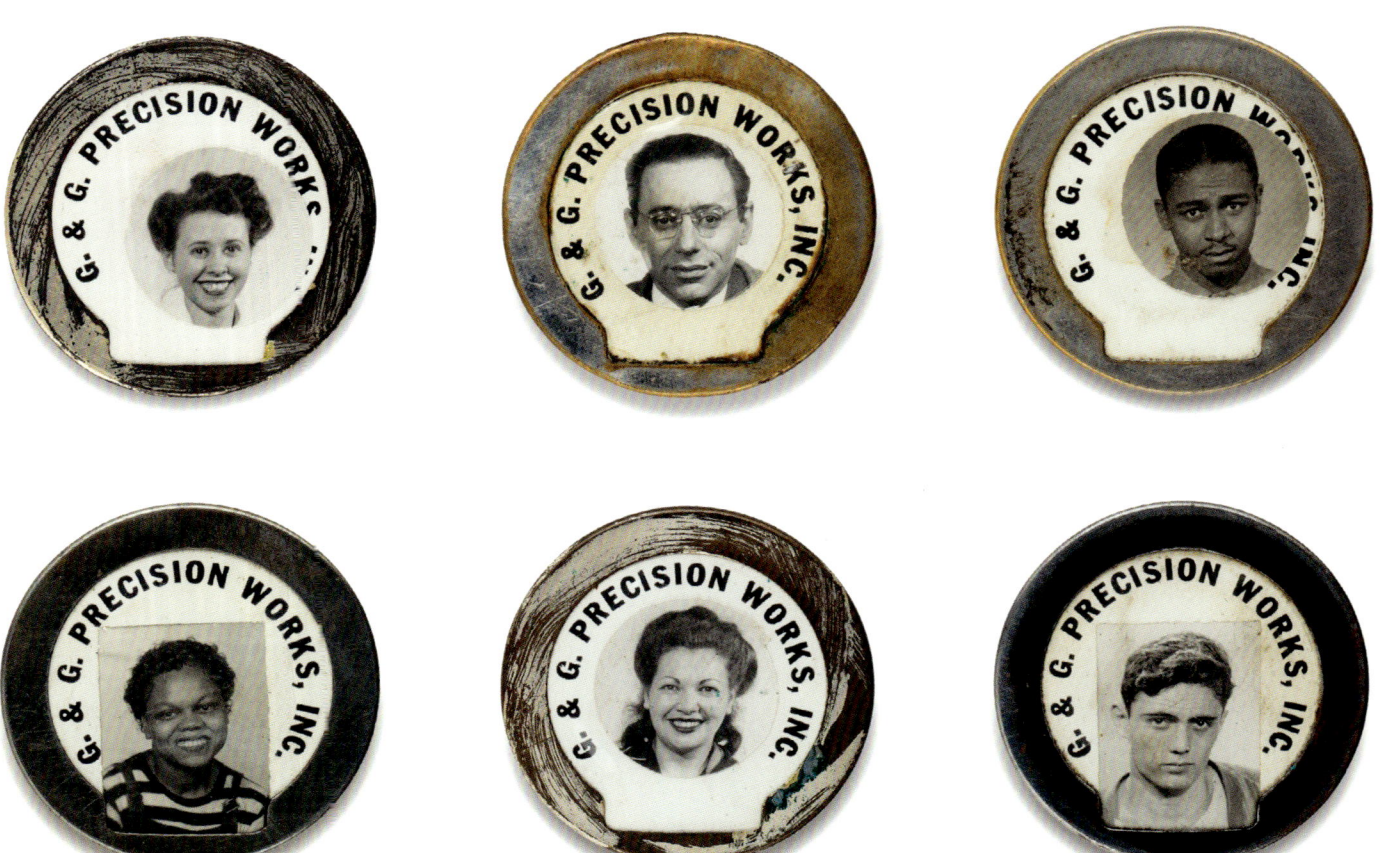

"I spent many days of my childhood in my father's and grandfather's offices at G. & G. typing nonsense on an old IBM Selectric while a hundred massive machines rumbled and roared in the adjoining shop," Ginny Levy recalled last year when her family's company, G. & G. Precision Works, Inc., shuttered. Incorporated in Queens in 1940 and relocated to Ardsley, New York, in 1954, G. & G. initially registered patents for small appliances and electrical signs. During World War II, the company became a subcontractor for Grumman Aerospace Corporation, producing parts for warplanes. When G. & G. closed in 2016, Levy swept through the midcentury office building in search of treasure.

"I became fascinated by the artifacts of my family's and the company's history," Levy said, "which so closely mirrors the experience of American manufacturing and our country's production heyday." Poking through a supply closet, she discovered a collection of eighty-three metal, pin-backed identity badges that represents the majority of G. & G.'s workforce in the early 1940s—a humbling contrast to today's multinational megacorporations that may employ well over a million workers in fulfilling U.S. military contracts.

Photo identification badges, now ubiquitous in large corporations, first gained popularity during World War II. A rudimentary form of security technology, they became integral to defense plans. How else could you be sure that Nazi spies or Communists weren't infiltrating your factory? In the 1940s and '50s, similar badges were used by employers as diverse as Campbell Soup Company, American Bridge Company, the U.S. Navy Fleet Supply Base, Sun Oil Company refineries, and even a prison.

At a time of nostalgia for the golden age of American manufacturing, the workers represented by these buttons— women alongside men, African Americans alongside whites— whose names were kept in an accompanying notebook, are powerful evidence of the diverse workforce essential to the war effort. Behind the imposing edifice of a military-industrial complex, the nation's countless small businesses formed the picture of modern America.
                                        —**The Editors**